The Unconquerable Spirit

A Mother's Love Forces A
Dynamic Struggle for Justice

To Sherry —
many thanks —

Kathleen Morton

The Unconquerable Spirit

A Mother's Love Forces A
Dynamic Struggle for Justice

Kathleen Morton

ISBN: 0-9749701-4-X

Library of Congress Control Number: 2004102891

Published by
Inkwell Productions
3370 N. Hayden Rd., #123-276
Scottsdale, AZ 85251
Phone (480) 315-9636
Fax (480) 315-9641
Toll Free 888-324-2665
Email: info@inkwellproductions.com
Website: www.inkwellproductions.com

Dedication

*I dedicate this book to our son, Michael,
who has shown extraordinary strength and endurance
over the years. His love and support for his little sister
was remarkable.*

Acknowledgements

My thanks to Bob Hope's comedy writer, Gene Perret, for his helpful suggestions during the writing of this book. Also my thanks to Greta Bishop for helping me to reduce the size of the manuscript, without affecting the integrity of the work. In addition, kudos go to Debbie Moyer, editor and Madalyn Johnson, designer for Inkwell Productions, for their efficiency and ongoing support.

Chapter 1

"Give up my child? Never!"

"You don't understand, Mrs. Morton."

"You've got that right."

"Michele has special needs and requires residential programming," the official said, "and in order to receive those services, you must give her up to the state."

I sat there, stunned by his complacency, and watched as everyone else in the meeting room nodded in assent. They seemed to be mystified by my reaction. Their behavior indicated a cold, unrelenting detachment, devoid of any feeling for parent or child.

"You're all crazy! Am I still in America or what?" Leaping out of my chair, I headed for the door.

"Don't go, Mrs. Morton! Believe me, this is the only way. It's just a simple case of relinquishment. All you need do is go to court, tell the judge you want to make Michele a ward of the state, and the court will issue an order to that effect. The court will decree also that the state must provide the services Michele requires within three weeks. Just think! In only three weeks, she'll be in the educational program that meets her needs." The official looked pleased.

Walking back toward the table, I looked at them all. "A simple case of relinquishment," I said, with a derisive laugh. "So simple. Except for one thing, what you're doing is illegal, and there's nothing simple about that."

"What do you mean illegal?" several of them demanded to know. "What law is being broken?"

"A federal law. Public Law 94-142, which is the Education of the Handicapped Act, enacted by Congress in 1975, where it specifically states that residential programming is to be given when it is required to meet the child's educational needs and at no time does it suggest, imply or stipulate that parents must lose custody of their child. On the contrary, this law gives parents more rights than they have ever had before. I'd suggest you bone up on it."

"I never heard of that law," the leader responded. "But if it exists, it doesn't apply to us. This is the Arizona Department of Economic Security (DES), charged with the responsibility when residential programming is required, and we've already told you what the process is."

"Ignorance is no excuse," I said. "I don't care who the Education Department places in charge of an educational issue in this state. That process does not free them, or you, of the responsibility of following the dictates of a clearly well-written federal mandate. As long as the Education Department receives federal funds under that Act, they must abide by the Act.

"So, you see, under no circumstances will I give up Michele! If I have to fight you, the legislature, and the governor, I will. Giving up Michele for services will never, ever, be an option."

I left the meeting feeling dejected. Their ignorance and insensitivity were astounding!

When I arrived home, I sat down and tried to relax, letting my jumbled thoughts take me wherever they chose. I thought about what had happened while we were living in New York, and how complicated our lives had become. I smiled as I vividly recalled the day the doctor announced that, after eight years, I was indeed pregnant again! When I got home, my husband, Arnie, and son,

Michael, celebrated with me.

Happily, the pregnancy was normal. I stayed busy volunteering my time at our church, and eventually was asked to chair the annual conference for the St. Kevin's Rosary Society. The conference date drew near as I entered my ninth month of pregnancy. One day, the moderator, Father Richard Brougham, approached me and said, "Kathleen, you have done a great job with this conference and we owe you a lot. But I'm not sure if you should come tomorrow night. You could go into labor at any time."

"Look, Father. A lot of hard work went into this conference. My presentation is ready, and I'm looking forward to attending. There's no way I'm going to miss it, unless the baby is delivered before the start of the conference, and that's unlikely since tomorrow is the 23rd and my delivery date is the 28th."

"Well, we'll see," Father Brougham responded with a nervous grin. "I have an 'in' with the Man upstairs, and I'm going to talk with Him tonight, and ask for the date to be moved up."

I shook my head and laughed. Over the years, Father Brougham had become a good friend of the family. He often came for dinner, which sometimes turned into debates on various issues, so I knew how determined and persuasive he could be.

The next day I woke up feeling great. I had all my material together along with a complete agenda written out for the evening's festivities. This was to be given to one of the officers of the Rosary Society in the unlikely event that I couldn't make it. Once done, I decided to relax until it was time to go to the conference. Father Brougham was scheduled to introduce me, if he didn't faint upon my arrival!

When my husband, Arnie, returned from grocery shopping, he asked how I was doing.

"Great!" I responded. "I'm feeling chipper. It's just becoming harder to get around."

"I know," he said sympathetically. "Well, just relax and don't do anything. Are you still planning on going tonight?"

"You bet I am! By the way, did you see Michael on the way in?"

"Yes. He's around the corner playing ball. We decided on pizza for tonight."

"Great choice," I said. "That's something you both enjoy." Feeling suddenly tired, I told Arnie I'd be upstairs resting. "In case I fall asleep," I requested, "wake me up at 5 o'clock. I plan to leave here by 6:30."

"Will do," Arnie said, "and I'm glad to see you're taking it easy."

In a sound sleep, I awoke with a start. The perspiration was dripping off me, yet I was cold and shivering almost uncontrollably. For a moment I was confused as to what day it was. I looked at the clock. It was almost five, and then I thought – 'The conference!' I could hear Arnie on the stairs, probably on his way up to wake me.

Suddenly, a searing pain hit me like a bolt of lightning. I struggled to get out of bed. Both the bedding and my clothes were soaking wet! Then I knew. My water had broken! I couldn't believe it! (Father Brougham's prayer had been answered.) Another searing pain forced me to cry out. I was definitely in labor.

When Arnie entered, he rushed to my side. "Are you all right, Honey?" I was doubled over. My face was contorted and my breathing came in gasps and he asks me if I'm all right! But knowing Arnie was excitable by nature, I tried to remain calm.

"I'm fine," I told him, "but I think the baby is coming. I really should get to the hospital."

"Oh, my God! Oh, my God! Oh, my God!" he shouted.

Then he began running around the bedroom yelling. "Where are my shoes? Where are my shoes?"

"Downstairs," I told him, as the pain momentarily subsided.

"Oh, that's right, that's right!" he said, then catapulted down the stairs. I half expected him to jump in the car and take off without me.

"Arnie!" I called down, "Get Don on the phone. He said he would drive us to the hospital, remember?"

"Yeah, that's right, that's right, he did. Great! I'll call him right away." Everything Arnie did now was incredibly accelerated. He made perpetual motion look relaxing and I was exhausted watching him.

Don and Betty Bunch lived across the street. They had four children, and our son, Michael, played with their two older boys, Mikey and Stevie. We were the best of friends.

When Don arrived I asked him to call the Doctor to let him know I was on my way, and then I requested he take care of Arnie. "I think he's lost it."

Don laughed and said, "Ain't that the truth. We men are all alike."

Once in the car, Arnie treated me like a china doll, which might break any minute. He gingerly placed his arm around my shoulders and said, "Here, hold my hand, and squeeze it as hard as you can when the pain comes." Knowing Michael would enjoy dinner with Betty and the kids, I finally let myself relax a little.

Headed for Physician's Hospital in Jackson Heights, Don made great time. When we arrived less than thirty minutes later, the obstetrician was already there. He asked how often the pains were coming.

"About every half second," I quipped.

He laughed. "Now that's pretty fast." And I was whisked

directly into the delivery room. Not too long afterwards, I heard our baby cry. I tried to sit up.

"Relax, Mrs. Morton," a nurse soothed, as she wiped my brow. "You have a beautiful baby girl. We'll give her to you in a minute, as soon as she's cleaned up. They're weighing her now. Wow! She's just one ounce shy of eight pounds. Have you picked out a name yet?"

"Michele Patrice Morton," I answered proudly. "That's 'Michele' with one 'l.'"

"Great! I'll make sure the records reflect that."

Moments later I cradled her in my arms. Bundled up in a pink blanket, she was indeed a beautiful baby. Her skin was milky white, with a touch of pink. She had dark curly hair, large blue eyes, and a little pug nose. Her cheeks were chubby. Yes, she would surely win the hearts of all who came in contact with her. I counted her little fingers and then opened up her blanket and checked her out thoroughly. She was perfect!

When they took me back to my room Michele's proud dad was waiting with our friend, Don. "How are you feeling?" they asked in unison.

"I'm deliriously happy. She's so precious. Here, Arnie, do you want to hold her?"

"Sure," he said, and removed her with great care from my arms. Looking down at her, he chided. "Do you have any idea what you put me through today, huh? Whew! What an ordeal. I almost didn't survive!" Don and I shook our heads and laughed.

After spending some special time with Mom and Dad, Michele was taken to the nursery. As soon as Arnie and Don departed, I called Michael. He'd been hoping for a baby brother. "Are you very disappointed, Michael?"

"Nah, everything is cool, Mom," he lied. "I'm excited

about the baby and I can't wait until you get home."

"You're lying, Michael, right?"

"Who me? Lie? Nooooo," he said. "Never happen."

"Michael, this is your mother you're talking to. Your mother! Remember me?" I laughed.

"Okay, okay," he responded, "I admit I'm a little disappointed. But the parts about being excited and missing you are true. Besides, I figure my little sister can learn how to play ball just as well as a brother would."

"I have no doubt you could teach her to do that, Son. You be good now, and I'll be home soon."

"Okay, love you, Mom, goodbye," and the line went dead before I could respond with any 'mushy' stuff, as he called it.

I put my head on the pillow, quite content with the way things had turned out. As I dozed, the phone rang. It was Father Brougham! "Hello. Is this Mrs. Morton?" he asked, with a great deal of formality, desperately trying to control his amusement.

"Funny, funny," I replied.

"It is funny, Kathleen. We were all expecting you to show up, so we waited around for a while. Finally, somebody called your house. No answer. The next call was to the hospital. You should have heard the roar and applause from the conference crowd when I made the announcement that you had just given birth to a baby girl."

"Well, you got your wish," I said. "The baby kept me from attending."

He chuckled and continued, "You also missed a surprise baby shower. One of the larger tables had been decorated and was loaded down with gifts."

"Oh, that is so nice," I said, feeling good all over. "I can't believe it! What a pleasant surprise that would have been!" Telling

7

Father Brougham to express my appreciation to all involved, I prepared for a good night's rest.

Since no children were allowed to visit the hospital, the first days of Michele's life were not easy for Michael. I knew he missed me as much as I missed him, and, he couldn't wait to see his little sister.

The morning I returned home several neighbors dropped by with their children. I didn't want Michael's young friends to see Michele before he did. Fortunately, the parents understood and arranged for their children to return later.

After school, Michael ran into the living room very excited. Greeting me with a hug, he asked with anticipation, "Where is she?"

"Over here, Sweetheart," I said, lifting Michele out of the bassinet.

"Oh, Mom!" he exclaimed. "She looks so tiny. Look at her little fingers and toes. Wow! Her skin's so soft," he said as he gingerly touched her cheeks.

"Want to introduce her to your friends, Michael? A few of them are waiting outside."

I gave her to him. He was a little awkward at first, but in no time she nestled in his arms. Then, I opened the door and he eagerly showed his baby sister to the waiting children. He was so proud, and I was equally proud of him. I felt this was an important step towards helping Michael accept the new addition to our family. After all, he had been the only child for nine years.

As time passed and friends and family lavished attention on Michele, we did the same with Michael. When gifts came pouring in, we bought him some extra things, or went on some special excursions with him. When we sent out birth announcements, I had one specially printed from him, which read in part:

"Master Michael Morton announces with pleasure the
birth of his sister, Michele, born on September 23......."

Every response sent to Michael we held for him to open,
and he was delighted. It made him feel important to be the recipient
of all the 'congratulatory messages.' A few even put some money
in the envelopes for him, which delighted him even more. He
thought this was great stuff!

Michele's birth made Kathleen and Arnie Morton (the
proud parents) and Michael Morton (the equally proud brother) an
American statistic, because a boy and girl and two parents were
considered the typical American family.

Because Michael was nine years older than Michele, I had
had plenty of time to practice before she came along. I always said
that Michael survived in spite of me, and that was with the help of
Benjamin Spock, the baby/child-care doctor who wrote all those
wonderful books.

My goal during pregnancy with Michael was to be the perfect mother — no slip-ups for me. I was probably the only mom in
all of New York City who set the alarm for the 2 a.m. feeding and
was upset when my son wouldn't wake up. You should have heard
the doctor's response when I called him at 2:30 a.m. to report my
concern.

Doctor Thomas L. Burns had been our family physician for
many years and we relied on his care and good judgment for all our
medical needs. An imposing figure with a deep gravelly voice that
barked out commands, he could be intimidating. But, under that
rough exterior beat the heart of a gentle man. He was a proud
Irishman who would likely view gentleness as a sign of weakness.
Although we had had our share of disagreements over the years
(I'm Irish also), our deep and abiding respect for one another led to
a lasting friendship.

Because I was so naive, I hung on to every word Doctor Burns told me. When Michael was three weeks old and had a constipation problem, Burns told me to pick up some suppositories. Never having heard of suppositories before, I didn't have the foggiest notion for what they were used. Noting my hesitation, Burns rolled his eyes but patiently said, "Go to any drugstore for them, Kathleen, and when the problem arises, take one out and slowly and carefully agitate the anus in rectum, without letting it go in."

That night, when Michael woke up crying, I felt relieved about being able to help him. My husband also got up because, after all, I needed all the help I could get with this delicate procedure. Michael was screaming and kicking and my husband held up his little legs while I started agitating the anus. Suddenly with a SWOOSH, the suppository disappeared inside. I screamed, "Oh my God, it's gone!"

"What's gone?" Arnie shouted.

"The suppository. It went inside of him." I was overcome with panic.

"WHAT! How did you let that happen?" he yelled as Michael lay there screaming his head off.

"What do you mean, how did I let it happen?" I replied in agitation. "You act as if I planned it." The idea that I may have hurt Michael was killing me.

"Let's try and retrieve it." Arnie ran and got the flashlight, shining it directly into the rectal area where the suppository disappeared. It was no use. I couldn't find it. The area was pulsating, but nothing could be seen. We both knew we were way out of our league this time and realized the doctor had to be called.

The only problem was, it was three o'clock in the morning. I knew he'd probably be upset, but I was sure he would understand when he realized the seriousness of the situation. When Dr. Burns answered, I blurted "Oh, doctor, you'll never believe this."

"Try me," he said, wryly.

Needing little invitation, I rapidly launched into some kind of incoherent speech. Dr. Burns soon interrupted.

"Kathleen, say it slowly and try to calm down"

"Well," I said, swallowing hard and trying to be calm. "Remember the suppository you told me to use?"

"Yeah," he said gruffly, "what about it?"

"Well, when I was agitating the rectum slowly and carefully like you said, it went swoosh and disappeared inside of him, and I can't get it out." After I was finished, immediate disbelief was in his voice.

"You mean to tell me that you called at 3 o'clock in the morning just to let me know that a suppository went into the baby's rectum? That's what the damn thing is supposed to do!" he shouted.

"But, you told me just to agitate the anus without letting it go in," I said, somewhat plaintively. I was already beginning to feel better now that it appeared Michael wasn't hurt.

"I did tell you that," Burns said, with as much calm as he could muster, "because he was only a little tyke, and I wanted you to go easy in the beginning to see if it would work. Bring him into the office tomorrow morning," he commanded.

My heart leapt. "Why?" I nearly shouted, trying to quell the panic rising within me. "Isn't he going to be all right?"

"He's going to be just fine," Dr. Burns replied with exasperation. "It's you I'm worried about!"

As time passed I learned that Michael was much more resilient than I assumed.

"You have to try and relax. "He won't break," Dr. Burns

assured me. "Everything he is doing is very normal and everything you're doing is abnormal. So, lighten up, and enjoy him."

I listened attentively and realized that what he was saying was true. I resolved to try and relax. As I left the office I commented, "Let me see if I understand you correctly. What you're actually saying is that when Michael starts cutting teeth, rushing over to the ER with him would be an overreaction ... right?"

"You got it," he said, laughing.

In time I relaxed and began to enjoy motherhood. I had no idea how important this would be once our second child was born.

With Michael we survived the chicken pox, measles, bumps and bruises. Then, we trudged through the "No homework, Mom," when he had about 10 pages to do. At age nine Michael entered the stage of entrepreneur. Deciding that he needed more money than his parents were willing to give him, he investigated several "for profit" ideas and finally latched on to selling Christmas Cards for a mail order outfit. That surprised me. He was certainly all boy. Give him a ball – baseball, basketball, football, bowling, and he was deliriously happy. It was more than difficult for me to picture him in a business venture like this.

"Who will your customers be?" I asked, with justifiable trepidation.

"All your friends in the neighborhood," he told me cheerfully. His blue eyes danced with delight at the thought of making a bunch of money and how easy it was going to be.

His first day out was a huge success. He came home flushed with pride running into the house yelling, "Look what I sold! Look what I sold! I must have about two hundred dollars here."

And indeed he did. He pulled crumpled dollar bills out of his shirt pockets, side pockets and back pockets, and with a grand flair threw them on the kitchen table.

"How about that for a good day's work?" he asked triumphantly.

The sight of the money all crumpled up like that startled me. However, I remained calm.

"Great," I said, with all the reserve I could muster. I just stopped short of pouncing on the bills and demanding who belonged to which dollar bill. They all looked so, so generic.

"Where are your orders, Michael?"

"Here they are," he said, and with loads of confidence he dumped out of his jacket pockets seemingly hundreds of minute torn, pieces of paper marked with indecipherable names, numbers and dollar figures.

I tried not to let the shock I felt register on my face. "Michael!" I almost exploded. "How in heaven's name can you tell who's who? Here, let me help you."

"NO!!" he shouted, looking at me in disbelief. "What's the matter? Don't you trust me?!"

"Of course, I trust you, Michael," I quickly reassured him, "but everyone needs help once in a while."

"Mom, I know what I'm doing. Please, let me handle the whole thing by myself. Okay?"

"Okay," I said smiling, impressed with his level of confidence.

He was as good as his word. A few weeks later, he handed me $472 and asked me to write a check for that amount. (I resisted the temptation to look at his orders). He mailed out the orders and within four weeks several cases of Christmas cards were delivered to Michael W. Morton, New Entrepreneur, Bayside, New York. I'm glad I took a back seat, because I saw a side of Michael I didn't think had matured yet. He was well organized and delivered all the boxes to the right people without a hitch. Mr. Entrepreneur continued selling Christmas cards for years (even in July!) and never lost a customer.

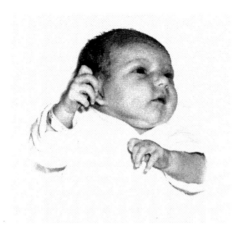

Michele - one day old.

Michael holding his new baby sister. How proud he was.

child. Happy, outgoing and bubbling with enthusiasm. Just what are your expectations of a five-year-old?" he asked.

"Well," I said with some deliberation, "it probably would be easier for me to tell you what I don't expect from a five-year-old. I don't expect her to lash out at me or strangers on the street or in stores. I don't expect her to throw herself down on the ground, screaming her head off, flailing her arms and kicking her legs while her face turns all colors, her breathing becomes labored, and who later denies, with vehemence, that it ever happened."

"Yes, yes we've been all through that," he said. "But, we have seen no signs of that sort of behavior."

"That doesn't mean it doesn't happen," I shot back. "Tell me you can't find anything! Tell me you don't have a clue, but, for heaven's sake, doctor, don't tell me you know it all, and be ready to close the door."

Dejected, I went back to Michele's room, but she wasn't there. Her two little roommates told me the nurse had thrown her out of the room because she was bad.

"What did she do?" I queried?

The little girl with sickle cell anemia replied. "The nurse said Michele was an instigator. We both got out of bed because Michele told us to, so the nurse got mad and told Michele she couldn't stay in a room with big girls any longer, and took her all the way down the hall to where the babies were."

I couldn't believe what I was hearing! Walking quickly down the hall in the indicated direction, I met Doctor Yang.

"Did you hear about Michele being moved out of her room?" I asked.

"No, what happened?" she asked with a look of surprise.

"Good question," I said and proceeded to tell her what I had been told.

23

"That's not right," Yang said.

"You bet it isn't," I told her. "She has enough to contend with as it is."

Looking over my shoulder Doctor Yang said, "Well, I'll be! Would you look at this!"

I turned around and saw Michele at the far end of the long hallway, pushing her bed by herself, along with her IV pole, which looked as if it might topple. Each time the bed hit the wall, she would straighten it and push on. It was obvious that nothing was going to keep her from doing what she wanted to do. We stayed on the sidelines where she couldn't see us, and as she passed by we heard her muttering to herself.

"I don't care what that nurse says, I'm not staying in a room with babies. It wasn't my fault that they got out of bed. I'm going back to MY room! So there!"

Her little face was set with determination and she was trying to be very brave.

I called out to her. "Michele, what are you doing?"

When she turned around and saw me, her brave stance began to falter. As the tears flowed she told me what had happened. I hugged her and wiped away her tears, assuring her that she didn't have to worry anymore. Doctor Yang also told her not to worry. "Just go back to your room," she said, "And I'll talk to the nurse."

"Are you mad at her for putting me in with babies?" Michele asked.

"Yes, I am," Doctor Yang said.

"I'm five years old!" Michele exclaimed. "That nurse is just plain stupid."

"Michele, that's not nice," I admonished.

"Well, neither is she!"

Both Yang and I struggled to maintain our composure as we walked Michele back to her room.

That afternoon Doctor Yang talked to me at length about Michele. She admitted that she didn't have all the answers and I respected her for that. Also, she never made me feel that I was crazy.

"I wish I could do more," she said. "The only other possible test is a pneumoencephalogram, but it's very invasive. And we haven't seen anything to warrant it."

"What's a pneumoencephalogram?" I asked.

"It's where fluid is removed from the brain through the spinal column. While the brain is suspended and still, pictures are taken."

I shuddered at the thought, yet I knew I was going to take the same child home again – without answers. Weeks of intensive tests had resulted in no diagnosis and no plan of action.

Upon my return the next day I was told that Michele's discharge was being arranged. Entering her room, I found her unusually withdrawn.

"Hi, Honey. How's my big girl today?"

"I'm fine," she said with no hint of her usual exuberance.

"Why the long face?" I asked.

"I'm just bored, Mommy. I'm glad I'm going home."

"I'm glad, too, Sweetheart." I said as I hugged her tightly.

Then, as we packed her things, her eyes became glazed over and she started grabbing at me. I realized she was going into one of her 'fits.' I called for help just as the doctor who had lectured me on how to handle a five-year-old walked down the hall with another doctor. I was trying to control her by holding her arms and she was screaming. I couldn't hold her any longer, so she ran into the hall, right into the arms of "Doctor Know It All."

As she lashed out at him, ripped his shirt pocket, and pulled on his stethoscope, he yelled, "Michele! Michele! Don't do that!" He tried to stop her, but to no avail. "Mrs. Morton!!" he shouted, "Do something!"

I was leaning against the wall calmly with my arms folded. "What's the matter Doctor? Don't you know how to handle a five-year-old child? You were such an expert yesterday. This is exactly the behavior I've been talking about. It comes intermittently and without warning."

Michele was now on the floor, screaming, kicking and flailing her arms. Then, as usual, the bizarre behavior suddenly subsided. She appeared dazed and confused. Looking at me somewhat apologetically, the doctor grimaced, shook his head, and walked off. A resident at the hospital, and undoubtedly well-intentioned, I hoped he had learned something from this experience. Not being 'absolutely certain' about anything in medicine would be a great start.

A pneumoencephalogram was scheduled for the following morning as Yang no longer hesitated. It was a dangerous test. My husband and I discussed it at length the night before, finally concluding that we had no other option. We held each other and prayed that we had made the right decision.

Conferring with doctors, nurses, and other medical staff personnel had by now become a way of life. Some experiences were pleasant, but many were not. I had always assumed that Nurse Ratched, domineering and obnoxious, in *One Flew Over the Cuckoo's Nest* was a bit of an exaggeration. Now, I learned she was real. I ran into a number of nurses who had an 'I'm in charge and you're nothing' attitude. I can still remember the haughty looks, the turning away as I approached to ask a question, the rolling of the eyes, and the snickering as they congregated in groups. Worst of all, I can remember being ignored. If I dared to interrupt these nurses always appeared highly insulted.

I thought about these things as I waited for the test to be done. What was taking so long? Was everything okay? Supposing everything wasn't okay? My God, I'd never forgive myself if anything happened! I tried to control my tears and choked sobs. I waited for what seemed an eternity. Finally, Doctor Yang came through the door. I immediately jumped up, my heart beating out of control.

"Mrs. Morton," Doctor Yang said, "there is definitely something wrong, but we don't yet know what it is. The test shows that the ventricles in the brain are dilated so much that there must have been times when Michele thought her head was going to explode from the pressure."

"Wouldn't that indicate a possible tumor?" I asked.

"No," Yang replied. "If there was a tumor, generally the ventricles would be dilated in that area only. In Michele's case, the ventricles are dilated symmetrically, which poses a greater problem for finding the cause."

I didn't quite know how to handle this new information. My feelings were so ambivalent. Part of me wanted to scream, 'I told you something was wrong, but no one would listen!' Yet, I felt no satisfaction in being right. A numbness began to spread through my body and I found myself thinking that knowing something was better than knowing nothing. Perhaps now we could find a treatment or cure.

"Are you all right, Mrs. Morton?" Doctor Yang asked, breaking into my thoughts.

"Yes, I'm fine," I assured her. "Just what does all this mean, Doctor?"

"Well, I believe Michele is taking temporal lobe seizures," Doctor Yang said, "which can manifest themselves in the way you

27

describe her behaviors. However, you need to know that she has no more control over this behavior than someone who is taking an epileptic seizure. The difference is, the epileptic child tends to draw sympathy and compassion from everyone around her, whereas, Michele, and YOU will probably draw only criticism. You need to be strong."

I didn't know it then, but that last remark would prove to be the under-statement of the century.

Doctor Yang placed Michele on Dilantin to control the temporal lobe seizures. The results were fantastic. We had our little girl back again and we were overjoyed! The nightmare finally over, normal family interactions became, once again, a part of everyday life. Michael was so happy also. He looked forward to taking his little sister back to the park and continuing to teach her how to play ball. He called her "shrimp" and teased her a lot, but he loved her to death. And although she tried to beat up on him, she doted on the attention he provided.

When Michael's friends called for him to go to the park to play ball, Michele jumped up and down yelling. "Let me go with you, Michael, let me go with you! Puhleeze!" It was hard to resist that little upturned face, and he rarely did. But not without a word of warning.

"Okay, you can come, but do as I tell you," he said in a no-nonsense tone. "You can play on the swings, the slide and the sand-box, and that's all. You hear?" His friends thought he was crazy, but he didn't care.

We had a great summer that year. No words could possibly express the wonderful feeling of joy that Arnie and I felt as we watched Michele run, play and swim again with her friends at the Club. One of them, Mary Ellen Monaghan, a little redhead who bubbled with an equal amount of enthusiasm loved the water as much as Michele. The two cavorted around the pool for hours, inventing games as they went along.

"Let's stand on our hands in the pool," they shouted in unison, as they jumped into the pool. Then, all we could see was four feet sticking up out of the water. When they came up for air, Michele shouted. "Mom, throw me a nickel!"

I did so and down they went again, this time for a competitive scramble to retrieve the coin. Peggy and Steve, Mary Ellen's parents, enjoyed their antics as much as we did. We were typical parents, happy and content to watch our children having fun.

As so often happens when children hit it off well, we parents became good friends, meeting frequently by the pool. Peggy, tall, with short dark hair, was very outgoing and possessed an engaging sense of humor which always lightened our conversations. Steve was quiet and introspective, but enjoyed a good laugh. With red hair and freckles he was quite fair, so couldn't take too much sun. We often played tennis together at the Club. Arnie was the only one in our little group who didn't learn to play. I kept telling him he didn't know what he was missing, but he couldn't be enticed. However, he encouraged me all the way and since I loved the game, I didn't need much encouragement.

September 23, 1971 was going to be Michele's 6th birthday. Because of all she had been through that year, we decided to give her a big birthday bash. Delighted, Michele chose to celebrate at the Club, where kids would be coming out of the woodwork. It was to be her day and everyone was invited!

Replete with a clown who tied balloons into knots and made funny looking animals for all the kids, we held the party in one of the large club rooms. The children yelled and giggled with glee as they requested different favorite animal figures. "Dogs! Cats! Lions! Tigers! Giraffes!" they screamed and, somehow, he met all their demands. The birthday girl stood beside him at the front of the room and he soon surrounded her with all different kinds of balloon animals. She smiled from ear to ear, loving all the attention. Finally, cake and ice cream were served and everyone sang 'Happy Birthday'. Michele couldn't wait to open all the presents!

"What a day, Mom!" she exclaimed excitedly on the way home. "I had so much fun! Thanks for giving me such a great party!"

As I looked at her, I felt happy and grateful. Things had worked out just fine. She would be starting first grade soon. Unbelievable. Stopping for a red light, I leaned over and gave her a hug. "I'm so happy you had such a good time on your birthday, Honey. No one deserves it more, and that's the truth."

"Thanks, Mom," she beamed. "Do you know what I'd like to do at the end of the summer?"

"No, what would you like to do?' I asked

"I want to sign up for the club's outdoor races."

"Sounds good, Michele, I'm sure you'll do well."

When race day arrived, Michele was very excited. So were all the other children. They all lined up and when the starter yelled, "On your mark, get set, go!" they took off like hares. The parents rooted for their own children as they tried to race to victory. When Michele crossed the finish line first, I scooped her up, swung her around, and both of us laughed with delight.

We raced to get to the phone, to call her dad. "Guess what?" she shouted into the phone. "I won the race. I took first place!"

When he facetiously acted as if he didn't quite believe it, she threw the phone at me. "Tell him!" she said. "Tell Daddy I won!" I could hardly contain myself as I confirmed that she had won indeed. It was a wonderful moment, which we would savor for many years to come. I had no way of knowing how much that memory would eventually mean to all of us.

Mom & Dad, dressed for a costume party with Michael.

Michele pointing to her Dad's fake mustache telling him he looks funny.

Dad, Mom & Michele
doing the Charleston.

Michele celebrating her
6th Birthday at Cresthaven.

Chapter III

Michele was enrolled at St. Kevin's, the Catholic school from which Michael had graduated. "I'm so happy to be going to the same school as Michael. It makes me feel so important," she declared, clapping her hands with pleasure.

Smiling, I said, "That's great, Michele. Now, why don't you go and try on your new uniform so we can see how it looks?"

"Okay," she said, and bounded up the stairs. Within ten minutes she returned, obviously delighted with herself. "Doesn't it look great, huh? Doesn't it?" and she paraded around the living room in full view.

Her Dad and Granny murmured complete approval while I commented "You look lovely, Sweetheart."

Then she looked over at Michael, who was taking all this in with amusement. Teasingly, he stated, "I think it looks ugly."

"It does not Michael!" she shot back. "What do you know anyway?"

"I know ugly when I see it," he responded laughing.

"Cut it out, Michael," I warned, trying to sound very stern. "Enough is enough!"

"Okay, okay, I'm only kidding Michele. You really do look great." Walking toward her, he reached out and, with one last teasing gesture, tousled her hair. As he ran upstairs and she after him, laughter ensued. I smiled. This could be the beginning of a great year.

The first day of school could not come quickly enough for Michele (or for me!). When it finally arrived, I took the day off from work to take her there. After all, this was a special occasion. Michele was ready to go two hours early (she didn't want to be late!). When I explained that the school wouldn't be open yet, she reluctantly returned to her room.

The first person we met when we arrived at the school was Sister Mary Electa, whose reputation preceded her. She always taught first grade and enjoyed working with the little ones. Since that is where the foundation for learning is laid, we considered it fortunate that Michele would be in Sister Electa's class.

"Good morning!" She cheerfully greeted us at the door. "And who do we have here?" she asked smiling and looking down at Michele.

"This is Michele Morton, Sister," I responded warmly.

"Hi Michele," the nun replied. "It's good to have you here."

I gently nudged Michele who smiled shyly and said, "Hello, Sister."

Loosening Michele's grasp, I gave her a hug and said, "I'll see you later, Sweetheart."

At that point Sister Electa firmly took charge and led Michele into the classroom. Turning to me, she nodded and smiled, then said in a soft whisper, "She'll be fine, Mrs. Morton. She'll be fine."

I shook her hand. "Thank you, Sister. Thank you very much."

Sister Electa was extremely perceptive. She knew intuitively, without knowing any of the circumstances, that the first day of school was harder for Mom!

Michele was bubbling with excitement when she came

home that day. "Sister Electa is so nice," she told me. "We did lots of things in class. We even played some games. Oh, and I have some homework that I want to get done right away."

Then she sat down at the kitchen table and didn't move until she had it finished. I thought I was in Fantasy Land. I was used to her brother trying to convince me that homework was against the law! What a difference!

Michele's enthusiasm for school continued through first grade and she did very well.

Reading was one of her favorite subjects and she enjoyed her trips to the library, especially after obtaining her own library card. We were alike in that way. As a child I had driven my mother crazy because reading interfered with my chores. While she placed a lot of value on reading she firmly reminded me, "Not to the exclusion of everything else! First things first!"

Michele didn't like that teachers sometimes spelled her first name with a double "L." Whenever it happened she would ask for an immediate correction, to the amusement of the school staff.

When school ended, we filled summer with fun and excitement at Cresthaven. The membership never seemed to change and it was a lot of fun seeing everyone again and catching up on life. Filled with excitement, the children acted like long lost buddies! With everything going so well for Michele, we had almost totally forgotten about her problem. The medicine was working and everything seemed fine.

The new school year started with the same excitement as the previous year. Michele's second grade teacher was Pat Boullianne. Pat and I were old friends, having been involved in many of the same clubs in the parish. Seeing me at school one day, she asked if we could talk.

"Sure," I said. "Is it about Michele?"

"Yes. I'm really worried about her."

"Why? What's the problem?" I asked.

"Her learning ability has dropped drastically and for no apparent reason. She has difficulty understanding the material and can't follow directions well. It has me stymied."

"Although I had noticed a change myself, Pat, I'd assumed it was just a phase that Michele was going through. Do you have any suggestions?" I asked.

"Well, I recently read an article about learning disabilities, something I have no first-hand experience with. The article was well-written and suggested certain tests. What do you think about that?"

"I think that would be a great idea, Pat. I'll certainly have Michele checked out."

Another problem! Who needed it? I was busy visiting my husband in the hospital after he was admitted with severe stomach pains. A couple of days later, my mother collapsed with a heart attack and was also hospitalized. Meanwhile Michael, reacting to everything around him, decided he hated school and would spend life giving his mother a hard time. He was a typical teenager who thought he was 'all-knowing.' Of course, that meant Mom didn't know anything anymore!

I realized that this behavior was Michael's way of attempting to assert his independence. Michele's behavior, however, was not so easily explained. I knew that, eventually, some action would have to be taken.

In the meantime, something very important was taking place at school. The children were preparing for their First Holy Communion. But before they could make their Holy Communion they had to master certain prayers. Michele was determined to keep up with her classmates. She studied incessantly until she had memorized them all including the most difficult Act of Contrition (the long form). Her determination paid off and she passed the test with ease. Now all we had to do was buy the perfect outfit, and she knew exactly which one she wanted.

"I saw it in a store up on Bell Boulevard," she said, smiling broadly.

"I bet you did," I laughed. "I can tell from that impish grin that the dress you have in mind is not run-of-the-mill."

"Right on," she retorted, her eyes dancing with glee.

"But, guess what Michele, dear. I had something else in mind first."

"Like what?" she asked incredulously.

"Like checking some department stores to see what they have."

"Oh, no!" she said, shocked at the very idea. "Mom, this dress is beautiful. I know you'll love it. Can we go to Bell Boulevard, please, please, please?"

I looked at her little upturned face, head to side, smiling with eyes pleading, and I thought, 'Why not? After all, it IS her day.' "Okay," I said with resignation.

"Yippee!" she yelled, and hurried me out the door before I could change my mind.

Bell Boulevard of Bayside was a popular strip of small local stores. Michele sprinted ahead of me, stopping at the children's store. Pointing to the dress in the window, she excitedly exclaimed, "There it is, Mom!"

I looked with admiration. I could see why she was so excited. The dress was made of a gorgeous white satin layered in exquisite detail with delicate lace. The head gear was gathered at the top with white satin ribbon and pearl diamond-shaped clips designed to hug the top of the head. The veil fell down over the shoulders with edging that matched the lace on the dress. The problem was, the price was also exquisite. I was about to tell Michele that this dress was out of the question, but when I looked at her little face filled with such excitement I melted. I agreed to let her try it on. 'Maybe it won't fit,' I thought. No such luck. She was transformed into a little princess.

The dress fit her to a 'T' and the veil set off her long, sleek, dark brown hair cascading past her shoulders. Her large blue-gray eyes danced with merriment.

"Can I get it? Can I get it?" she pleaded.

I had no more arguments to offer. Michele got her dress!

On the day of the ceremony, Father Martin Tully, Pastor of Our Lady of the Blessed Sacrament Church, (where I did some part-time work) surprised us all and showed up on the altar. As the other children walked up in solemn and silent procession, they each received their First Communion from the pastor of St. Kevin's. When it was Michele's turn, Father Tully walked down, took the Host, and as soon as he said 'Body of Christ,' Michele looked up and exclaimed, "Father Tully! What are you doing here?!"

So much for the solemnity of the occasion! After receiving Communion, she jauntily marched back to her seat, grinning from ear to ear. She could hardly contain herself. After all, her favorite priest had shown up just to give her her First Holy Communion! Father Boccio, her other good friend from the same parish, whom she dearly loved, also attended. She was so happy!

After the Holy Communion celebration, I arranged to have Michele tested. This was done several weeks later. Her learning had not improved.

Checking around, I learned that the New York Child Development Center had a good reputation for doing comprehensive evaluations on children with learning problems. Although the cost was high, I made the appointment. It was more than important for us to know what was going on with Michele. Their program included all-day sessions for a period of two days, after which we waited anxiously for the results.

A few days later, I got the call. "Mrs. Morton, this is the Child Development Center. Michele's test results are complete and we need to make an appointment for you to come in. How about tomorrow morning at 10:30?"

"That'll be fine" I said. I immediately called Arnie.

"Do you need me to go with you?" he asked.

"No, you're working," I said. "I'll go by myself. I should be home before Michele gets home from school."

The next morning, when I arrived at the center, I was ushered into a room where a man rose to greet me. "Good morning, Mrs. Morton," he said. "I'm Mike Jelson and this is Mary Ward." He gestured toward the woman sitting by the desk. Shaking hands with each of them I sat down.

Smiling, Mr. Jelson began. "Michele is a very interesting young lady. She is a very smart little girl, yet the tests show she is learning disabled across the board."

"Across the board? " I was astonished.

"For some reason," Jelson continued, "Michele is having great difficulty in processing the information received. We can't seem to figure out why."

Now we were back on familiar ground. "Don't feel bad," I said. "No one ever seems able to figure anything out where Michele is concerned."

"Mrs. Morton," Mary Ward interjected forcefully, "It is very important that everyone working with Michele not treat her as though she were retarded, because she is not. If she's treated that way in a learning environment, she'll become totally frustrated."

"I'm sure," I said with a thoughtful nod of my head. "So, where do we go from here?"

"Well, the center has put together a teaching method for use both at home and school. It should work very well. For example, she has difficulty understanding directions. Instead of saying, 'Michele, get me a glass,' your directions will need to be more specific. Something more effective would be, 'Michele, go into the kitchen, open the second door of the closet on the left side, first shelf, and get me a glass.' She will be much more responsive to this approach."

"That sounds encouraging," I said, promising to follow their instructions. I left feeling somewhat better about things.

Realizing that this was a special education approach to learning, I was worried that the Catholic school might not be able to deal with it. I was right.

When I spoke with the principal, Sister Suzanne, she said, "Unfortunately, as much as we'd like to keep Michele, special education is not part of our teaching program." Placing her hand on my arm she added, "I'm sorry, Mrs. Morton, I really am."

"But St. Kevin's is so much a part of our lives!" I protested. "And you know Michele will be upset if we have to take her out. Oh, Sister, I just don't want to do it!"

"My hands are tied." Sister Suzanne said. "If you can figure out a way to make it happen, that would really be wonderful."

"Well, I'm certainly going to try." I slowly got up to leave.

They knew me well at the parish for I had been active for years, even before our son entered first grade. Over the years, I'd served on the Parish Council, chaired the children's tennis and bowling programs, and held the positions of President of the St. Kevin's Bowling League, and President of the Rosary Society. Additionally, Arnie had coached the children's baseball and basketball leagues. Now that Michele didn't quite fit into the 'norm,' she would have to leave. It made no sense to me.

The pastor, Father Powell, was also very sympathetic when I met with him. "You know I'd love to help you," he said, "but the school just isn't equipped to deal with that kind of challenge."

"Then get equipped," I told him.

He slowly shook his head and said, "It's not that easy, Kathleen."

"I didn't say it would be easy, Father, but it can be done. Do you think what we've been dealing with is easy? Not on your life!"

"No, I know it hasn't been easy, Kathleen. I'm sure it has been rough going. But I'm not in a position to change anything. If you can convince the Superintendent of Schools for the Catholic Diocese, then maybe, just maybe, some changes can be made."

"Okay," I said, "I'm game."

So off I went to see the Superintendent of Schools. If I wasn't successful on this level, my next step would be the Bishop.

I argued my point with the Superintendent, telling him, in addition to all the other reasons, that a special education approach would help children other than Michele. It was time for the Church to recognized this.

Having listened intently, he suddenly said, "I agree with you. You make some very valid points. I'll arrange for a special education teacher to be brought in for the start of the third grade to work with Michele and any other children at St. Kevin's who may have learning disabilities. You'll be contacted over the summer for a meeting with the new teacher before school starts in September."

"Thank you so much, Monsignor," I replied exuberantly. "I can assure you that you have made one little girl very, very happy!"

I had talked to Michele briefly about the possibility of

transferring to another school next year and she hadn't liked the idea. I couldn't wait for her to get home to break the good news. She was her usual happy self when she came running into the house.

"Guess what?" I asked, as soon as she'd thrown her book bag on the floor.

"What?"

"You're going to be able to stay at St. Kevin's. A new teacher will be brought in and we'll meet with her over the summer."

"Oh, that's great, Mom!" Giving me a hug, she asked if she could go over to Eileen's house to tell her.

"What about your homework?"

"I don't have any today! Can I go? Please, Mom."

"Oh, alright, Honey, go ahead. But, please be back in an hour." Before I could finish, she was out the door.

'Another milestone crossed,' I thought. Happy with the outcome, we made it the topic of conversation at the dinner table that night. We all listened attentively to what Michele had to say, applauding after her declaration about staying in St. Kevin's.

The anticipated phone call from the new teacher came in August. "Is this Mrs. Morton?" she inquired.

"Yes, it is."

"Hi, I'm Sister Jan Marie, the new Special Education teacher for Michele."

"Hello, Sister. I'm delighted you're here."

"So am I. I'd like very much to meet Michele, if that could be arranged."

"Of course. Whenever you say. She's looking forward to meeting you." We arranged to meet the next day at the school.

The next morning, as we prepared to leave, Michele asked if Sister Jan Marie sounded nice.

"Yes, very nice," I said. "Why?"

"I'm nervous about meeting her. I mean, suppose she doesn't like me?"

"What? Not like you? You've got to be kidding." Laughing, I held her face in the cup of my hands.

"Oh, don't be funny, Mommy," she said, pushing my hand away. "You know what I mean."

After a mere five minutes with Sister Jan Marie, Michele began to relax. Her new teacher was a big hit! The two got along famously.

"Yippee!" Michele yelled as she got into the car. "You were right, Mom, Sister Jan Marie is nice. When does school start again?" she asked.

"Oh, no, you're not going to bug me every day about that now, are you?"

"No, I'm not," she swiftly responded. "I'm just curious, that's all."

I smiled, and said softly. "It will start in about three weeks, Honey. In the meantime, let's enjoy the rest of the summer while waiting for that day. Okay 'little girl'?"

"Stop it," she said, laughing. "You know I'm not a little girl any more."

The new approach to education seemed to help Michele tremendously, as it did the several other children who qualified. However, because she wasn't quite sure what was happening to her, Michele needed constant reassurance that we could work through this. I bought all different kinds of educational materials and worked with her at home and at her own pace. We made a kind of a game out of it, which helped. For recreation, Michele rode her bike with her friends and went bowling. Her interest in bowling developed out of my involvement with the children's bowling league, held on Saturdays. Michele always came along to help out. It made her feel important and familiarized her with the game.

Michael had learned to bowl in the same league and by the time he graduated from St. Kevin's he was a very good bowler. Michele knew this. Each Saturday after the league we worked on her bowling. When she finally started knocking down some pins, she was hooked! And when she got her first strike, she thought she was ready for the PRO leagues! Nothing could dampen that indomitable spirit of hers.

"I got a strike at bowling today," she boasted to her brother at dinner time. "Soon I'll be as good as you."

"Never happen," he jokingly retorted.

"It will, too," she said with vehemence. "You watch!" and to punctuate her fervor she screwed up her little freckled nose and jutted out her chin for emphasis ... "YOU WATCH!!" she repeated with finality.

Arnie and I looked at each other, feeling good about this moment of normalcy. As a matter of fact, we felt we had come a long way from the 'crisis' situations that had intruded into our lives.

Both Michael and Michele quickly settled into the routine of school, homework and play. Michele continued to be happy with her class and her teacher. Sister Jan Marie seemed to be very effective in reaching all of the children with the programs she introduced. Fear and frustration were removed, primarily because of this individual approach to learning. The excitement of the children was obvious as they began to comprehend what they were doing.

Each day after school Michele sailed through the door talking non-stop about her daily activities. Because my life had become somewhat humdrum, I was always eager for her to arrive.

Then, one day, she walked into the kitchen without a word,

looking despondent.

"What's wrong, Michele?" I asked with immediate concern.

"Nothing," was her curt reply.

When I pressed her for a better explanation, she told me to leave her alone. Mystified by her sullenness, I walked into the living room where Michael was doing his homework.

"What's wrong with her?" he asked.

"I don't know," I told him. "She won't talk. But, I'm sure she'll eventually come around." The silence that followed was disturbing. It was finally broken by Michael calling out to Michele to tell him the time.

"NO!" she yelled, "I'm not giving you the time."

By now I had had enough, and ordered Michele to tell her brother the time. The clock was located in the kitchen on one of the upper shelves.

"I CAN'T!" she screamed, with a crack in her voice. And with that I heard her dragging the kitchen chair along the floor.

"What do you mean, you can't?" I asked, as I ran into the kitchen. I found her standing on the chair looking up at the clock and sobbing.

"I can't see! she said with an anguished cry. Then, bowing her head, she repeated, "I can't see, I can't see."

As I lifted her off the chair, I could feel her entire body trembling. "Okay, Sweetheart, you'll be all right," I said in a soothing voice, while tenderly kissing her tears away. I held her until her sobs subsided. Now Michael also tried to console her. We were both trying to make her feel better when we were startled by the ringing of the phone. When I picked it up, it was one of Michele's teachers reporting that Michele hadn't been able to see the board that day. Within minutes the phone rang again and another teacher reported the same thing. After the third call, I finally took the phone off the hook.

"Michele, Honey, come here," I said as I put my arms around her. "This doesn't make any sense. I know you're upset, and I don't blame you, but we need to try and understand what is happening."

I called Arnie and he said he'd leave the office right away. I then called a friend who gave me the name of an ophthalmologist. But the ophthalmologist couldn't see her for two months. I tried to explain that this was an emergency. When the doctor finally came on the phone, he listened to what I had to say.

"Severe vision loss just doesn't happen that way." he told me. "It's probably something that can be corrected with glasses. I'll make arrangements to see her in a few weeks."

"A few weeks! That's not good enough, doctor " I said. "I believe this is a true emergency." He was not convinced.

As I hung up the phone, Arnie walked in the door. The look we exchanged with each other said loud and clear, 'WHAT NOW?'

"Did you hear what has happened to me, Daddy?"

"Yes, Mom told me, Sweetheart." Picking her up in his arms, he carried her into the living room. We sat in silence for a few minutes, then all started talking at once. There were questions, hundreds of questions to which no one had any answers. But we asked them anyway. How could this happen? Was this really an emergency? Could it be hysterical blindness? Why so suddenly? Was this related to what happened in the past?

I suddenly remembered the Manhattan Eye and Ear Hospital, an extremely busy center where it usually took months to get an appointment. I called them and told the receptionist my name, adding that I believed I had an emergency situation with my daughter. I asked to speak to the Chief of Ophthalmology. To my surprise, the doctor came on the phone.

"Doctor," I said, "Thank you for taking my call." Then, taking a deep breath, I plunged right in. "I'm not sure what I'm dealing with here, but it has all the earmarks of something truly devastating." There was a catch in my voice and I knew I was talking too fast.

"Slow down – slow down," the doctor finally said. "Now, tell me what happened with your daughter."

"That's just it. I don't know what happened! She just came home from school and said she couldn't see."

"Just like that? No pain? No redness? No inflammation in the eyes?"

"No, none."

"What's your daughter's name, Mrs. Morton, and how old is she?"

"Her name is Michele, and she's eight years old."

"Has Michele had any other medical problems in the recent past?" the doctor asked then.

"Yes. She's been diagnosed with temporal lobe seizures. She takes Dilantin, which has brought it under control."

The voice on the other end of the line suddenly became more serious. "Mrs. Morton, I think you should bring Michele into the hospital right away. Explain at the desk that it's an emergency.

I hung up the phone, took several rapid breaths and sat down on the kitchen chair. Arnie quickly came into the kitchen and asked what the doctor had said. I told him.

"We're to bring her into the hospital right away as an emergency case."

"Did he say what he thought it might be?"

"No, he can't do that until he sees her."

"Where are the kids?"

"Michele is upstairs and Michael is outside playing with his friends."

"I'll take her to the hospital while you stay home with Michael. You guys can go ahead and eat."

At the hospital, she was seen right away. For the next three days she returned for more intensive tests, consultations and discussions about her background. No information was to be given to us until the end of the three days when a meeting with the doctors was scheduled. The meeting was led by a specialist who had been brought in to examine Michele. As luck would have it, his particular area of expertise was Neuro-Ophthalmology!

I was gripped by an icy feeling at the thought that neurology was involved. There was a connection to the nightmare we thought was behind us. The specialist related his findings in a solemn and somewhat formal tone.

"What we have here is a little girl..........."

"Big girl," interrupted Michele.

"Okay," the doctor said patiently. "What we have here is a big girl, eight years of age..."

"Eight and a half," Michele quickly interjected.

While the specialist tried to control his annoyance at these interruptions, the other doctors laughed. And so did I. It added some much-needed levity to an otherwise grave situation. Eventually, even the Neuro-Ophthalmologist sported a hint of a smile on his face. The meeting continued without incident.

"What we have here is a big girl, eight and one half years of age (Michele smiled nodding her head in agreement) reporting sudden severe vision loss. The tests show that the eyes themselves are normal, but there is no doubt that severe vision loss exists, which is probably coming from the brain. At present, the etiology is unknown."

"Mrs. Morton," he stated, "this is very serious and I strongly recommend that Michele be transferred to New York Hospital, Cornell Medical Center, for a neurological workup as an in-patient."

So, there it was! The problem was real. And serious. There would be no simple solution. What in heaven's name were we facing here? My heart was heavy, but I couldn't let Michele know. I mustn't lose hope.

"When should she be admitted, doctor?" I asked.

"Right now," he said. "Arrangements can be made from here."

I nodded my head almost absent-mindedly. "Give us a couple of hours, doctor. I'd like to take her to lunch first."

Michele normally enjoyed eating out. She was much like her mother in that way! But the doctor's report had dampened her spirits. She didn't act hungry and toyed with her food.

"What's the matter, Honey, aren't you hungry?" I asked, just to have something to say. Even small talk didn't come easy.

"I'm scared Mommy. And I don't want to go to the hospital," she said. "I want to go home."

"I'm sure you won't be in the hospital very long," I told her. "And I'll stay there with you." This seemed to reassure her. She smiled and began to eat her lunch.

More history was taken at the new hospital, followed by a number of doctor consultations and a variety of tests. But these doctors were just as perplexed as all the others. The results just didn't fit into the neurological diseases with which they were familiar.

"What do we do now?" I asked the neurologist in charge.

"Well, the immediate problem is the vision loss. With your permission, we'd like to start aggressive cortisone therapy, that should last about a week."

"What would it do?"

"Sometimes it can reverse the trend."

"You mean restore Michele's vision?" I asked excitedly.

"Perhaps. The therapy has been effective in some instances. But, remember, we don't yet know what's wrong with Michele, so we don't know if the response will be the same."

I gave them the go-ahead and called Arnie at work. For the first time we felt there was hope. It put a spring in my step as I walked back to Michele's room. She had achieved a level of comfort and even suggested that I go home.

"Are you sure?" I asked.

"Yeah, I'm sure, Mom. I'll be okay. They're very nice here."

"Okay, Honey," I said, pleased with her comfort level. "The staff will start an IV with a medicine that might help you. Every two or three hours they'll take you to the Ophthalmology Unit so a doctor can check your vision."

"Okay," she said, with a casual shrug of her shoulders.

I gave her a hug and told her what a good girl she was.

The Cortisone therapy kept our hopes high. We prayed that the trend would reverse itself. Each day I arrived at the hospital in high spirits. On the third day, Michele was in the Ophthalmology Unit when I arrived. The chief of ophthalmology was examining her. I leaned against the wall inside the unit waiting for the examination to be completed. Suddenly, I heard the doctor raise his voice and shout.

"This is ridiculous! Where is the mother of this child? Where is the mother of this child?"

"I'm Michele's mom," I said as I quickly walked toward him, my stomach doing somersaults "What's wrong?"

"We can't do anything for her here. I'm stopping the therapy."

"WHAT?!" I exclaimed in disbelief. "WHY??"

"Because it's not working, that's why," he said in anger and frustration. "There's no hope of saving her vision."

"But it's only been three days. We still have four more to go. Please Doctor," I said, unable to keep the tears from spilling out. "Give her a chance. Let her have the benefit of the doubt."

He brushed me off like a fly on his shirt sleeve, turned on his heel and walked away. I couldn't believe it! Hopes dashed to the ground in just a matter of seconds. I leaned against the wall and sobbed. The nurse had taken Michele back to her room without her seeing me.

I stopped at the neurologist's office, where he saw me immediately. Aware of what had happened, he apologized.

"The specialist has a very good reputation and is well respected in his field," he said by way of explanation.

"And that excuses his behavior?!" I almost exploded. "He's an insensitive clod! That's what he is. With something so serious, how could he act that way? Does he think parents are made of stone?" I ranted angrily, pacing back and forth. The pent-up feelings seemed too much for me. I wanted to SCREAM!

"Mrs. Morton, I don't blame you for being upset and angry. But, to be honest with you, the therapy isn't showing any signs of working. Since cortisone is a very potent drug, we could actually hurt Michele if we were to continue with it. In other words, the benefits don't outweigh the risks, and there is some evidence her vision is actually getting worse."

"*Now* you tell me! If I had known the therapy would end in a few days, if no change was noted, it wouldn't have been such a shock. Here we were, thinking there was still a chance. Someone should have explained all this to me before the therapy began. Would that have been too much to ask?" I demanded.

"No, it wouldn't have been, and we were remiss, I'm sorry."

"No one has even told me what level of vision she presently has."

He looked at me with some deliberation and said, "Mrs. Morton, there's no easy way to say this. Michele is legally blind now, and we can't correct her vision since the loss is coming from the brain."

"Legally BLIND! My God!" I shook my head in disbelief. I sat down staring into space, immobilized. The doctor informed me that Michele would be in the hospital for a few more days while they ran more tests. In the meantime Social Services would get involved to help me with information regarding organizations for the blind. I didn't say anything to Michele except that the therapy was being stopped and more tests would be run.

"Any more IV's?"

"No, Honey, no more IV's."

"Good," she said emphatically.

Arnie stopped by the hospital after work and Michele was delighted to see him. I didn't tell him the news until we went out to dinner on our way home. He was as devastated as I was.

"Good Lord," he said. "What do we do now??"

"I don't know," I said dejectedly. "They're having Social Services help me with organizations for the blind. Isn't this unreal?"

Arnie seemed stunned. He did his best to absorb the things I was telling him.

We both sat in the restaurant with our own thoughts, trying to unravel something that couldn't be unraveled. The nightmare was beginning again. It was like a hurricane, hitting us when we least expected it, knocking us over with unexpected twists and turns. Common sense didn't exist and predictions were out of the question. The only thing we knew with great clarity was how formidable this neurological disease actually was. And, since the etiology was still unknown, no prevention or cure was available, rendering us vulnerable every step of the way.

"When Michele realizes the vision loss is not reversible she's going to be very angry, I said, finally breaking the silence between us. "And Michael. He'll never believe this. You know how crazy he is about her, and how protective. It's this feeling of helplessness that's so difficult to cope with."

"You can say that again," he responded with fervor. "What about school? Will she stay in St. Kevin's?"

"No, I don't think so. She'll need more specialized education than they'll be able to provide. I know she won't be happy with that either. I'll have to wait until tomorrow to find out from Social Services what my next move will be. But I will call the principal at St. Kevin's and let her know the latest developments. The staff there are all very kind and caring. I'm sure they'll be very helpful during this difficult time."

The next day I went to Social Services at the hospital as the doctor had suggested. I still felt somewhat numb and very emotional. There was no one in the reception area when I entered. 'Good,' I thought. 'No long lines.' However, whatever level of contentment I felt was short-lived. No one greeted me, although they saw me standing there waiting. They were too busy bickering amongst themselves. Voices grew louder as they moved in and out of their offices. I couldn't believe it! This was the place that was supposed to help me, embroiled in personal pettiness!

After about fifteen minutes of waiting, I finally walked to their office. "Excuse me. My young daughter has just lost her vision and I am emotionally distraught. The doctor sent me here to get help. What a joke! You apparently need more help than I do. Without question, you're the most unprofessional people I've ever met." I looked at each one of them with disgust, turned, and walked

53

purposefully out the door.

"Wait!" a young woman interrupted, jumping up. Moving toward me, she apologized profusely. The other two, just as contrite, stared at the floor. "Please. Let me help you," the first woman said motioning me to come back. Turning around, I looked at her, and saw that she was sincere. I followed her to her office.

After I'd introduced myself, I provided background history on Michele. This woman conveyed empathy and compassion. I felt much better. Laden down with their overwhelming donation of reading material, I got up to go.

"I'll contact the Lighthouse for the Blind, Mrs. Morton, and tell them about Michele, and they'll contact you directly. Also, you should contact the public school as soon as possible, so Michele can be placed in a program for blind children. And again, Mrs. Morton, please accept our sincere apologies for such a scene. It's not typical behavior for us."

"No, I'm sure," I said warmly, extending my hand. "You ultimately handled everything extremely well, and I really appreciate that. As far as I'm concerned, none of the rest of it ever happened."

"Thank you so much," she said with a smile, "And remember, if you need anything, anything at all, you know where to come." I smiled and left the office, feeling that something had finally been accomplished. The representative from the Lighthouse for the Blind also proved quite helpful. Her first question was "Do you have a son?"

Quizzically, I replied, "Yes. Why do you ask?"

"Because this is the third call I've made to you. The first two times I left messages with him."

"Oh, no! He never told me."

"That's what I figured," she said. "Denial isn't unusual in

situations of this kind. He's hurting too." She proceeded to give me names of different programs for blind children and encouraged me to call for assistance at any time.

I chose not to discuss the issue with Michael just then. He had always been very good about taking messages and the fact that he had ignored these two from the Lighthouse suggested that he was hoping that the problem would just go away. Working with the Lighthouse was just too much reality for him to handle.

I forced myself to concentrate on getting Michele into the right educational program. Contacting the public school's administrative office, I made an appointment to discuss our situation. I figured it would take a few weeks to affect a transfer. Meanwhile, I assumed, she would stay at St. Kevin's.

When I arrived I was ushered into a waiting area, but it only took ten minutes for them to call me. I went into the office and was introduced to a Miss Carling.

"Sit down," she commanded.

I obliged, trying not to be turned off by her curtness. Officious in her approach, she asked what she could do for me.

I told her about Michele's sudden blindness and how I needed a special educational program for her now. She looked at me with a bewildered expression.

"Don't you realize the child has to be evaluated first?" she asked, as if I were being ridiculous.

"Yes, of course, I realize that. I can bring her in any time, just name the day."

"Well, obviously, you don't understand the process."

"Then, why don't you fill me in," I said with mounting exasperation. "I've just been catapulted into the world of the handicapped and I admit I don't yet know my way around. What I do know is that Michele requires a program that meets her needs. And she needs it right away. So, how do I go about getting that for her? Am I in the wrong place?"

"No, you're in the right place," she responded with a slight chuckle.

"Did I say something funny?" I asked.

"Mrs. Morton, placing Michele is not that simple. She'll have to be put on a waiting list."

"A waiting list," I said. "What kind of waiting list?"

"For newly-diagnosed children. It will probably be a year or more before we can finally place her."

I looked at her in disbelief. "OVER A YEAR??.....NO WAY! I want her evaluated and placed within a few weeks."

"It can't be done, Mrs. Morton. Possibly within a year, but that's the best we can do."

"We'll see about that." I got up to leave, desperately trying to maintain my composure. As I reached the door, I turned "You know, Miss Carling, my child is legally blind now, and there's nothing I can do about that. But there is _definitely_ something I can do about appropriate and timely education. Michele may have lost her vision a few weeks ago, but she has not lost her citizenship."

"I'm sorry," Miss Carling said. "That's just the way the system works."

"Then, the system's got to be changed." And with that I walked out the door.

Although, I didn't need another fight on my hands, I now knew I would have to take on the New York City Board of Education.

Meanwhile, Michele reacted poorly to her vision loss. She resisted both activity and outings, St. Kevin's included. She behaved as totally helpless, claiming repeatedly that she could not do anything for herself. I was determined to train her to be more independent, but she sabotaged my efforts at every turn. Even so, I continued to encourage her to act for herself. Whenever she insisted she couldn't do it, I showed her how. One day, she decided she didn't want to go to school because she couldn't put on her uniform. I patiently explained again and then left her alone. A while later, she stomped down the stairs shouting, "See! I told you I couldn't put this on!" As I looked up, I observed her arms where her head belonged and her head through one of the arm holes almost choking her.

I stifled a laugh, because it actually looked comical and because I was stressed. But before I could get to her she ripped the uniform all the way down the front and pulled it off.

"THERE!" she said, dropping it to the floor. "Now I _can't_ go to school."

"Oh yes you can," I said. "And you're going."

"No! I can't get in without a uniform," she replied almost gleefully. "I'll get in big trouble."

"Then I'll call the principal," I told her. Reaching Sister Suzanne, I explained the situation. We both laughed at Michele's determination to have her own way.

"Just bring her in," Sister Suzanne said. "Tell her I said it's okay for her to wear regular clothes. Also, make sure she knows it's okay to be late. Otherwise, she'll use that as another excuse."

"I know," I said. "Poor kid, she's really struggling."

When I hung up Michele asked me what Sister Suzanne had said.

"She said you could wear regular clothes and you won't get in trouble."

"Not even if I'm late?"

"She said that would be all right, too."

"I can't believe this!" Michele argued and began chanting,

"You can't be late, you must wear your uniform. You can't be late, you must wear your uniform ... That's all you ever hear in school, and now it doesn't matter? Why don't they make up their minds?!" she said. Throwing up her hands in disgust, she stomped up the stairs.

Michele's First Holy Communion portrait.

Chapter IV

No one I knew could believe what I told them about the educational process for the handicapped. Had this happened in the non-handicapped world, parents would have been up in arms. I was learning quickly that the same rules didn't apply to the handicapped child. The appalling thing was that no one in the 'system' saw this as a problem. My reactions merely seemed to convinced them that there was something wrong with me! Why couldn't I just accept the fact that Michele would be in the system and that they would eventually reach her name on the waiting list? So desensitized to the immediate educational needs of the newly-diagnosed handicapped child, no amount of persuasive arguments could make a dent in their armor.

In the end, I did what every red-blooded American parent would do in the face of stalemate. I called in the troops – people in power who knew me due to my years of involvement in community services and politics. Within a couple of weeks, I got a call from the local education agency telling me to bring Michele in for her evaluation.

"What's wrong with this picture?" I asked both myself and Arnie. Why should parents have to know someone in order to get what the child rightfully deserves in the first place? The process should be automatic. Equal treatment for all and all that good stuff. Yeah, right! But this is altruistic thinking, foreign to a city bureaucracy." I decided to continue my fight with the local education agency. My intention was to change the 'system', much to the chagrin of the bureaucrats with whom I had to deal.

At one point one indignant bureaucrat demanded, "What's wrong with you, Mrs. Morton? You got what you wanted for Michele."

"What I wanted for Michele is something she should have received automatically," I retorted, with equivalent indignation. "I can't seem to get that point across. Michele is not the issue here. The issue is discrimination being leveled at the newly-diagnosed handicapped child. Such children must wait interminable lengths of time for placement, which is in violation of their rights. Other children have no wait at all. Parents can move into a neighborhood and get their child registered. Bingo! Just like that," I said, snapping my fingers for emphasis. "They're placed immediately. Somehow, the handicapped child seems to immobilize the **entire** system! This has to change."

Over the course of the next few months, I set about doing exactly that. I plied every State Education officials with letters, and follow-up phone calls. I lobbied political figures and legislators. I attempted an appointment with the State Education Commissioner, but was denied access to him. However, as the battle continued, I sensed a softening of the State's position each time I spoke to another official.

One morning, the phone rang "Is this Mrs. Morton?" the voice asked.

"Yes it is," I replied.

"This is the commissioner's office from Albany. I'm calling to tell you that your complaint has been reviewed. The commissioner agrees that a change in the process should take place."

"Wonderful!" I responded enthusiastically.

"Effective immediately," he continued, "each child current-

60

ly on the waiting list must be evaluated as soon as possible. Every newly-diagnosed child after that will be evaluated and placed within three weeks."

"That's great. Thank you so very much!" I responded excitedly. Hanging up the phone, I could only wonder about this sudden unexpected turn of events.

Michele was evaluated and immediately placed in a public school that had a class for the visually impaired. She was not a happy camper.

"I don't want to go to that stupid school," she exclaimed vehemently. Anything Michele didn't agree with was considered stupid in her estimation. "I want to stay at St. Kevin's."

"I thought you didn't like St. Kevin's anymore," I said.

"Is that why I'm being changed?" she immediately wanted to know.

"No, Honey, it isn't. It's because the public school can provide a special class for children with vision loss. They have a special program to better meet your needs."

"But I'll miss my friends" she said with a glum look.

"I know you will, Michele," I said softly, "and I also know that friends are very important. But you'll make new friends. I'm certain of it. Just wait and see." Putting my arms around her, I drew her close, and rocked her from side to side for a few minutes. "Will you at least give it a try?" I asked.

"Oh, I guess so," she said resignedly.

Upstairs in her room, she listened to her favorite recording, "The Wizard of Oz." She knew it by heart. I rightly envisioned her holding her stuffed dog, Toto, in her arms, becoming lost in the story.

Although there was a public school only a block away, Michele had to attend one outside of our local area. Every public school, we learned, did not have staff specialized to teach blind children.

I conferred with both administrators of her new school and her teacher. Although my plan had been to drive Michele, the staff insisted she take the bus the first day. I finally agreed when they promised to call me when she arrived. This was not going to be an easy day for Michele – new teacher, new bus, new area, new school – all within her new blind world. Not an easy day for anyone, much less a child. It made me uneasy. Amazingly, she survived!

As the days progressed, Michele continued to react to her severe vision loss. The unfamiliar surroundings only aggravated the situation, but the teacher was very patient. To help ease Michele's anguish, I was often present in class. Some of her frustrations, I learned, were legitimate. One day she came home complaining that she was not allowed to participate in gym class.

"What do you mean, you're not allowed to participate, Michele?"

"I'm NOT," she exclaimed indignantly.

"What do you do?"

"I sit on the side of the room doing nothing until the bell rings," she said, with her hands on her hips. "Some school!" she declared, showing her frustration.

"I'll talk to the teacher in the morning," I promised.

"Well, while you're at it," Michele said, "tell her to let me go to the bathroom by myself. She always sends someone with me. I hate that."

I had a feeling that this was not going to be one of our better years.

The next morning I informed the teacher of Michele's concerns. While she didn't deny these things occurred, she claimed for good reason. If Michele was allowed to participate in gym class she might get hurt.

"And you think isolating her is the answer?" I asked. "I think you'll have to be a bit more creative than that."

"I agree. A lot more has to be done with Michele's program, Mrs. Morton, but she does present quite a challenge for us."

She said this without any defensiveness. I had always respected this teacher. She was sharp, and apparently tried her utmost to do what was best. She demonstrated understanding and compassion. Though she knew that not allowing Michele to participate in gym was wrong, (and that WAS changed) she noted other concerns. "Michele complained bitterly in school about her eyes hurting," the teacher commented. "It's clearly impossible for me to ascertain whether this discomfort is organic in origin or psychologically based. However, it's my feeling that the distress is 'real' regardless of the cause."

She was right! There was no question. Michele reacted severely to the vision loss and all the other changes forced upon her young life. She tried desperately to keep up with her friends in the neighborhood, but it was so hard. No one came around any more. It was as if she were contagious. She often sat by the window crying because she was no longer invited to play. My heart went out to her. On one occasion when she was outside by herself, several of the neighborhood kids came around and started to play hopscotch. I watched from the window.

"Can I play?" Michele asked.

"No, you can't," they said in unison. "You're blind."

"I'm NOT blind!" Michele replied indignantly. I can see. "Let me play, and I'll show you," Michele pleaded.

"Okay, go ahead," the leader of the group said, throwing her the bunch of safety pins they were using instead of a coin.

Michele caught them, surprisingly. Her face was wreathed

in smiles at the thought of participating. I was happy, too.

"Please God, don't let her falter." I prayed. However, when Michele threw the pins down and was hopping on one foot, one of the kids kicked them out of her reach. Of course, she wasn't able to find them when she bent down to pick them up. Jeering and mocking her, they taunted. "See, you are blind, you are blind." Sobbing, Michele came running into the house. My heart was breaking with hers. How cruel children could be.

"Mommy, they said I couldn't play hopscotch because I'm blind. But I'm NOT completely blind. I can still see a little, can't I Mommy? Can't I?"

"Yes, you can Honey, you can still see some things." I drew her to me and wiped her tears.

"I was so sure I could have picked up those pins," she lamented. "I can't believe I couldn't do it."

"You could have done it, Sweetheart, except one of the kids kicked the pins out of your reach before you bent down to pick them up."

She looked at me with big round eyes and said slowly. "What a dirty trick."

With so much going on in her little life, was it any wonder that her behavior got out-of-hand? The enthusiastic, bubbly, out-going little girl didn't exist anymore. Each day brought some new trauma for her, and for us. And since the doctors didn't know the cause, none of us could anticipate when the next problem would arise, or what it would be. Michele hated everyone and everything. And we felt we were on a merry-go-round completely out of con-trol.

One evening I was in the kitchen cooking supper and Michele was upstairs playing with her dolls and doll house. I heard a noise that sounded like something falling. I called upstairs to

Michele, but received no answer. Running upstairs, I called to her, asking if she was all right. Still no answer! As I opened the door, I saw her lying on the floor, unconscious, her mouth open, tongue hanging out the side. Her eyes were rolled back, showing only the whites, and her entire body was writhing in some constant grotesque motion.

I panicked! I screamed at the top of my lungs, but no one was home to hear me. I didn't know what to do next. Then I heard the door. Arnie was home from work. I screamed again. He immediately came running.

"Holy God! What the hell happened?" he exclaimed.

Neither of us could think straight. Only a few minutes had elapsed, but it seemed like an eternity.

"Let's pick her up and put her on the bed," I said to Arnie, "and then I'll call Doctor Solomon." I felt suddenly energized.

When I reached the doctor and described what was happening, she told me it sounded like Michele was taking a grand mal convulsion.

"What in God's name is that?" I asked. "I know nothing about these things. What do we do now?" She told me to relax until the seizure subsided. Then, when she came out of it, I could take her to the hospital.

It took longer than anticipated, but Michele finally opened her eyes. She looked at us blankly without any sign of recognition. And she said not a word.

Leaving a note for Michael, who was out with his friends, we took off for the hospital. Although Michele's eyes were open, they were blank, staring straight ahead, devoid of emotion. No matter what we said to her, there was no response, just the same relentless blank stare. We were beside ourselves by the time we reached the hospital.

"She doesn't respond to anything," I explained fearfully. The doctor explained that Michele was in a post-dictal state, common after some seizures. Expressing concern about the length of time elapsed since Michele came out of the seizure, she admitted her to the hospital for observation and more tests and conferences. The intent was to come up with a medical regime to counteract the unexpected seizure condition.

I was holding Michele's hand and wiping her brow when the doctors returned.

"Has she responded yet?" one of them asked.

"No, she doesn't seem to know who we are. Her eyes are open, but that's all. It's as though she doesn't even hear us."

"What's going on here?" my husband interjected. "Do you have any answers at all?"

"I'm afraid not, Mr. Morton. You see, Michele doesn't seem to fit any particular pattern. This makes diagnosis difficult. We are working hard to determine why these setbacks are taking place."

"We appreciate what you're saying, Doctor," I said. "But from a parent's point of view, it seems implausible that the medical profession is still in a state of quandary, given the severity of the symptoms. Severe uncontrollable behaviors, sudden devastating vision loss, and now this horrible manifestation of a seizure condition. These clues are not mild. They scream at us with their intensity."

"I realize that," the Doctor said, "and I don't blame you for feeling as you do. Unfortunately, there are some cases that just don't provide easy answers. Our job with these is to treat the symptoms and go from there. In the meantime, we'll increase her Dilantin."

"I suppose you're right," I paused to take a deep breath. "But, I'm sure you can appreciate the level of frustration for any family faced with this kind of perpetual trauma. What should we do now?"

"Let's see how she does first with the extra Dilantin." Then we heard a slight murmur. "Oh! She seems to be coming out of it now," the doctor said. "How are you feeling, Michele?"

"Fine," she said, looking bewildered. Where am I?"

"In the hospital."

"Why?"

"You got very sick and your mom and dad brought you in. They're right here in the room with you."

Seemingly reassured by this, Michele immediately asked if she could go home.

"Yes, I think we can manage that," the doctor responded with a smile. Michele smiled back.

In the months that followed, she responded well to the extra Dilantin. There was no more evidence of any kind of seizure activity. We began to relax and slipped back to ordinary living.

Barnum and Bailey Circus was in town. Weeks prior, before Michele suffered the severe vision loss, I had bought tickets for her and her little friend, Eileen. The two were neighborhood friends and both went to St. Kevin's. Eileen was a little doll, always helpful to Michele. Even at age eight, she showed great understanding and compassion.

Now I was faced with a dilemma. Although, we had box seat tickets, Michele would never be able to see anything from that distance. 'How would she handle it,' I wondered. 'Was I game enough to find out?' I decided to give it a try, so I brought up the subject.

"I want to go," she exclaimed without hesitation, "and Eileen's going too – right?"

"Yes, she is, but I wasn't sure if you would want to go since you probably won't be able to see very much."

"I still want to go. It'll be fun with Eileen."

"Okay," I said. "Then go tell Eileen. Let her know we'll be leaving Saturday at 11:00."

"Great," she replied.

Arriving at Madison Square Garden that day, we learned the children could go to a certain area and pet some of the animals before the show. The elephant delighted Michele the most; she couldn't believe its size. The constant movement of its trunk caused both girls to laugh. It was a nice beginning and I said a silent prayer, desiring the day to continue as it had begun.

Inside, we found our seats and sat down. Music blared from loudspeakers, and horses pranced around the arena, and the show hadn't even started yet! Both kids were highly animated. The main feature of the show was Snow White and the Seven Dwarfs, a huge favorite of Michele's. Suddenly, a uniformed staff member approached Michele and placed a hat on her head. She was delighted.

Laughing, I requested, "Could I please have another hat for her friend?" I immediately produced my wallet.

"No," he said. "Unfortunately, I can only take one child from each section."

"What do you mean?" I asked.

"The hats aren't for sale," I was told. "Is this your daughter?"

"Yes, this is Michele."

"Well, Michele has just been selected to be part of the show. Have her down by the railing and one of the clowns will come by, lift her over, and take her to Snow White."

I couldn't believe what I was hearing. Countless times I had taken the kids to the circus and nothing like this had ever happened before. Michele couldn't believe she was going to be right up there with Snow White. I hoped my mention of her vision loss would not change anything.

"Is there one specific clown for each child?" I asked.

"No, the clowns will move around the arena and so will the kids. Don't be concerned. She'll have a ball!"

"Yes, I'm sure," I said. "But you see, Michele is legally blind. She couldn't be left by herself to move from place to place."

"I'm glad you told me. No problem," he said. "I'll arrange for the same clown to be with her at all times. Don't worry, he won't let her out of his sight."

When the clown came to get Michele, he also reassured me that she would be perfectly safe and that he would seat her next to Snow White. Michele was in seventh heaven. Glancing up, I said, 'Thank you, God, for our little miracle.' At that moment, no one **EVER** could have convinced me that Divine intervention was not at play here.

Eileen was so happy for Michele. There was not a jealous bone in that child's body. As they moved the children (along with Snow White and the Seven Dwarfs) around the arena on a large open-type colorful train, replete with whistles, Eileen yelled Michele's name over and over again, so she would look in her direction and wave. Michele responded with the same high level of excitement, finally blowing her a kiss. I laughed at the antics of both of them. It was going to be a wonderful day after all.

KATHLEEN MORTON

Chapter V

Michele's behavior in the public school grew progressively worse. She created some chaos in class, would not do as she was told, and resisted any attempts to make her behave. Her teacher called one day somewhat apologetically. "We're going on a school outing tomorrow and I was wondering if you could possibly keep Michele home since she may be too difficult to control."

I said I understood and I agreed this would probably be for the best.

As a result of Michele's behavior, difficulties multiplied. I experienced severe problems getting her on the bus each morning. One day she was almost impossible, screaming, crying, resisting all attempts to get her out the door, but the teacher said to send her anyway because she generally became quiet once the bus moved. However, not long after her departure, the teacher called. "Mrs. Morton, Michele was so upset she threw her shoe at the bus driver, hitting him on the head. He's furious."

I was flabbergasted. Michele had never done anything like this before. I told her I'd be right over.

When I arrived, I learned there was more to the story. The teacher said, "The other kids on the bus told us that it was the bus driver's fault, because he made fun of Michele when she was crying. He cried louder than she did, mimicking her, while calling her a big baby over and over again. She yelled at him to stop, but he simply taunted her all the more. Finally, they said, she threw her shoe at him. We're extremely upset that a driver would do something like this, and we're already processing a formal complaint against him."

"It is certainly incredible that a driver would behave in this manner," I told her. "But Michele's behavior is also very serious. I can't let it go on. Michele's anger at the vision loss is very profound and if it's allowed to continue, there's no telling what will happen. I have to take some action. I'm pulling her out of school."

"I hope you don't feel the school is to blame," the teacher said, with some concern.

"Oh, no, not at all. You've been wonderful and very supportive, which I really appreciate. But I have to get her anger under control somehow. I'll have to consult her doctors."

I decided to call Doctor Yang. She listened intently and then recommended a child psychiatrist by the name of Doctor Wing. "I will call and tell him about your concerns, Mrs. Morton, and also give him Michele's history. You will find that he's a very good child psychiatrist. I believe he'll be able to help Michele."

Doctor Wing called the very next day, stating he wanted to meet with the whole family, but not in Michele's presence. After arranging for my mom to take care of Michele, we went to the doctor's office. Once there, we discussed her behaviors in detail.

Doctor Wing responded, "Michele's severe behavior is a predictable reaction to both the unexpected blindness and all that followed. You're right about intervention being essential, Mrs. Morton. However, what I'm about to suggest to you will be extremely difficult. You'll need to be very strong. For that reason alone, I rarely recommend this behavior modification program. Doctor Yang tells me that you are an unusually strong parent. That is what's required to see this through to the end. I asked to meet with the whole family because it's absolutely essential that everyone agrees and buys into this program."

"What do we have to do?" I asked apprehensively.

"You'll be mostly involved, and your husband and Michael need to support you. There can be no disagreements. All of you must be of one mind." We sat impassively, staring at the doctor as he looked at each of us in turn. Then he continued. "The minute she sees one of you falter, she'll capitalize on it. We're dealing with a very smart little girl here. What she wants is attention. It doesn't matter to her whether it's positive or negative. When situations like this occur, it is generally the negative behavior that gets the attention. What we're going to do is reverse that, providing attention only when she's behaving positively. It sounds simple, but believe me, it isn't."

"What am I to do when she exhibits bad behavior?"

"You'll ignore her. Don't speak to her, don't even look at her. She's to be treated by all of you as if she wasn't there."

"Are you kidding?" I asked in disbelief. "She'll go crazy!"

"That's the point. Michele is very angry. She needs to get rid of that anger. This is the way to do it. Remember, and I emphasize this, only pay attention to her when she is good. Every one of you must understand that. Also, anything you value must be locked up. Otherwise, it will probably be destroyed. That is because when you ignore her she will try everything she can to get your attention, breaking and throwing things along the way."

"And what should I do while she's on a rampage?"

"Never react. Make no eye contact. Say nothing. Just sit down, pick up a book or magazine, and leaf through it. But be sure you don't care about the book or magazine, because she'll probably pull it out of your hand and rip it to shreds. If she does that, just pick up another old magazine and start reading it. Not easy to do, I grant you. But again, the only time she's to get any attention is when she is good. This will ultimately reinforce the good behavior. And, that's the goal of which you can never lose sight in order to be successful."

"Suppose, in her anger, she tries to hurt me? What do I do then?"

"I was just coming to that," the doctor replied. "If that happens, just walk over, pick her up like a sack of potatoes, and give her a couple of smacks on the rear. Put her down and walk away without a word. There'll be times when you think you're losing your mind, but you can't give in. If you do, you'll confuse her even more. Consistency is the key. Ignore her when she's bad, and give her lots of attention when she's good. Think it over and call me tomorrow."

"Well, what do you think?" I asked Arnie, after we left Wing's office.

"I don't know what to think. It certainly will be quite an ordeal for you."

"Yeah, I know. But in the long run it might be worth it. I know of no other alternative."

"What about you, Michael? You're unusually quiet."

"I think it sounds hard to do, especially if she starts breaking things. She'd better not break any of my stuff," he said gruffly.

"Put everything that's important to you in your closet and keep it locked. I'm going to lock away some things as well."

"So then, you're really going to go through with this?" Michael asked rolling his eyes.

"Not unless I have your full cooperation. That's essential. You heard Doctor Wing."

"Okay, okay, you can count me in. He laughed. Guess I can always run outside and escape when the going gets rough."

I gave him a playful poke in the ribs. "Keep laughing,

Michael. Something tells me we're going to need a sense of humor to get through this. So, it's settled then. I'll call Doctor Wing tomorrow."

We liked Doctor Wing and his approach, so that was a plus. After I spoke with him, he gave me a phone number where I could reach him at any time. He told me that I would probably need to talk during the process, and boy was he right!

He was also right about Michele's probable reactions to being ignored. Before I started the program, her behavior was unacceptable, NOW, it was utterly revolting! Ignoring her only accelerated her behavior to outrageous levels, leaving a path of destruction along the way. Nothing was sacred. Dishes, vases, table lamps, standing lamps, all went down for the count. I talked to Doctor Wing daily by phone asking him if he was sure this was the right way to go. "She's breaking everything in sight," I lamented. "It's not just knick knacks, we locked those up. It's furnishings as well."

"I know it isn't easy," Doctor Wing said, " but remember, you can always replace furnishings. You can never replace Michele." He reassured me that things were going along just fine and urged me to be patient. "You're doing great," he said.

Well, I didn't feel great. I felt anger, frustration, and despair. There seemed to be no let-up. Michele behaved for periods, wherein I paid a lot of attention to her, but then, without warning, her tirades began again. One night as we all sat down to dinner, she started shrieking at us at the top of her lungs. We all ignored her and continued talking. Then, she began to take her food in her hands and throw it piece by piece on the floor. Casey, her dog, immediately came over and scooped it up.

When we continued to ignore her, she stood up, still shrieking, leaned over the table, and put her face between Arnie's and mine, yelling her head off and looking from side to side. We paid no attention, simply moved our heads to the side of hers so we could see each other again, without ever interrupting our conversation. Michael rolled his eyes, looked at us in disgust and was about to react when a warning look from me stopped him. Then, with a swiftness that took us all by surprise, Michele pulled the tablecloth as hard as she could, sending our dinner plates flying.

As Casey came running, Michele ran upstairs to her room, crying.

Arnie jumped up and said. "This is insane. How do you stand it all day? We can't go on this way." Then he went into the kitchen to clean the food off his clothes.

Michael started to run upstairs after Michele, but I stopped him. He turned around at the bottom of the stairs and said, "You know, Mom, you're all crazy. You, Dad and that stupid doctor. She's worse now than ever!"

"I know, Michael, but remember, the doctor warned us. We all agreed that we would not only try this, but see it through to the end. Need I remind you that you were part of that agreement?"

"I know. But, did you really expect things to get this idiotic?" he asked with typical teenage belligerence. "Why, just the other day, she got into my closet and ruined everything in there, including my train set!"

"You were supposed to keep your closet locked," his father yelled from the kitchen.

"Oh, sure, he said, "I'm supposed to be Mr. Perfect while she ruins dinners, screams her stupid head off, and breaks everything in sight. And to make matters worse, five minutes later, we're supposed to run up there and tell her how wonderful she is. If that's not crazy, I don't know what is!"

"If it makes you feel any better," I said, "I've harbored the same doubts, as has Dad. We've talked about it frequently. I've also shared our doubts with Doctor Wing, who says all of this is to be expected. But it should end soon. Since we're almost there, let's not throw in the towel just yet."

Michael looked at me, shaking his head. "Okay, okay, I'll try harder. Now, is this the time and place I go tell her how WONDERFUL she is?"

"Yes! That is if she's behaving appropriately. Are you up to it, funny guy?"

"I suppose so" he said, with a hint of sarcasm and then ran up the stairs two at a time.

I knew I could trust him once he gave his word. He was sick of the whole business and had every right to be. Our family was living in an environment where the abnormal had become normal. The only member of the family who didn't want anything to change was Casey! He was having too much fun cleaning up the mess!

The next day brought even more havoc. While Michele was relentless, I continued to follow the program to a 'T.' By mid-afternoon, I'd finally had it.

The rampage started upstairs and moved down when she did. Ignoring her, I did as Doctor Wing suggested. I picked up some old magazines and started reading them. True to form, she pulled the magazine out of my hands and ripped it to shreds, throwing the pieces all over me. Showing no reaction, I picked up another magazine, and the same thing happened again. When I picked up the third magazine, Michele was enraged, and stomped out of the living room into the dining room. I heard her muttering, "I'll show her, I'll show her!" I was dying to know _what_ she was going to show me, but I didn't want to react or even act mildly curious, so I kept my head down, 'reading' the magazine.

I heard a rustle of paper and wondered what she was doing. I looked up a second too late. Bag of apples in hand, she started throwing them at me one by one. Before I could stop the barrage, one had hit me on the head, another on the breast, and a third on the shoulder. For someone who was blind, she sure had good aim! When I finally reached her, I picked her up like a sack of potatoes, gave her a couple of smacks on the rear, put her back down on the floor, and walked away without saying a word.

She ran upstairs to her room screaming bloody murder. After slamming her door shut, she reopened it and screamed downstairs, "You stupid, shit-fuck!" Then she slammed the door again. I couldn't help but laugh at this sudden unexpected outburst of profanity, although her teacher had warned us about a new boy in class who used a lot of colorful language. Later, when talking to some friends I facetiously said, "Profanity was bad enough, but STUPID! Now that really got to me." We all had a good laugh, shaking our heads at the insanity of it all.

But, at that moment I wasn't laughing. Anything but. I called Doctor Wing, yelling on the phone, making no sense at all. I had definitely reached the end of my rope.

"Calm down, Mrs. Morton. Calm down," the doctor said. "Remember when I told you there would be times when you would feel you were losing your mind?"

"Yes, I remember! I shouted. "But, you know something, Doctor, I don't think I'M going crazy. I THINK YOU ARE!!!"

"Mrs. Morton," he intoned, quietly and gently, "Take it easy." Suddenly, our conversation was interrupted by a noise. "What was that?" Dr. Wing asked with concern.

"She just threw the large corner table on the upper landing down the stairs. I don't know how she could even pick it up, much less throw it. It's now in a million pieces."

Although I was out of control myself at this point, he kept saying to me, "Calm down, Mrs. Morton. Calm down. You're almost there, believe me. You're almost there. What is she doing now?"

"I don't know. But she'd better be hiding, because I'm going to kill her!" I screamed.

"No, you're not, Mrs. Morton. No, you're not. Just go to her. If her behavior is appropriate, touch her gently and tell her how wonderful she is."

"This is ludicrous!" I told him. "We're at totally opposite ends of the spectrum."

"I know how you feel, but after going through all this, you don't want to give up now, do you?" (This was beginning to sound like the argument I'd had with Michael.)

I processed what he was saying and, in my heart, I knew he was right. Taking a deep breath, I said, "Okay, Doctor, I'll give it another shot."

"Great! And don't forget, you're almost there."

I hung up and leaned against the kitchen wall as tears tumbled down my face. Silently, I prayed for the strength to continue. I was just about to go upstairs when I heard Michele coming down. As she walked from the living room into the kitchen she looked at me with those big beautiful eyes of hers. "Mommy?" she asked.

"What is it, Sweetheart?" I asked, not knowing what to expect.

She stood silent in the doorway. After much hesitation, she solemnly stated, "I think I may be able to do something with my life after all."

"Oh, Honey!" I exclaimed as I reached out and hugged her tightly. Here she was, all of eight years of age, saying that she thought she could do something with her life after all. My heart went out to her.

Then she pushed me away and looked up at me. "But I still hate this blindness!"

"I know you do, Sweetheart," I said, wiping away her tears. "But, I'll be with you all the way."

"Promise?"

"I promise, Honey. I promise. Cross my heart and hope to die," I said, making the sign of the cross over her heart. She fell into my arms, laughing. I knew then, just at that moment, that we had indeed made it.

I called Doctor Wing, who expressed delight at the news. I thanked him profusely for his patience and fortitude. He said he knew I would succeed, if given a little encouragement along the way. However, he gave me a lot more than a little encouragement. He gave me hope, guidance, and a firm belief, under incredible odds, that I could succeed. He exercised enormous patience during one of the most difficult periods of Michele's young life. In my book, he was truly a saint!

It was as though Michele had crossed a new threshold. She couldn't wait to make plans. Her life had taken on new meaning and her energy level was high. She didn't want to waste time talking about her interests and what she wanted to accomplish. She wanted to jump into action right away.

"Okay, Michele, what would you like to do first?"

"I'd like to take swimming lessons so I can swim in the big pool."

"Fine. How about discussing it with one of the lifeguards when we go to Creathaven?"

After Michele told the lifeguard what she wanted, lessons were undertaken. She enjoyed herself immensely and couldn't wait to try swimming laps in the big pool. But she found out that swimming within the confines of the straight course to complete the lap was too difficult. Because of her vision loss, she frequently strayed over to the other area without realizing it. She tried to conquer this problem by periodically touching the rope on the right side as she swam straight ahead, but it didn't work. However, she kept on trying and, without a doubt, enjoyed the experience. At the end of the summer, the club awarded Michele a trophy for her valiant effort and she was thrilled beyond words.

Michele's happiness was contagious. Things progressed so well, euphoria began setting in. Her energy was boundless, and directed in a very positive way. And, she had more on her agenda.

"What?" I asked with a chuckle.

"Well, the next thing I'd like to do is learn how to roller skate."

"Roller skate?" I said surprised. "That would be quite a challenge, Michele."

"I know," she said with a laugh, thoroughly enjoying herself.

"Okay, let's see where we can find a roller rink."

Perusing the phone book, I found one on Long Island. I gave them a call and they put me through to an instructor right away. We set a date for our first meeting within a couple of weeks. Michele listened intently to the conversation and smiled when I made specific plans for private lessons. I didn't go into her vision loss over the phone, and Michele was grateful for that.

"I don't want you to tell the teacher I'm blind," she said with some vehemence.

"Why not?" I asked.

"Because then they'll treat me differently."

"I guess that's true, but how do you suppose we'll get away with it?" I asked.

"Well, first of all, I don't look blind, and no one knows me there, so why tell them?"

"Great! I'm game if you are, Michele."

"And anyway, you'll be there all the time, won't you, Mom?" Now that I had agreed, she wanted reassurance.

"Of course," I said. "I wouldn't miss it for the world. Now, how about going out a few times before the first lesson to get yourself oriented. You can exercise some independent movement, learn where the skates are, where you put them on, and how to get from point A to point B. How does that sound?"

"That sounds great!" she said. Looking at me steadily, her face filled with emotion, she tenderly reached out and touched my arm, "Thanks, Mom. I love you."

"I love you too, Sweetheart. Now, run along so I can get dinner ready."

"I'll help you," she immediately responded.

"That'll be fine, Michele. But a little later. I'll call you and you can set the table."

Although Michele's behavior had improved tremendously, the public school still had some reservations about meeting her educational needs. They felt they lacked appropriate programming. A faculty member at the school referred me to the New York Institute for the Education of the Blind located in the Bronx. It was a residential school, but they also had a day program, which was what I wanted for Michele.

I'd already had my arguments with doctors about not sending Michele to an institution in upstate New York, which they strongly suggested I do, so that I could "get on with my life."

"She is my life!" I said, astounded. "Do you think I can put her away some place and just go visit her on holidays?" I was so upset that day, that the doctors sent for the resident psychologist to calm me down. I knew they meant well, but I wasn't ready for that kind of suggestion.

Michele's seizures were difficult to control and I was constantly at the hospital, where the doctors worked hard to control them as well. Tests revealed she no longer could take Dilantin because her blood workup showed some possibility of her developing systemic lupus erythematosis, a serious skin disease which also could involve the internal organs. This was a rare reaction to Dilantin. We all agreed she didn't need any more complications.

Finding a medication that worked for Michele wasn't easy. Her system rejected Phenobarbitol, Mysoline, Tegretol and now Dilantin, all popular anti-seizure medications that worked well for most children. The worst was Tegretol. She hated to take it because it made her feel dreadful and she became hallucinatory and extremely agitated. Once it was removed, she was back to her old self, vowing never to take that medication again. I couldn't agree with her more. Of course, all this made it very tough for the doctors at New York Hospital, but they always came up with some answer. They decided to try Celontin and Valium combined, after she was slowly removed from Dilantin, and it worked! Her seizures were again under complete control.

In the meantime, we had been out to the roller rink a couple of times, and Michele was becoming more adept at moving around the facility, getting skates, putting them on, and lacing them! (That last certainly not a simple chore)! She was really pleased with herself. When her lesson day arrived, she was happy and excited. There were no other skaters at this time of the morning. Joan, her instructor, was very nice, taking her out to the middle of the rink. Holding Michele's hands, she instructed her on how to move her feet. Slow and awkward at first, Michele soon began to get the hang of it.

We went through this process twice a week for several

months without a hitch, and soon she was very good on skates. After only a month of lessons, she decided she needed to get her own skates.

"What's wrong with the skates they rent you?" I asked.

"They don't fit right and they're old. And the wheels don't turn the way they should."

"Okay, I tell you what. Once you're able to skate the entire length of the rink, I'll buy you your own skates."

"It's a deal," she said with delight.

Well, I didn't have long to wait. She attempted the task several times not quite making it. Undaunted, she kept trying, and one morning, less than a week later, she succeeded. She quite obviously couldn't wait to reach my seat. She skated with arms raised in triumph.

"Mom, did you see me?" she yelled

"See what?" I asked with amusement.

"I skated the whole length of the rink!" she exclaimed.

"Really? I didn't see that," I teased her.

"What! You weren't watching me?" she said incredulously. "You must be kidding. You are kidding, right?"

I couldn't contain myself any longer, and started to laugh. "Yes, I'm kidding you, Sweetheart. You did a great job. Good for you," and I hugged her enthusiastically.

Her new skates actually made a big difference. She was becoming very proficient at turning and skating backwards to a dance number. But one morning at lesson time I could tell that something was amiss. The teacher gave instructions, stopped Michele, talked to her, gave additional instructions, and then stopped her again. I couldn't hear the exchange, but I knew something wasn't going right. Finally, the teacher skated over to me.

"Michele doesn't seem to be following directions this morning, Mrs. Morton. It's as if there's something wrong with her hearing."

"What were you asking her to do, Joan?" I asked.

"The figure eight. But although I've drawn a large eight on the floor of the rink, she just doesn't follow directions. I point out where to start, but she seems to ignore what I'm telling her."

"Okay, Joan, let me talk with her alone. Tell her I want to see her."

Michele skated over, looking frustrated. "You know what the problem is, don't you, Michele?"

"Yep," she said, throwing up her arms. "Why did she have to start teaching me that stupid figure eight? Things were going along fine."

"It was bound to happen Michele. If it wasn't the figure eight, eventually it would be something else. That's what happens when you become more advanced. Seems to me, you have only two options. Either tell Joan you are blind, or today's your last lesson. Your decision."

She looked at me without flinching, weighing her options. "Oh, okay," she said. "I don't want to quit, so I guess I'll have to tell her."

I motioned for Joan to come over and told her that Michele had something to tell her.

"What is it, Michele?" Joan asked.

Michele hesitated, struggling for the right words. Finally, she said, "The reason I couldn't follow the figure eight is because I'm blind."

"BLIND!" Joan exclaimed, and looked at me in disbelief.

"It's true," I said. "When people know, they usually treat her differently, so she never tells anyone unless she has to."

"In that case," Joan said, "I'll help you find the beginning of the figure eight, and we'll go on from there. How does that sound?"

Michele was happy again. Every week I practiced with her. Then her skill surpassed mine and I could no longer keep up. She could skate backwards now and dance, while I could only skate straight ahead. Since she needed me with her to keep from colliding with others, she had to stay with me. I was her buffer, and a very boring one she told me one day, rolling her eyes in frustration.

"Okay, Michele, I said, laughing. "I'll take some lessons too." Michele was ecstatic!

It turned out Joan was free the hour before Michele's lesson, which worked out fine for us. Michele listened to tapes on her recorder while I struggled on the roller rink. Ten minutes into the lesson, I took a flop. I was sure every bone in my body was broken. Joan assured me they weren't and helped me up. Still, lying there, I had questioned the wisdom of my decision. Here I was, in my forties, taking skating lessons for the first time, trying to keep up with a kid whose energy and enthusiasm were boundless. Was I crazy or what?

Bouncing off the floor a few more times, I finally got the hang of it. After that it was fun. Eventually I became pretty good and Michele and I both had a ball dancing around the rink to the waltzes of my favorite Viennese composer, Johann Strauss.

The doctors were very pleased with Michele's progress. Her seizures were completely controlled. They were not, however, very happy when I told them she was changing schools and would probably be traveling to and from the Bronx every day. They felt this daily round trip in highly congested traffic would be detrimental to good seizure control, and they didn't want us to take that chance. They agreed that the N. Y. Institute for the Education of the Blind would be a great school for Michele, recommending the residential, rather than the day program.

The more we thought about it, the more we realized this program would be in Michele's best interests both medically and educationally. I was even more enthused after meeting with Noble Wiltshire, their assistant director. He outlined an effective academic program along with science, art, mobility training, and activities of daily living. In the afternoon, Michele would participate in music appreciation, music therapy, and individual piano lessons. In addition, the institute offered off-campus trips in the spring. And, most importantly, parents were welcome at all time.

There was one problem. All children had to be appointed by the State before the school could offer admission.

"So, how do I go about getting that appointment?" I asked him.

"You need to contact the Commissioner for the State Education Department in Albany," he told me. "It probably won't be easy, because the appointment of children to our residential program depends upon where the child lives."

"Why would that have anything to do with it?" I asked.

"Good question, but unfortunately it does. It's an amendment to a state regulation by the Commissioner that's been in effect for several years. It stipulates that the child must live at least twenty miles away in order to qualify for an appointment to a residential school."

"But we don't live 20 miles away."

"And that may be a problem. We feel that Michele could benefit greatly from our program, and that it's what she really needs, but many appointments have been denied based solely on that factor."

"This is crazy!" I said. "Everyone says that meeting the needs of the child is of paramount importance. Many educational materials from the Commissioner's office speak to this important issue. Yet, an amended regulation runs counter to that! Isn't that just like a bureaucracy? Well, I've got news for them. Where Michele lives has got absolutely nothing to do with her needs. Whether she lives a million miles away or across the street from the school, her needs remain the same. There is no such thing as a geographic cure! Ask any parent."

Noble Wiltshire held my gaze with obvious interest. "Does that mean you're going to fight it?"

"Yes, I am. What choice do I have? No child should be denied admission based on where they live. I feel very strongly about this."

I left the Institute feeling somewhat weary. We'd finally found a program that would really meet Michele's needs. Emotionally, I was prepared to let her go since it was a 4-1/2 day school week. That meant she would be home every Friday for the weekend as well as Easter and Christmas holidays, and all summer. If she didn't do well, we could just take her out. And, the open door policy for parents was very inviting.

The local education agency supported Michele's transfer to the N.Y. Institute, sending a letter stating they couldn't meet Michele's educational needs in the public school. I forwarded that letter to the N.Y. State Commissioner of Education, along with a medical report from N. Y. Hospital. This material was ultimately forwarded to a Mr. John San Fratello, Associate in Education of the Visually Handicapped for the State. This began a senseless stream of letters back and forth. He remained adamant about the fact that the commissioner's amendment to the regulation was inviolate and must be followed. My contention was that rules were made to be broken for good causes, such as meeting the medical and educational needs of a child. There was no meeting of the minds. Time was running out. I wanted Michele to start the new school year in September at the Institute. Although months had elapsed in fighting this issue, there was still no progress.

I finally got fed up, called the Commissioner's office to make sure he wasn't out of town, I called an airline, and made reservations to fly to Albany the following day. I also called my commissioner friend to see if he could help me get an appointment with the Education Commissioner. He laughed at my determination and said he was sorry I was still fighting this battle. He urged me to stay put because he had to go to Albany on business anyway, and he promised personally to talk to the Education Commissioner.

A few days later I received a call from Mr. San Fratello telling me approval had been granted for Michele's appointment to the Institute.

"Great!" I told him enthusiastically. "That's wonderful." I could have danced around the room, I was so happy.

"You are indeed very tenacious," he said. "But what bothered me during this whole process was being contacted by every commissioner in N. Y. State regarding Michele Morton. If every parent were to do that to me, I wouldn't be able to do my job."

"Mr. San Fratello," I said evenly, "I make no apologies for exerting pressure, especially when it means that blind children will no longer be denied services, simply because of where they live!"

"TOUCHÉ," he quickly responded. "I'm not sure when Michele can start since it's so late in the summer, but I'll get back to you on that."

In a determined, no-nonsense tone, I said, "Mr. San Fratello, I expect Michele to start on the first day of school in September."

"But time wouldn't permit that," he insisted. "Why, the paperwork alone.........."

"I hope you'll forgive me for saying this, Mr. San Fratello, but I don't really care about the paperwork. It can follow her, if need be. I care about the child, and I really believe you do too. Think about it. The State has been arguing this case for months. If the decision to place Michele had been made when it was initially brought to your attention, you would have had all the time in the world to process paperwork. So my question to you is, why should she suffer? It wasn't her fault that the State took all this time. All kids have the right to start the first day of school. It's so much easier for them that way. They all get to know one another at the same time and no one has to play catch up. As it is, Michele's had so much to deal with in her young life. I don't want to add anything else. I hope you understand."

"Well, all right," he replied with a heavy sigh. "I suppose it could be done that way. Initially, I'll provide an informal approval to get her started."

"Thank you very much, Mr. San Fratello. I know you have worked hard on this, and I do appreciate your efforts." That ended our conversation and we never spoke again. But I shall always remember a man, initially stalwart in his desire to do what a bureaucracy dictated (which was his job) then doing a complete about-face, with a great deal of equanimity, when the rules were changed.

I called Noble Wiltshire and told him Michele had received the State appointment and would be starting the first day of school. He was delighted to hear it. "Wow! You'll never know what you've done for other children and parents. We can now contact those who were previously denied admission and tell them to reapply based on the needs of their child, rather than where they live."

"Yes, I know, Mr. Wiltshire. That's what's so great about this outcome. It opens the door to all blind children requiring this kind of programming. I feel a sense of relief that it is over. Now I can concentrate on trying to convince Michele that this is the best decision we ever made. Something tells me that 'residential' is not going to be one of her favorite components. Wish me luck."

Michele with her dog Casey, who was always very protective of her.

Michael at age 14.

KATHLEEN MORTON

Chapter VI

In the meantime, Michele was still having a great time skating. The lessons had ended, but we went out to the rink on a regular basis to skate, sometimes for hours. It was definitely good exercise. On the way home one day, she started to tell me about another item on her 'to do' list, then stopped.

"Why did you stop, Michele?" I asked.

"You'll laugh," she said, making a face.

"Now, why would I do that? C'mon, tell me," I coaxed her.

"Let's stop for lunch first, and then I'll tell you."

"Oh, oh, hold on. Is this a BRIBE?"

"Noooooo!" she said, throwing her head back and laughing. "It's just that I'm hungry."

"Yeah, sure. Tell me about it, Michele."

"It's the truth, Mom," she said, extending her arms in mock appeal.

"Okay, lunch it is. You're lucky I'm hungry too." I smiled at her antics.

Once settled in the restaurant, we played our own private little game. I told her what was on the menu, so she could decide what she wanted. Then, pretending to read the menu, she gave her order to the waiter. Here again, she was striving for independence.

"So what's on your mind, kid?" I asked, a hint of amusement in my tone.

She looked up at me with an impish grin. "You're gonna love it," she said, smiling broadly. "I want you to teach me how to play tennis."

"TENNIS?" I said, astounded. "Are you kidding me?"

"No. I want to be just like you. It'll only be for fun, anyway," she said, her eyes wide and appealing.

I sat there deep in thought. After all, I had told this kid she could accomplish anything she wanted. The whole world was open to her for the asking. All she had to do was think positive. Many people, I had told her, placed limitations upon themselves because of negative thinking, but once their feelings of self-worth improved through positive action, they felt good and a better quality of life resulted. The one thing always to remember, I reinforced, was that we all have choices. When I gave this lecture, she had not appeared too receptive. So, she certainly had come a long way from the feeling that her life was over.

I finally said to her, "Alright, let me give it some thought, Michele. I know they have beep softballs, so maybe we can get beep tennis balls too. I'll check it out."

I called a dozen sports places, manufacturers, and administrative offices during the next few weeks. Most were negative in their response. The idea of making a beep ball so that blind people could play tennis was way beyond their comprehension. Only one said it had some possibilities, but because the demand would be minimal, it wouldn't pay for them to manufacture it.

Dismissing the special equipment possibility, I decided to teach Michele at home. We had a very large room upstairs that would do for now. Having her own racquet and tennis outfit made her feel quite proud. We practiced daily. She would not give up and neither would I. It was a lot of fun.

It didn't take her long to learn ready position, turn, racquet

94

back, step in front, and follow through. That was all mastered before I introduced the ball. "Okay, Michele," I said to her one morning. "Your timing and footwork are good. Now, I want you to stand back here, and I'll throw the ball to you."

"Okay, Mommy, I'm ready," she said, standing in the ready position. She looked so cute.

"I want you to listen intently for the ball, as I constantly repeat, bounce, hit, bounce, hit." She went through all the steps very well, but couldn't seem to connect with the ball, no matter how many times she tried. This only increased her determination. She practiced valiantly. Finally, the day arrived when she connected! She fell into my arms squealing with delight.

"How about that for a shot?" she exclaimed, her eyes dancing.

"It was awesome, Honey," I said, hugging her as we danced around the room. I was as much a kid as she was.

After she hit the ball a few more times, Michele decided she wanted to try it at the Club. Our friends at Cresthaven were amused when I signed up to play with Michele. Once on the court, we discovered something we hadn't anticipated. The exterior noises, wind, planes, and birds chirping, cancelled out softer sounds, such as, the bounce of a ball. And at Cresthaven all the courts were clay. This did not help.

Michele did the best she could. A beep ball would have come in very handy that day. When we finished our play, I said encouragingly, "Hey, kid, you did very well under the circumstances. Good job!"

She smiled enthusiastically. "It was great, Mom. Thanks."

I knew she felt very good about herself as she jauntily walked off the court with her mom, holding her racquet over her shoulder. So all was not lost. Realizing that Michele wouldn't be able to hear as well outside as indoors, an idea hit me. I worked with an indoor children's tennis program on Saturdays. That would be a better location for our play. When I mentioned this to Michele, she thought it was a great idea.

As a result of Michele's involvement with swimming, skating and tennis, her life became more meaningful again. Because of her accomplishments, her self-esteem soared. Her indomitable spirit caused her to feel most everything was still within her grasp. Her sense of humor had returned, and she was very happy.

At the indoor tennis facility, I talked to Bob, one of the pros. I asked him if any courts were available.

"As a matter of fact, there is one Kathleen," he said. "I won't have a lesson for another forty-five minutes and you can use it until then. Who is this pretty girl you have with you?" he asked with a smile.

Michele was beaming. "This is my daughter, Michele," I said proudly," And she's just learning how to play."

"Fine. The court's yours. Have fun, Michele!"

Michele was excited and couldn't wait to get started. What a difference the indoor tennis made. The ball resounded when it hit the ground. There was no problem hearing it at all. Michele moved with ease on the court, returning the ball well. Time flew by until the pro showed up with his lesson. Watching, he invited us to finish playing. As we were hitting back and forth, Michele whistled one past me!

Laughing, Bob applauded, "Good shot, Michele! You should be teaching your mom."

Michele was in seventh heaven, especially since Bob had no idea she was blind.

A few days later she came bounding in the door all excited about a camp some of the kids from Girl Scouts were to attend.

"It's a sleep-away camp!" she exclaimed, thrusting the application into my hands. "Can I go?"

Perusing the material, I found it to be a good program, but when I saw how expensive it was - $1600, I knew it was out of the question.

We had already gone far beyond our budget. Experimental medical research that some doctors told us would help Michele had required tests with repetitive blood draws on many occasions. After which, we waited for a breakthrough.

One day while at N. Y. Hospital, Doctor Dorothy Pietrucha, the pediatric neurological resident, said, "Mrs. Morton, I know you have Michele in some research program and that's fine, but you shouldn't be paying for it."

I looked at her, surprised at her vehemence. "But, Doctor Pietrucha," I said, "the research is experimental. I need to pay. Otherwise, Michele can't be part of the program."

She looked at me. "You're right, it is experimental, but, to put it bluntly, Mrs. Morton, I don't believe the type of research they're doing will ever help Michele. I'm sorry."

I sat looking at her in dismay, letting this all sink in. "And they know that?" I asked.

"I don't know," she said with a shrug. "I can only tell you what I believe after having been involved with Michele's case. I just don't want you to have false hopes."

"I can't believe it!" I said. "I've always had the highest respect for the medical profession. I thought doctors were all so sacrosanct." I felt my lips quiver as tears welled up in my eyes. "I was such a fool!"

"No. You're a mother who loves her child very much and that's what made you extremely vulnerable. I'm truly sorry. I know this is disappointing after all the money you spent."

"Oh, it's not the money so much, Doctor. But I'd placed so much faith, trust and hope — especially the hope in this research. Learning that it may all have been for nothing is hard to accept." I stared into space and thought. Here was another chink in the armor with which we were trying to insulate ourselves. A chink big enough for this kind of one-two punch to get through with devastating force.

My thoughts returned to the present. Here was Michele, still eagerly waiting my answer regarding the expensive sleep-away camp. In all honesty, I wasn't that receptive to the idea because of their lack of experience with blind children. I finally told Michele that although it sounded great, we just couldn't afford it this year. Surprisingly, she took it very well. I expected one of those dramatic reactions like "my life is over" routines, but the opposite happened. Kids! Who can figure?

A few days later a surprise came in the mail. It was a letter from the N. Y. Institute inviting Michele to attend their sleep-away camp in Vermont for three weeks. Camp Wapanacki, with outside railings throughout, was designed for blind children. The cost? Thirty-five dollars to cover incidentals! Now, THAT, we could handle. Was this Divine Intervention again? I really did believe in miracles — and with good reason.

The next morning when Michele came down for breakfast, I broached the subject of going to sleep-away camp. "Do you still want to go?" I asked after our discussion.

"Oh yes!" she said emphatically. "Can I go now? You said it was too much money."

"Well, there may be a way around the high cost," I said.

"Wait a minute, Mom, are you talking about another camp? The only one I want to go to is the Girl Scouts camp, with my friends."

"I know which one you're referring to, Michele. But I've just received a letter from the school for the blind we were checking out, and they have a great camp. It would be better for you because they have experience with blind children and they've invited you to attend."

"But I won't know anyone there!" she protested.

"I know, but it won't take long for you to make friends. I think it's a great opportunity. I'm sure you'll love it, if you'll only give it a chance."

Michele sat quietly, giving it some thought. I could see she was receptive to a possible new adventure in her life, but there was also a fear of the unknown. "If I go, can I call you if I want to?"

"Of course you can, Michele. As a matter of fact, I'll get a long distance card for you to use with your own number on it. How about that?"

"Okay," she said. "I'll give it a try."

And so, arrangements were made for Camp Wapanacki. Excitement mounted as the day drew near. We went shopping to buy all new things for this anticipated camp experience. God forbid she would take a used 'anything' with her. Packing the night before was an absolutely frenetic experience. It was a family affair. Everybody joined in to help. Her questions were endless. Were we sure her pj's were in her suitcase? What about her toothbrush? Her hairbrush? Her stuffed animals? She needed constant reassurance that all was well.

The next morning we were all exhausted, especially since Michele had stayed up most of the night, too excited to sleep.

On our way to Pelham Parkway in the Bronx, where the school was located, she suddenly said, "Stop the car! We need to go back!"

"Why?" we asked in unison.

"I forgot my 'OFF!' And I can't go to camp without it."
'Off' was her favorite mosquito repellant and she carried it with
her to every outdoor activity.

"It's probably packed away, Michele," Dad assured her.

I was driving and Michele and her dad were sitting in the
back. We both exchanged glances, knowing that she was feeling
some anxiety as arrival drew near. Arnie put his arm around her
and she seemed to settle down for the rest of the trip. When we
arrived we found the 'OFF' in her small suitcase and she expressed
relief and happiness.

There was a tug at my heartstrings as the bus pulled away.
The camp was in Hardwicke, Vermont, and it was a long trip for
her in new surroundings. We didn't have misgivings about letting
her go, but we certainly did feel some apprehension. The staff at
the school and those going up to the camp with the children were
both sensitive to our feelings and very supportive. That helped us a
great deal.

After three days of camp, I wanted to drive up to Vermont
to see how Michele was doing. The Camp Director, Joe Ingram,
thought it was too soon. He asked us to give her a few more days
to adjust. We agreed. Ten days into Michele's camp experience, we
made reservations at a local hotel, then set out to visit her at camp.
We would meet with Joe Ingram first.

When we arrived we were greeted warmly by Joe. He was
very affable and we chatted a bit about the 'mountain' we had just
climbed.

"We didn't think the car would make it!" I said.

He laughed and replied, "Most people feel that way the first
time around, but eventually they get used to it."

"So, how is Michele doing?" I asked.

Joe hesitated, gave a little smile, and said, "She's doing

okay."

"Just OKAY? Not wonderful? Not having a great time and all that good stuff?" I asked, laughing.

Still smiling, he said, "No, I'm afraid not, but that's to be expected. She's been through a lot, having just lost her vision after being able to see for eight years. And I must urge you not to take her home. I know she'll ask you, possibly even beg you, but it would not be in her best interests to do so."

"Why not?" her father asked. "We want her to be happy here, but if she isn't, what's the point?"

Neither of us liked what we heard, and we both felt a bit frustrated.

"The point is, Mr. Morton, if you and your wife take Michele home today, chances are she'll never have a good camp experience again. I can't emphasize that enough. Also, the first two weeks are the hardest for any child. Let me reassure you, she's not unhappy all the time, but she'll probably try to convince you she is and that this place is horrible. If you don't give in to her, I believe you'll never regret it. I know that may be hard for you to accept since you know neither myself nor the reputation of the camp very well. That's why I'm taking this length of time to talk with you and, hopefully, persuade you that it's in Michele's best interests to stick it out."

We listened attentively and believed what Joe was saying was probably true. We suspected it wasn't easy for Michele to be away from home for the first time. We would have expected such a reaction even if she had not had all the recent problems. Kids are usually excited about going away, but get homesick within a few days. We felt we were actually dealing with a pretty normal situation.

In addition, we liked this guy. He was forthright, friendly and caring. After Arnie and I had a chance to discuss it privately, we decided to let her stay and not let our 'hearts' dictate what we would do. This turned out to be easier said than done.

"Let me take you to where Michele is," Joe said, "and you can spend the day together." When we arrived, there was lots of noise coming from inside the building. The campers were playing a game. Michele was participating and looked like she was enjoying herself. Joe called to her, telling her someone was here to see her.

"Where?"

"Right here, Honey," we said in unison moving toward her. She jumped with delight, falling into my arms and then into her father's. "How're you doing, kiddo?" I asked, ruffling her hair.

"Not too good," she whispered, looking askance at where she figured Joe was standing.

I looked up and exchanged glances with Joe and Arnie. Joe smiled, waved, and told Michele he'd see her later.

We sat on Michele's bed to chat. She talked non-stop. According to her, this camp had no redeeming qualities. We just sat and listened and let her get it all out of her system.

Once she was finished, we empathized with her, hugged her tightly, and told her we wanted this to be a very special day. Maybe she'd like to help make it that way for all of us.

"I know," I said enthusiastically. "How about taking us around the campground, and showing us where everything is?"

She smiled, jumped up and said, "Okay, let's go!" We went out the door laughing.

The campground and the surrounding area were beautiful. The camp sat, almost majestically, high on top of a mountain. It boasted a softball field, lake, and hiking trails. Michele seemed proud to show us around and talked animatedly about the various programs.

Her favorite spot was the cafeteria. Anywhere there was

food, Michele was happy. She loved to eat and her appetite was insatiable. We always said that any program would lose money on Michele if part of the deal was to provide food. Lunch was ready and we were invited to eat with Michele. Several counselors came over to say hello and chat with us for a while. Michele showed no signs of distress. Arnie and I were delighted, feeling that perhaps the worst was over.

Joe had told us that after lunch there would be a quiet period followed by a softball game. We decided the best time for us to leave would be when the campers and staff got themselves ready for that. When the time came for Michele to walk us to our car, she became suddenly upset.

"NO!" she protested. "Don't leave me here." She clung to me with all her might.

"Michele," I said consolingly, "we've had a great day, haven't we?"

"Yes, but, I don't want to stay without you! They beat me up when you're not around."

I glanced at Joe, who was standing on the sidelines. He shrugged, smiled and shook his head.

"Michele," I said, "I can't believe that's true." I motioned to a couple of counselors to help separate us. They practically had to peel her off me, she was holding on so tight. Arnie hugged and kissed her after she let go and we both got into the car.

As we drove quickly away, we could see tears streaming down her face. She yelled, "Don't go! Don't leave me! Take me with you!"

I couldn't stop my flow of tears and Arnie wiped his eyes as well. We consoled ourselves by telling each other that it was the best thing for her, but I knew 15 minutes later, when we reached the bottom of the road, that I had to go back.

"Are you crazy?" Arnie asked in disbelief.

"No, I'm not," I said defensively. "How do I know they don't really beat her up?"

"You don't really believe that," Arnie said.

"No, I don't, but I still have to go back." I turned the car around and began the return drive.

Once there, I left the car by the top of the road rather than driving into the parking area. Arnie and I quietly walked onto the campground site again, this time unnoticed. There was a lot of activity, but we couldn't see Michele. Then Joe turned around and spotted us.

He walked toward us smiling. "I kind of thought you would be back."

"It was hard to leave her like that," I said, shaking my head and smiling. "Where is she?"

"On the softball field having a good time," he said, laughing. "There she is, up at bat."

Sure enough, there she was, happy as could be, waiting for the ball to be pitched to her. She connected, whooping for joy and ran to first base. Her face was all smiles.

"She's going to do just fine. Don't worry." Joe comforted.

"Okay," I said. Joe shook hands with us and we left feeling like a million bucks. Even Arnie admitted he was glad we had returned.

We stayed in Vermont for a week and called Joe several times. He said Michele was doing great. He advised we not return to the camp, but arranged for us to talk to her. On the phone, she sounded happy and contented breathlessly telling us all about her activities. When she actually cut us short because of another program beginning, we knew we had nothing to worry about.

Michele's first residential camp experience ended within a

few days of our return home. When we picked her up, she was filled with wonderful stories and memories. Joe Ingram had been right. It turned out to be a very positive experience and something we looked forward to every summer. Eventually, Camp Wapanacki became a household word and a family ritual during the summer. We made reservations and drove up to Vermont each summer to visit her without fail.

One summer she was incredibly animated about the boating session. There were three boats: a canoe, a sailboat and a motorboat. The staff involved the campers by teaching them how to use the different boats.

"It's my turn to start the motorboat this morning," Michele declared. "If whoever is scheduled can't get it started, nobody goes that day."

"Wow, that's really putting on the pressure. How do you feel about that?"

"Fine," she said with a shrug. "It's a lot of fun and I know I can do it."

At boating time we went down to the lake to see for ourselves. The staff member, Mike, and the other kids were already there.

"C'mon, let's go, Michele," Mike called out to her. "Get us started."

"Okay," she yelled excitedly, running in his direction. We were right behind her.

He handed her the cord. "Pull hard," he instructed.

She took the cord from him and pulled. Hardly a noise emitted. We were both rooting for her, along with everyone else. She pulled again, and revved the motor this time, then pulled once more, and the boat roared into action. As Michele jumped in, all the kids shrieked with delight, including Michele. With Barry at the helm, the boat sped away, leaving water spraying from every direction. She'd made it. What a thrill! Arnie and I hugged each other and laughed excitedly at her success.

Later in the summer another new 'first' in Michele's life was to take place. She knew she would be attending the New York Institute for the Education of the Blind (NYIEB) in September, but we had not yet talked to her about the residential component. I broached the subject with her after breakfast one morning.

"Stay at a school? Sleep there?" she said, wrinkling up her face. "Whoever heard of a school like that?"

"I know it's not easy to accept, but the doctors feel traveling every day to the Bronx in stop-and-go traffic will not be good for your seizure condition, and that has to be taken into consideration. For the first few weeks I'll see you every day to be sure things are going along fine. Also, you can always call home at any time after classes are over for the day. In addition, you'll only be staying four nights at the school, and the other three nights at home. Think of it as an adventure."

Michele shrugged with an air of resignation, as if to say, "Do I have a choice?"

Fortunately, her mood soon changed. She liked the school even more when we visited it again to get her schedule. The director of the school was Roger Walker, and he and his wife, Cindy, lived on campus. Nobel Wiltshire, the assistant director, also lived on campus with his family.

Cindy Walker taught at the school and was going to be Michele's teacher. Michele liked her right away. Slender, petite, and neat in her appearance, Cindy exuded care in her approach, making Michele feel relaxed in her presence.

As a result, Michele now looked forward to attending the Institute. She was actually becoming intrigued with the residential part.

The New York Institute for the Education of the Blind had been serving blind children since 1831. Michele was admitted September 8, 1975. The school enjoyed an excellent reputation programmatically with Academics, Physical Education, Social and Recreation programs, as well as more intensive support services and programming for the children, both those blind, and multi-handicapped. Staff had at their disposal the latest information and technology required to teach the blind child how to function as independently as possible.

The first day of school went well. We dropped Michele off at class in Van Cleve Hall. She was well received by her new teacher, and when we left we could tell she felt very comfortable in her new surroundings. We attended a parent meeting on campus. The meeting started off with a welcome from Roger Walker. Later, staff and parents mingled while parents' questions were answered over refreshments. Finally, the children were assembled in the auditorium to entertain us with songs. Michele was initially in the last row, but when they were instructed to turn and face the audience, she was in the first row. It was wonderful, and she looked great.

Back home, we missed her terribly. The house felt so empty. I walked around aimlessly. Arnie touched my shoulder and asked, "Are you beginning to have doubts?"

I shook my head. "I really don't know what I'm having. I guess you could say my feelings are pretty ambivalent. Everything is so new. Michele being away from home is the last thing I ever wanted. Yet, it seems to be the best decision in order to meet her needs. When I'm with the doctors and educators everything seems crystal clear. Now that I'm not, the crystal has become cloudy. Suddenly, I have this urge to jump in the car, drive like the wind to the Bronx, and bring her home."

"I know," Arnie said, putting his arm around me. "It's never easy. But you're the best mom that any child could ever have. I would never try to second-guess you when it comes to what is right for Michele. Your decisions are always solid and I'm sure you know that deep inside."

I smiled. "Thanks, Honey." I was pleased at his sensitivity. Feeling a little perkier, I turned and said, "Right now I'm going to call the Institute to see how she is."

When Delores, the evening supervisor, answered, she was very responsive and went to get Michele immediately. Animated and happy, Michele told me all she had done that day. Then she told me she loved me and off she went to be with the other children. Delores returned stating that Michele fit in very well and that, so far, things were going smoothly. She encouraged me to call any time. Feeling really good after I hung up the phone, I sat down to relax and watch a little TV without feeling guilty.

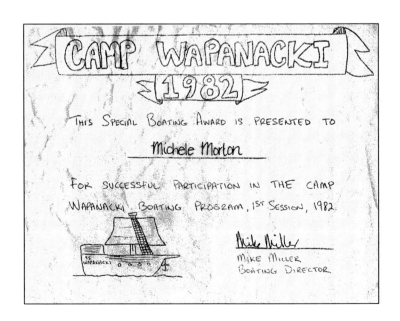

CAMP WAPANACKI 1982

THIS SPECIAL BOATING AWARD IS PRESENTED TO

Michele Morton

FOR SUCCESSFUL PARTICIPATION IN THE CAMP WAPANACKI BOATING PROGRAM, 1ST SESSION, 1982.

MIKE MILLER
BOATING DIRECTOR

Chapter VII

Now that Michele was a student at the N. Y. Institute, I was interested in knowing everything about the school. Roger Walker answered all of my questions without hesitation and expressed pleasure when I offered my services for committee involvement. One of the committees that sparked my interest was the Curriculum Committee. Roger granted my wish to join it, much to the chagrin of some of his staff, who felt uncomfortable with a parent on such a committee. But he said having an interested and involved parent participating in decision-making strategies should be actively encouraged and that was the end of it.

Interestingly enough, the majority of parents felt the same way about some of the staff. At one meeting I noticed the general consensus of the parents attending seemed to be never to question or make waves. When I asked why, the response surprised me. "Because they can throw your kid out," they said, nearly in unison.

I looked at them, astounded. "You don't really believe that!"

"Oh, yes," some said. "They can do whatever they want."

"I'm not getting those vibes at all, and certainly not from Walker or Wiltshire. Look, if any one of you have a question about your child's programming, it's not only your right, but your responsibility to ask. I certainly don't foresee any problem."

"It's all right for you to say that because you don't have to be as concerned as we do," came a voice from the back. It was

Phyllis Roth, one of the first parents we had met when Michele enrolled. "Your child is only blind and is in the academic program. If they threw her out, you would have other options. But I have two blind children here at the school, both with multihandicaps. Tell me, Mrs. Morton, what would I do if they threw them out? Where would they go? Do you think there's a whole bunch of schools out there just waiting to accept them?"

I was dumbfounded at the depth of fear that prevailed. My eyes swept the group of parents and I made eye contact with most of them. I stated, with some deliberation, "No one is going to throw any child out of this school because a parent questions a program. That's archaic thinking! You have my word on that.

"From your perspective, your fears are real. But my experience has been that the minute we allow ourselves to become intimidated, is the minute we weaken our position. So, what shall we do to strengthen instead?" No one responded. "What do you think about establishing a Parent/Staff Association within the school, where parents and staff deal with issues together? Such an organization could do some fund-raising for the school as well." There were murmurs of approval. They seemed to like the idea of this organized approach. "Okay, then, it's settled. I'll talk to Roger Walker and get back to you."

The next day, armed with their support, I took up the issue with Walker. Sitting at his desk, he motioned for me to enter his office. He wore a gray business suit with a white shirt and gray and red striped tie, and was as affable as ever. Standing, he greeted me warmly, with hand outstretched. I shook his hand and smiled as he ran his fingers through his hair, trying to control the strand that kept falling over his forehead. That was a battle he never won!

"I met with some of the parents yesterday," I said, pulling up a chair and sitting down.

"That's good," he declared. "Was it a positive exchange?"

"Yes, I came away feeling it was a good meeting. But I was surprised to find out how intimidated most of them were. They feel if they make waves, their children could be thrown out of school."

He looked at me with an incredulous expression. "That's preposterous! Where would they get an idea like that?" he asked, falling back into his chair with arms raised.

"Beats me," I said shrugging my shoulders.

"Grant you," Walker continued, "I suspected a general feeling among some parents that they harbored fears, but I have no idea where that originated. They never really talked about it."

"What do you think of the idea of starting a Parent/Staff Association? The board could be comprised of five officers (all parents), who would be the voting members. You and Noble Wiltshire would be permanent members, and a different member of the staff could be rotated in each month. Its purpose would be to encourage good communication among parents and staff, and to organize fund-raising activities for the school as a whole."

"That's a wonderful idea!" he responded exuberantly. "How do the other parents feel about it?"

"They liked the idea," I told him, "and supported my coming to talk to you today."

"That's a great start," he responded with a smile. "Let's do it!"

I left Walker's office feeling satisfied and excited about this new challenge.

Additional meetings were held, followed by officer nominations and elections soon after. So, in the year 1976, the PSA (Parent/Staff Association) became both a reality and a positive driving force of the N.Y. Institute of the Education of the Blind. And I became its first president.

Obviously, the school was very well run with Roger Walker at the helm. He was down-to-earth and easy to work with and welcomed parents' ideas, and suggestions. Noble Wiltshire, his assistant, was also very supportive. When something didn't run smoothly, the problem was immediately addressed and quickly resolved.

At first, adjustment to life away was difficult for Michele. That was only to be expected. Missing us seemed to last only a few weeks. The school had a good recreational program and other children to play with, both big pluses for her. Another big plus was the food – she loved it! The variety of delicious food served daily, may very well have been the turning point for her.

For several weeks, I visited daily, observing classroom activities, outdoor playtime, and evening recreational programs. Sometimes we walked around the campus, just the two of us, and chatted for awhile. This eased some of her anxieties and her comfort level improved. Typically, when it was time for me to leave, Michele would walk me to the car, give me a kiss and hug, and go on her way. I looked after her and thought, 'So many major adjustments in her young life and she handles them like a real trouper.' A few times, in the beginning, I was the one who cried once I got in the car to drive home, because my heart was heavy. I loved her so much, and missed her terribly. But I couldn't dwell on that, because I knew in my heart that this was a great program for her, and one of the best decisions we had ever made on her behalf.

However, the continuous whirlwind of changes in Michele's medical condition took a hold of us, seemingly never to let go. Every time we thought we could shake it off, it held us tightly, daring us to escape from its vise-like grip. The constant hospital visits and admissions were never-ending, and at this juncture we still had no idea of the cause of her illness. Since we didn't know if or when something would occur, all we could do was react when it did. In a sense, we were being held hostage by a disease that continued to baffle even the most learned experts in the neurological field of medicine. The New York Hospital, Cornell Medical Center, was known as one of the most prestigious institutions in the world, yet the answers eluded them as well.

My way of coping was to take each day and hope for the best. I took whatever positive steps I could to handle the situation. My job, as Michele's Mom, was to do the best, the very best, I could for her. Meeting her needs was a challenge, but that was the key to success. And isn't that true of all of us? Once our needs are met, we become highly motivated, bringing meaning and excitement to our daily activities.

There was no question in our minds, although we didn't always voice it, that we were dealing with some kind of disease that showed signs of a puzzling physical deterioration, with some mental aberrations. Although the evidence of deterioration was subtle at times, the frustration was great once the discovery was made. One day, while playing with her dolls up in her room, I heard her cry out.

"Michele" I called up to her, "are you okay?"

"No! No! No!" came the anguished cry.

When I reached her room she was sitting on her bed sobbing, with Barbie doll clothes strewn all around her. The doll had been thrown across the room.

"What's going on, Honey?" I asked, as I walked across the room and put my arms around her.

"I can't dress Barbie anymore," she said through tears.

"Why not?" I asked.

"Because my fingers don't work right! I can't put Barbie's arms in the sleeves and I can't open and close the buttons on her dresses. What's wrong with me, Mommy?" she asked in an anguished tone.

I hugged her tightly and dried her tears. "There are some things we don't always immediately know the answers to," I told her. "I'll call the doctor tomorrow. In the meantime, let's do something that's fun!" I started tickling her and she fought me off as best she could. Eventually she stopped struggling and threw herself down on the bed, laughing. I laughed with her and we carried on until her father arrived.

"What's going on here?" he asked, smiling broadly. He turned to me and mouthed, "Having a problem?"

I nodded.

Turning to Michele he said. "What is this? Are you guys on strike, or what? There's no supper made downstairs, no table set, nothing." That brought more peals of laughter. "I bet it's because you want pizza tonight. Is that it?"

"Yes! Yes! Can we, Mom? Please?"

"Sure. Let's go." And so, we hurried down the stairs together, holding hands and looking like the typical American family, with not a care in the world.

Another episode. Another problem to check out. Would it ever end?

I soon realized I would have to have a plan B to implement for situations like this. The shock element caught us constantly off guard, and I relied heavily on Michele's amazing sense of humor to get us out of tough situations. She wasn't given to depression, thank God, and ordinarily was a very happy kid who loved life. It was our job to try and maintain her love of life and her self-esteem, so she could continue to feel good about herself.

We found out that her inability to dress Barbie was because her fine motor coordination was now affected. I was advised of this as if it were run-of-the-mill information for a parent. But it wasn't. I had never thought in terms of fine motor coordination before, or about how it worked or didn't work. We take so much for granted. We walk, we talk, we sit, we kneel, we stand. We do a zillion other things, all at the dictates of the brain. We never think twice about these movements until something misfires, creating chaos throughout the system.

At times, the depth of frustration I felt made me want to scream my head off. But then I reasoned, what good would that do? The problems would still be there. Also, for Michele's sake, I was determined to put my best foot forward, to never let her see me in a despondent mood. Optimistic by nature, and armed with belief in the power of positive thinking, I was determined to ride through the neurological tempest that swirled incessantly around me.

Meeting once a month, the board of the Parent/Staff Association made plans to hold its first annual dinner-dance to generate additional school funds. Excitement and enthusiasm dominated the planning stages.

The longer Michele attended the N. Y. Institute, the more she loved the school. It was good to see her level of excitement each weekend. She talked incessantly about Joanne, one of the child care workers (CCWs). We had met her and agreed that she was pretty wonderful. This young lady was kind, considerate, caring, and funny, all wonderful attributes. Her responsibilities with Michele began when the school day ended. Michele had really lucked out with Cindy Walker, her teacher, during the day, and Joanne after hours. We all relaxed a bit. I continued to travel back and forth several times a week due to my involvement with the PSA and other meetings.

The school's decision to establish a coffee shop and teach

the kids how to make sandwiches, operate the cash register and wait on customers was a big hit with the students. Michele was excited about the prospect of operating the cash register. Anything to do with money turned her on – big time! The students were divided into groups and each group was scheduled to work on a different day of the week and at different times.

A couple of months into the program, I received a report from the school that Michele had become uncooperative there. I was surprised since I knew she had been looking forward to participating. When I picked her up that day I asked, "How was school this week, Honey?"

"Fine," she replied, shrugging her shoulders.

"Any problems that I should know about?"

"Nope," she said in a clipped tone, looking totally indifferent.

"That's not what I heard, Michele." She turned and looked at me quizzically. "They told me you were uncooperative when scheduled for the coffee shop program. Is that true?"

"Oh, that!" she said, screwing up her face. "We learn nothing there. All we do is clean up after everyone and pick up garbage."

"Really, Michele!" I said in disbelief. "Everyone has to take their turn cleaning up. That's all part of the program."

She sighed, showing some frustration. "Mom, they have us just cleaning up every time we go, and I'm not doing it any more, because it's just not fair!"

"Okay, I'll look into it," I promised her. "Let's drop it for now, and have fun this weekend. Is that a deal?"

"It's a deal. But, you'll see, I'm right, Mom," was her solemn declaration. "Yes!" she declared emphatically. "You'll see."

When we arrived home I called Frank Simpson, director of pre-vocational services. He was equally surprised at Michele's insistence. He told me he had the schedule in front of him and that it indicated one week for sandwiches, the next week cash register, and so on. Wearily, I informed him I would come for lunch the next time she was scheduled. I requested he not tell Michele because I wanted to observe without her knowing I was present.

When I arrived on Michele's scheduled day, her class had not come down yet. While waiting, I ordered lunch and was impressed at how well the students handled the order, took my money, and gave me the right change. Very little supervision was needed. 'Wow!' I thought, 'This is a great program.' About an hour later when Michele and her classmates arrived, I was the only one left. Guess what? It was clean-up duty for them!

Michele promptly refused, sat down at one of the tables, and stated that she had been told that she would be working on sandwiches or the cash register. The employee working with the kids was aware of my presence and tried to get Michele to cooperate. But Michele held her ground stating, "No cash register, no sandwiches, then no garbage."

"It's too late to work on sandwiches or the cash register now, Michele," the staff member pointed out. "We're getting ready to close."

And there was the crux of the problem! It was closing time for the coffee shop, so all that was left to do each day when Michele's class came down was the clean up and garbage detail. Michele was right! Although, the schedule indicated that a different activity would take place each week, it couldn't happen with her class because they came down at the same time every week. I had to laugh at Michele's refusal not to lift a finger. She had to go on strike, for heaven's sake, to get her point across. She was something else, I tell you. And I was proud of her!

I walked over to Frank Simpson's office. "We have a problem, Frank," I stated.

"Why? What's going on?" he asked.

"The problem is what is not going on." And I proceeded to tell him what I discovered. He looked at me in disbelief, slowly shaking his head in embarrassment.

"I can't believe this wasn't picked up. I was remiss myself for not investigating more closely. I'm sorry. I can assure you, it will be corrected right away."

"These things happen, so don't worry about it. The programs you run here are second to none. Of course, Michele may argue that point right now," I added with a laugh.

"Who could blame her?" he said smiling. "In the future, we'll have to pay closer attention to what she's telling us."

Returning to the coffee shop I found Michele still sitting at the table, the same determined look on her face. This time I made my presence known. As she began to relate the same story, I interjected that I already knew, having witnessed it all.

"I've already discussed this with Mr. Simpson," I told her. "He didn't realize your class came down when the coffee shop was closing each time. The time will be adjusted in order for each of you to learn the other coffee shop duties."

Michele's face was wreathed in smiles. "Thanks, Mom. See, I told you!"

"You did indeed, Michele, but sometimes mistakes happen. In the future, let me know sooner, before there's a standoff. Can you do that?" I asked, laughing.

"Oh, I think so, Mom," she said with a smile and a devilish look in her eye. After we hugged and kissed and she went back to her class, I returned home, feeling very satisfied with the way things had turned out. When I related the situation to Michael and his dad that evening, they weren't at all surprised at the stand that Michele had taken.

Although things seemed to be going well, I noticed something in Michele's speech pattern that was puzzling. She seemed to have momentary lapses. Occasionally, certain words in her sentences were absent, although she seemed not to notice. For instance, if she wanted to say, 'Let's go to the store,' it might come out like, 'Let's to the store.' When I asked her to repeat the sentence, she would insert the word 'go,' but miss another word. Since the problem wasn't obvious, I just made a mental note to ask the neurologist about it.

However, before our next appointment, she started falling every so often, skinning her hands and knees. Now, this was a kid who was on the track team, so dismissing it as clumsiness was not easy to do. A few days later, the next call was not so easily dismissed either. Michele was walking with Joanne and, without warning, fell down hard on the concrete, hitting her head. The laceration was deep and wide and blood spurted everywhere. She was rushed to the nearest hospital. After I got the call, I jumped in the car and headed for the ER, only to find out she had already been discharged. I then made a beeline for the school, and arrived just before they did.

When the van pulled in, I was some distance away. I walked over just as Michele got out. My heart leapt as I stared in dismay. Her head was swathed in bandages. "Michele!" I called out. I ran toward her and drew her to me for a big hug. "How are you, Honey?"

"I hurt, because I got a bunch of stitches."

"I know, Sweetheart," I said soothingly, hugging her again. "Why all the bandages?" I asked the staff member who accompanied Michele to the hospital. She informed me it was just a precautionary measure so Michele wouldn't touch it overnight. A nurse observed Michele during the night, and the next day I took her to see the neurologist. Doctor Solomon was out of town, so she saw the neurological resident on duty. When he examined her, he said, "There's nothing wrong. She's fine."

I was surprised at his casual attitude. "I don't think so doctor, she has a big gash on her forehead from a fall yesterday. She's had some interrupted thought processes. And I'm concerned it may be some type of seizure that's not apparent to us. I would like to have an EEG done, just to be sure."

"I'm not ordering an EEG," he said curtly. "It's not necessary. I can't see any kind of seizure activity in my examination."

"Then how do you explain her falling when there is no stumbling or tripping involved?"

"She probably did trip, but nobody saw it."

"No, Doctor, that's not true. The report I received indicated she just keeled over without warning. I trust this staff. Believe me, they're just as interested in getting to the bottom of this as I am."

He stood. Slowly he emphasized each word, "Mrs. Morton, there is no need for an EEG here and I'm not ordering one. Do you understand?" Then he closed her file with finality and we were promptly dismissed. I stood, but did not respond. After all, Doctor GOD had just spoken. It was hard for me not to bow, before I walked out of the office.

I left the clinic thoroughly frustrated. How could I make an EEG happen? My mind raced a mile a minute and then, suddenly, it dawned on me. Her speech was also affected, so why not make an appointment with speech pathology?

There, the receptionist greeted us warmly. When I told her I was there to make an appointment, she informed me that they had just had a cancellation. Would we have time to have the evaluation done now? Would we?! I thought, with amusement, 'The real God must be handling this one'.

"Sure," I said. "That would be great."

The testing took about an hour. Afterwards, we waited in the reception room while the results were evaluated. Eventually, the speech pathologist told us that the speech pattern showed Michele might be taking some small seizures.

"But the neurologist said there was no sign of seizures when he checked her," I said.

"The kind I think she's taking, and which would explain the missed words, are called subliminal seizures, and wouldn't show up on a clinical exam. We really need to do an EEG right away.

"I thought so myself," I said, "although I didn't know there was such a thing as subliminal seizures. Since Doctor Solomon is out of town, what can I do?"

"We can order it from here. I'm going to see if I can get it done now. Michele told me all about falling yesterday, and that's quite a head injury, so it wouldn't be wise to delay this."

'My sentiments exactly,' I thought. Now, here was a woman after my own heart. She was successful in getting Michele in right away. The doctor would call me the following day after the results had been properly interpreted.

The next day, as promised, Dr. Pietrucha called. "Mrs. Morton," she began, "the results of the EEG show that Michele is in big trouble with subliminal seizures. She's taking over a 100 a day. We need to get her on medication immediately. We'll get her started on Zarontin which is very effective for these types of seizures. Would you be able to pick it up and take it to her?"

"Of course, I'll take it to her right away!" I said. I was shocked at what I'd just heard. "Over a 100 a day?" 'So, Doctor God was wrong,' I thought. 'What a blow to his ego.' I told Doctor Pietrucha what had happened with the resident and she thanked me.

Hanging up, I breathed a sigh of relief. Now something could be done about the recent developments. It had begun to feel that I was always on an extended learning expedition. Some of the teachers were knowledgeable and some weren't. Generally, doctors weren't trained well enough to listen to parents. Medical schools failed miserably there.

Parents of sick children have to be tenacious and learn to circumvent the system, if necessary, when that system works against the best interests of their child. Many times, it is bureaucracy at its finest that drives the system. This, actually, should play no part in the life of a sick child. One thing all parents know for sure is that it is they who must deal with the consequences of what does or does not happen to their child. So, why then shouldn't the parent be considered an equal partner in this decision-making relationship?

Fortunately, there are many men and women who become doctors who need no special training in this regard. It is they who make parents such as myself forever grateful for their presence in our lives.

In addition to being placed on Zarontin for the subliminal seizures, Michele was also fitted for a medical helmet. (Yes, there is such a thing!) They're designed to protect one's head in the event of a fall. To my surprise, it looked really good on her. The inside was soft and fluffy, the exterior leather. We laughingly called her our little football hero!

As time passed, I learned that resilience is the key to coping with constant emotional turmoil. Changing my behavior became commonplace. For instance, one of my absolute declarations had been that I would never drive into Manhattan. Parking was impossible and traffic was a nightmare. But I had to face the fact that I could no longer take the subway with Michele. While waiting for the train one day there was so much pushing and shoving that she lost her balance and fell down, even with me holding her hand. It was then I realized that I would have to drive.

After several months of fighting thousands of yellow cabs for a few feet of space, listening to the incessant honking of horns and screeching brakes while timidly trying to move forward, I was getting absolutely nowhere. I realized I had to change my driving behavior and stop being intimidated. Otherwise I wouldn't survive. Though I continued to be fearful of being hit, I eventually realized that cabbies didn't want accidents on their records either as this was their livelihood. Armed with this new attitude and a pounding heart, I plunged in, moving ahead quickly and forcefully, ignoring the yellow cabs just an inch from my car, trying to swallow me up. I jockeyed around them successfully until I had moved ahead. I felt exhilarated! 'New York! New York! What a wonderful town!' I said to myself with a laugh.

Though the hospital had valet parking, a huge sign reading 'Parking Lot Full,' invariably greeted us as we entered. Continuing around the circular driveway and out of the complex, we searched for the lone available spot that possibly a hundred other cars were vying for. Since it was becoming increasingly difficult for Michele to walk long distances, especially during winter with snow and ice on the ground, a distant parking place presented a true problem.

The valet parking concession for N. Y. Hospital was run by a cheerful, young black man. He always had a big hello for Michele, to which she responded in kind. I decided to talk to him one day. As I approached, he gave me his undivided attention. I explained the difficulties we were encountering, especially now that Michele was blind.

"When did that happen?" he exclaimed. "She sure doesn't

look it."

"It's been a few months now," I said, "and we're still trying to find out what's going on. I thought maybe you could help us with parking. The lot is always full when we get here."

Rubbing his chin and directing his attention to Michele he said, "I tell you what I'm going to do for you, young lady. The next time you come in, signal to me, drive out and around the block, come back around, and I'll have a parking spot for you right here."

Michele and I were delighted to hear it, and he was as good as his word. After that, for hundreds of hospital visits, we drove directly to the front of the building, got out of the car, gave the valet my keys, and left the parking to him. Boy, did that make our lives easier! There are so many good people in the world, and he was right up there with the best of them. My response to his kindness was to tip the workers well and to buy lunch from time to time.

At the hospital, Michele continued to have her eyes checked on a regular basis since the cause of vision loss remained unknown. Since neurological problems were also apparent now, it was the leading neuro/ophthalmologist we saw. He had an enviable reputation in his field, but his behavior outside of that arena left much to be desired. He was egotistical and extremely demanding. Rumor had it that all the residents feared him. He was what you could call a Doctor God, with credentials. We always had to wait over an hour to see him.

On one such appointment I decided to take Michele for her EEG test after I found out from the receptionist that, as usual, the waiting time would be over an hour. The test was completed within that time frame and the sticky substance used to keep the electrodes in place was also removed from her hair and scalp. I brushed her hair well, and she looked fine. We quickly returned to ophthalmology.

When we got off the elevator, I immediately noted the receptionist appeared flustered. "Oh, Mrs. Morton, I'm so sorry. They called your name a few minutes ago. When you didn't respond, the doctor demanded to know where you were. I told him you were at EEG and would return in a few minutes. He was furious with me for letting you go, but I told him I couldn't stop you."

"Of course you couldn't stop me. That's ridiculous!" I exclaimed. "Don't worry about it. We're here now and I'll explain it to him."

"He won't see you now," she said.

"Didn't you say this happened only minutes ago?"

"Yes, just before you arrived. But the doctor won't see Michele now."

"This is insane!" I said. "I'm going back there." Walking back into the examining area, I saw the doctor leaning against a wall, reading. He looked up as I approached and icily told me that he was not seeing Michele. When I tried to explain, he deliberately turned his back on me. Throwing up my hands, I began to leave the examining area. A staff member asked if I wanted to make another appointment.

"No!" I said, emphatically. "I don't care if he ever sees Michele again. His behavior is appalling."

Suddenly I heard his voice. When I turned, there was Doctor God, with credentials, in the middle of the reception area, pointing his finger at me and yelling, "Mother! Mother! I heard what you said in there and let me tell you, I'll never see that child again. Never! You understand?" he shouted, his voice shaking with fury.

Holding my ground, I looked him square in the eye, and calmly stated, "You know, Doctor, that decision has *got* to be in Michele's best interest. Furthermore, the most important person on this floor right now is this child and the second most important is her mother. And don't you forget it!" With that, I turned around and walked into the waiting elevator with Michele.

I later learned he took his rage out on the residents that afternoon, but they didn't care once they heard what happened. They secretly applauded the mother who stood up to him. As for me, I couldn't believe that anyone, much less a doctor, would take exception to a parent using an hour productively instead of sitting idle in a waiting room. Fortunately these things didn't happen too often.

I never did bring Michele back to see him at the hospital clinic, but as fate would have it, we were destined to meet again.

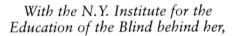

*With the N.Y. Institute for the
Education of the Blind behind her,*

*Michele shows how happy
she is to be there.*

Chapter VIII

The PSA had just completed its first annual dinner dance at the school. It was a huge success thanks to the hard work of the committee. It also brought in several thousand dollars, which we turned over to the school. This made Roger Walker very happy and he expressed this at our next board meeting.

Then, the issue of transportation came up. The City of New York, it seemed, transported all special ed children to their schools on a daily basis, but refused to transport those who needed busing on Mondays and Fridays only. When I asked Roger Walker about this, he replied that it had been a problem for many years. Every attempt by parents to fight the City had proven unsuccessful.

Because of this, one of our Board members, Angelo Perrone, along with two other Staten Island parents, hired a lawyer to raise the issue with the City. Angelo wondered aloud if he should invite this lawyer to our next parent meeting. Perhaps he would be interested in representing all of the children. The decision to extend the invitation was unanimous.

After that meeting, the lawyer said he would take on the case as a class action suit. He wanted $1,000 up front and another $1,000 at a later date, to be paid in $500 increments. He told us the class action approach would include all children needing the same type of bus service. We were initially elated. However, as time passed it appeared he was actually only working for the first three children. Because only those parents were included in all correspondence. Concerned about this, I brought it to his attention. He told me not to worry, that he was in there fighting for all the kids. I responded that I was not happy with this arrangement. If he felt the need to copy three parents he should copy all parents. OR, he could copy the board and we could pass the information along to all the parents.

While we tried to resolve this matter word came down that transportation was approved, but only for the initial three children. Upon checking, I found out that this lawyer had never even requested a list of the other children. Somewhat forced to finally request the list, he expressed shock. "I had no idea so many children required this service!" he exclaimed.

I was stunned. Almost two years and $1,500 later he was saying he had no idea that so many children required this service. I strongly stated that it was his responsibility to find out how many children there were. Though our initial agreement called for another $500 I was determined to see that he didn't get another penny. As far as I was concerned, he owed us money!

Not long after that exchange, he called to say that the Bureau of Pupil Transportation had agreed to transport our children, but on a second shift schedule only. This meant a 10:00 a.m. arrival and a 4:00 p.m. pick up time, which would throw the school's schedule into chaos. We rejected the proposal, stating that all the children should be treated equally, arriving on time for class and being picked up when classes ended. By the way, the city's proposal applied to all boroughs except Queens. This caused a round of laughter from my colleagues because, of course, Queens was where I lived, as did 16 other families from the school! The reason provided was insufficient funds. Now the city was really being selective.

'There's gotta be something illegal going on here guys,' I

mused. 'Unequal transportation for residential school children and none at all if you happen to live in Queens – C'mon!' It was truly laughable. I wondered how naïve they thought we were. Anyway, this was the additional reason why we turned down the offer.

I called an emergency board meeting to discuss the issue. Once assembled, we talked primarily about our 'legal counsel.' The majority agreed that he should not proceed with the case and that the lawyer needed to be informed.

"Since I'm the treasurer," Angelo commented, "I'll write out a check for $500 to cover his latest bill."

"I don't think so," I shot back. "No more money need go to him.

He looked surprised. "Kathleen, we have to honor the contract."

"What contract?" I asked. "We had no written contract with him. What we had was a verbal agreement which appeared in the minutes of our meeting. Nothing was signed by either party. In any case, he didn't fulfill his part of the agreement, which was a class action suit against the city, so that ALL children would receive appropriate transportation. Instead of that, he obtained transportation for the initial three children, one of whom doesn't even attend school here!

"That was the very issue, Angelo, I had doubts about when he repeatedly sent copies of the legal procedures to you and the other two parents, while ignoring the remainder. When I asked him about this, he told me who he copied was insignificant because he was working for all the children. We now know that wasn't true. Also, are you aware that in addition to the $500 he wants more money to continue with the case? There's no way he's getting another cent from us!"

Angelo was obviously upset.

"Look, Angelo, I continued, I know you have a personal relationship with this lawyer. You, along with the other two parents succeeded in obtaining appropriate transportation through a private arrangement with him. That's fine. But over that same period of time he did not live up to his agreement with all of us. We're still in the same boat we were in two years ago. Do you think he was entitled to take $1,500, given to him in good faith, and do nothing?"

An uncomfortable silence followed. We stared at each other. I sighed audibly, shaking my head and finally said, "This isn't getting us anywhere. We obviously will never agree on this. As you know, both the treasurer and president must sign all checks and, to tell you the truth, I will resign as president before I sign another check to him. That's how strongly I feel about this."

After some heated discussion involving the entire board, the majority agreed with me and the issue was closed. Thanking them for their support, I concluded, "This problem is far from over. I'm going to continue the fight until every child in this school receives appropriate and equal transportation. It won't be easy, but if we stick together, we can prevail." They agreed enthusiastically and the meeting was adjourned.

Around this time, the New York City's Special Olympics sports program was getting underway. The board thought it might be a good idea for our children to participate. Initially, the officials turned us down because our children were blind. But persistence paid off. We finally received an invitation to participate. This created a lot of excitement among the children and staff. Vicky Tripodi, physical education director for the school, prepared the children well for the upcoming events. Michele was to participate in the softball throw and broad jump.

When the day arrived, Arnie took off from work to join me

in the stands. Everything went well, adding to the overall enthusiasm. Suddenly, it was Michele's turn to appear on the field for the softball throw event. There was obviously a problem. Afterwards we found out what actually happened:

As Michele approached, the umpire handed her the ball telling her to throw it.

"Now?" she asked.

"Yes, now," the umpire responded.

So, she did as he asked, and threw the ball while facing him, missing his head by a hair. He was about to disqualify her when Vicky ran onto the field waving her arms. When she reached him, she explained that Michele was one of the blind children who needed special assistance with the set up. He shook his head looking chagrined and said he had no idea. Then, he apologized.

Ball in hand, he walked Michele to the marker, turned her so she faced the field, and told her to throw the ball from there. Meanwhile, one of the staff members in the field yelled, "Michele! Michele! Throw the ball out this way." Winding up, she threw the softball as hard as she could, to a backdrop of cheers from the stands.

The broad jump competition went off without a hitch and Michele was pleased with the results. She knew she had made a very good jump. Most of the children did well in the various competitions and won prizes. Michele came in second in the softball throw and took first place in the Broad Jump. Boy, was she happy! Just witnessing her excitement made us feel terrific.

A year later, as the children prepared for another competition, our broad jump champ discovered something that left her reeling.

"What's wrong, Honey?" I asked when I saw how despondent she was.

"You won't believe it!" A look of sadness crept into her eyes as she pursed her lips before continuing, "I can't jump."

"What do you mean you can't jump? The school won't let you jump or you're not able to jump?"

"I'm not *able* to jump!" she yelled in frustration.

"Okay, let's not get excited, now. Here, give me your hands. When I count to three, try and jump. Ready? Let's go – one, two, three – jump!"

As hard as she tried, Michele could not lift her two feet off the floor simultaneously. We practiced this method with relentless intensity until we were both sick of it.

"Forget it," she finally said. "I'm going upstairs to my room to play records." A few minutes later I heard the music from the Wizard of Oz and knew she would be happy for a while. No matter how many times Michele listened to the record, it kept her enthralled. For many years it was broadcast on TV. Each January she pestered her father to call the TV station to find out the day and time, so she was sure to be home. The entertainment value from that one production was phenomenal.

I thought back to last year, when she'd come home from Girl Scouts and announcing that they were going to do the Wizard of Oz play. Auditions were to take place the following day.

"I'm going to try out for Dorothy," she said happily.

Her father and I looked at each other, amused. She certainly wouldn't need a script because she knew the story by heart. But there was one small problem. She couldn't carry a tune to save her soul. She was tone deaf, just like her father. Still, nothing could dissuade her. We tried to soften the blow by telling her not to be too disappointed if she wasn't chosen, as a lot of girls would be trying out for the leading role.

"So what?" she said. "I'm still going to try."

After auditions I could tell by her face that she didn't get the part. "How did it go?" I asked.

"I tried so hard, but they gave the part to someone else."

"So, does this sad face mean you didn't get any part at all?"

"No, it doesn't. I got a part. I'm going to be a Munchkin."

"Why, that's great, Michele! Just think! We're going to see you on stage!"

"Do you think I'll make a good Munchkin?" she asked.

"The best in the world!"

"Where's Daddy?"

"Upstairs. Go tell him the good news."

"Okay!" she said and made a beeline for the stairs.

The production was wonderful. And, there was her dad, up by the stage, taking pictures as if she were the star. Two Dorothys had been cast and I could understand why. Both were beautiful singers. It would have been very hard to have chosen one over the other, so one child played the first half and the other child the second half. Smart move.

Now, here was Michele upstairs, probably mulling over what was going to happen next. I went up to chat with her. She told me she was fine, that jumping wasn't all that important anyway. Funny, that was going to be my persuasive argument with her, but she had come to the conclusion on her own.

At one point during Michele's stay at the school, one of her roommates was a little black girl named Dwella. Always in a great mood, Dwella's smile lit up her whole face. She and Michele became fast friends. When I drove Michele back to school after summer vacation Dwella had usually already arrived. One of the staff would invariably say to her, "Here comes Michele."

Dwella then would yell at the top of her lungs, "Michele! Michele!"

Michele would jump out of the car and run in her direction responding with, "Hi Dwella!" and continuing her pace until they almost collided. Then, they would hug each other, jumping up and down with excitement.

A few weeks after this recent reunion, I received a call from Delores, the evening supervisor at the school. "Just thought you'd like to hear the pillow talk between Dwella and Michele tonight," she said.

"I was making my rounds to be sure all lights were out when I heard Michele and Dwella discussing Snow White." It went like this."

"I'm going to try out for Snow White tomorrow," Michele said to Dwella.

"So am I," Dwella replied.

"What? Michele exclaimed. "I don't think you can be Snow White, Dwella.

"Why not?!" Dwella demanded.

"Because Snow White is 'white' and you are black," Michele explained matter-of-factly.

"Aren't you black also?"

"Who, me?" Michele cried out, now laughing. "No, Dwella, I'm white! "I thought you knew that."

"I can't believe that," Dwella said astonished. "You're white?!"

I could just picture this exchange between the two of them, and I appreciated Delores relating it to me. Poor Dwella. Throughout her young life, she'd assumed everyone was black and evidently the subject had never come up. The next morning, both of them tried out but, neither got the part.

The 'I can't jump' syndrome, I knew in my heart, was symptomatic of something more serious. We didn't have long to wait to find out. One day the school called and said Michele had a lot of difficulty walking, and couldn't accompany the other children on their regular afternoon walk to the store with some staff members. The next day when I picked her up she was walking fine. That's what was so puzzling, I was told by the staff. Suddenly all the mental signals for gross motor movement seemed to stop. Her legs and feet would move as if she were riding a bike but was unable to move from the spot at which she stood. Then, just as suddenly, the signals returned, and she'd start walking – fast at first, and then at a more normal pace.

I immediately called Doctor Solomon, who said she wanted the chief of the rehabilitation center to see Michele. An appointment was set for the following week. Meanwhile, I observed some gross motor difficulties while she was home. It was as though she had to 'rev up' before taking a step. After a minute or so she would walk with no further difficulties. Encouraged by this, I began to think the problem would gradually subside.

When appointment day arrived she was feeling perky. I told her since she was such a good girl we would stop at the Gertz Department Store in Flushing for dinner on the way home. That was Michele's favorite place to eat. Everyone there was nice to her and she especially liked the cashier. Michele always paid the bill on the way out, and the cashier would give her a big hello. Then they would exchange some funny story with both of them laughing while saying goodbye.

Now, here we were pulling into New York Hospital, once again in search of answers. As we exited the car to walk into the hospital, Michele suddenly could not move a muscle. No matter how much she tried, she could not take a step. I held her hands and encouraged her, but to no avail. Even the horns of the cars behind us and the shouts of angry motorists were unable to propel her forward. She looked up at me, tears streaming down her face, and said, "Mommy, I just can't walk." She cried from the depth of her soul.

I drew her to me and hugged her tightly, and there, in the middle of the of New York Hospital rotunda, we stood locked in an embrace and wept unashamedly, oblivious of the clamor around us. This was one moment we had hoped never to share.

The doorman came running over, and after assessing the situation said, "I'll get a wheelchair."

"No!" Michele screamed. "No wheelchair!"

He turned and looked at me quizzically, arms outstretched and eyebrows raised. I nodded my head in assent to his offer and whispered to Michele, "Honey, just go in the wheelchair until we get upstairs. Then you can get out of it."

She looked up at me and after a few moments reluctantly agreed.

When we arrived at the rehab center, Michele got out of the wheelchair, falling to her knees. She quickly pulled herself up by holding onto a chair. We continued to practice trying to walk. Suddenly, her motor movements responded and she started to walk with ease.

When it was her turn to see the doctor, she walked into her office without faltering. The doctor examined her thoroughly, released her to a staff member to conduct another test, and then spoke with me privately.

"Mrs. Morton, whatever disease Michele has is now severely affecting her gross motor coordination. She needs to be in a wheelchair."

"You've got to be kidding," I replied. "Isn't there something you can do in rehab?"

"Michele's not a candidate for rehabilitation."

"Why not?"

"Because she has the earmarks of a deteriorating illness, and that cancels her out."

"But couldn't she be helped by rehabilitation?"

"She no doubt could."

"Then why not do it? Give her a chance, for heaven's sake! No one even knows what in blazes this disease is. So how do you know that therapy won't have a lasting effect? Plus, Michele wants no part of a wheelchair. She's adamant about it. So, where does that leave us?"

"I don't know. Believe me, I really sympathize with you. I've called Doctor Solomon and she is on her way to meet with us."

"I don't doubt that you sympathize, Doctor, but what I need is support, not sympathy. We need to throw the book away for this kid and do what we think would give her as much quality of life as possible. She doesn't fit any mold, so why try to have the mold fit her?"

By the time Michele returned from her test, her walking had become quite labored. The elevator door opened and Doctor Solomon walked out with a wheelchair which she left by the door, unseen by Michele. She gave Michele a big hello, to which Michele responded pleasantly. She liked Doctor Solomon very much. I then addressed both doctors. "Unless you can think of a way to help Michele out of this gross motor problem there's no need for us to discuss anything further. Michele does not want to go into a wheelchair."

"That's right," Michele piped up. "No wheelchair!"

"Mrs. Morton," Doctor Solomon asked, "are you sure that you know what you're doing? There's a safety factor here."

"I'm not shoving her into a wheelchair, if that's what you mean," I said angrily. "I'm telling you, intermittently this kid can walk and walk well. She's going to be given every opportunity to do exactly that."

Frustrated, we left the hospital. Though the parking attendant brought our car around within minutes, Michele was already leaning on me for support and I had to half carry her to the car. Once settled, Michele said, "Thanks, Mom. I really want to try to keep walking more than anything."

"I know, Sweetheart, and I'm going to put you through my own kind of therapy. Before you go into a wheelchair, everything possible will be tried. But it *will* be hard work. Are you game?"

"Of course!" she replied, happy to know she might still have a chance.

That night at dinner, Michele told her father and Michael about what had happened at the hospital. "I told them no wheelchair!"

Since I had already discussed it with them before Michele came down to dinner, they weren't at all surprised by her declaration. We all admired her determination and spirit, and I felt I'd be letting her down if I didn't do everything within my power to help her.

Arnie had some reservations. "We have to keep in mind that two highly respected specialists are saying a wheelchair is the only option for safety's sake. Do you think it's wise to ignore them?"

"I'm not ignoring them, Arnie. Neither of them said she couldn't be helped with therapy. ('not' is the operative word here). It's just that she is not a candidate due to this strange, mysterious and unknown disease. I feel compelled to give Michele the benefit of the doubt. While I have high regard for Solomon's opinion, medical doctors generally go the traditional route, and that's just not good enough for Michele. They see a child showing evidence of deterioration, so why bother with rehabilitation? Complacency sets in. As a Mom, I see a determined child trying desperately to hang on, warding off every assault on her system. And despite it all, she still keeps smiling. How can I give up on that? No, until I turn over every stone, turn every corner, and have gone down every avenue on her behalf, I can't allow myself to fall under the spell of complacency. Besides, I have a plan."

Arnie looked at me, eyebrows raised, "You do?"

"While doing some research on degenerative diseases, I picked up a book by John Ott called *Health & Light*. I found it very interesting. He talks about how the ultraviolet rays of the sun can affect biological systems. Ultraviolet rays filtering through the eyes affect the pituitary and pineal glands which, in turn, influence the endocrine system. This doctor is convinced that removing his sun glasses while relaxing on the beaches of Florida cured his arthritis. He no longer needs a cane. Ott's doctors and some friends believed he simply had a great imagination. Here's a direct quote from Ott's book:

"It was gratifying to have my doctor advise that the x-ray pictures showed a definite strengthening and improvement in the area of my hip joint that had been causing so much trouble. A physical examination revealed the complete disappearance of a 30 per cent restriction of the movement or rotation of the hip joint which my doctor commented on as being wonderful but quite surprising and most unusual. For six months I had been imagining I felt better, and it was a great relief to have these x-ray pictures and examination confirm my imagination."

Arnie looked at me shaking his head and laughing. "This sounds great! Michele is lucky to have you for a mom. You never give up."

"She won't let me," I replied with a laugh. "I also read that water therapy is very good. I plan to take her to the club each day from early morning until dinner time. That way she'll have a combination of water therapy and direct sunlight."

"But you can't get into the club at this time of year until later in the day, due to the children's camp program," Arnie reminded me.

"I know. I've already taken care of that. I called and told them what I'm trying to do. They told me to bring Michele down anytime. They're rooting for her too! I've also registered her at the Y. I understand they have a great water therapy program."

We got up the next morning to a nice, sunny day. Pulling the drapes aside, I opened the window to enjoy the gentle breeze moving through the trees. The birds chirped almost rhythmically. I felt refreshed and ready to tackle whatever came my way.

After breakfast we headed for the Club. We changed in the locker room and made our way down the incline towards the pool. It was then that her movements became sluggish. She leaned on me, unable to make much independent movement. Dropping our pool bags, I half-carried her to the pool area and placed her on a chair before going back up to retrieve our bags.

Once she got into the pool, Michele could walk without a problem. She walked from one side of the pool to the other, thoroughly enjoying herself! We spent the entire day there, and enjoyed lunch and dinner. We repeated this plan of action daily. Sometimes we even arrived early enough to have breakfast!

After several weeks, Michele was still enjoying the experience, but there had been little progress. There were times when I wished I had borrowed the wheelchair just to get us back and forth to the pool area. I repeatedly asked myself if I was being unrealistic. When members were present late afternoon or evening, they often helped me with Michele. I appreciated this. Most of them felt sorry for her because they remembered her from days gone by, running up and down with all the other kids – jumping, laughing, and playing without a care in the world. They admired her determination, and were rooting for her all the way.

One day, as I extended my hands to help her up the pool steps, she declined and started walking without the slightest hesitation. Grinning from ear to ear she said, "I feel great!"

She walked around the entire pool, testing her ability. I had no idea what was happening or if it would last, but I had to enjoy the wonder of it all. I gathered our things, and started walking towards the locker room. Michele walked ahead of me, striding up the incline with strong, purposeful steps, waving arms in the air and shouting, "I can walk! I can walk!" She held her head back and turned herself around with glee.

Members started cheering and gave Michele a standing ovation. This was indeed the moment. The moment we had to savor without reservation. How long it would last I had no idea, but nothing was going to take away the enormous pleasure I felt watching her prance up that incline in triumph! This was the quality of life I'd been fighting for.

I called Doctor Solomon, who warned me not to get my hopes up. She didn't buy into Ott's theory regarding health and light. Still, what was becoming more and more obvious as time went on was Michele's enormous capacity to endure and survive.

In spite of the doctor's doubts, months passed with no signs of the walking difficulties Michele had encountered earlier. In fact, after the summer she was one of the children selected by the school to go cross-country skiing in Vermont. And what a time she had! When one of the counselors threw a snowball and caught her on the side of the head, she immediately retaliated laughing. They got a perfect picture of that moment.

So, what had really happened that summer to bring such positive results? Was it the extended exercise in the pool? The concentrated daily involvement? Or was it the ultra violet rays of the sun filtering through the eyes? We may never know. It did reinforce my belief in John Ott's theory of health and light. Michele had always liked to wear sun glasses, but when I told her it might help if she didn't, she took them off and never wore them again. As a matter of fact, Ott was the reason I followed the course I did, and the end result was remarkable. Who would have thought, when others were ready to put Michele in a wheelchair, that she'd be cross-country skiing within a few months?

One of the Broadway shows Michele really wanted to attend was Peter Pan, starring Sandy Duncan. I hoped I would be successful in obtaining front row aisle seats, since when Michele was in the first row she could follow the show better. When I learned that the front row belonged to the star of the show, I wrote to Sandy Duncan, explaining my reasons. I received a prompt reply from the theatre informing me that there would be two tickets, front row aisle seats, waiting for me at the box office when we arrived.

Michele's enthusiasm for the upcoming event was boundless, especially when she found out we would be chauffeured by her dad and Michael, with her Big Brother behind the wheel. Although still a teen, Michael was a very good driver, so we gave him the opportunity to drive into Manhattan. He was pleased because he knew it meant we had total trust in him. After dropping us off at the theatre, father and son went off on their own.

The show was great and Michele was enraptured. Sandy Duncan did a superb job as Peter Pan. At the part in the show where Peter Pan was struggling to recall the name of Tinkerbell, Sandy dramatically reached out to the audience asking, "What is the name? What is it?" You could have heard a pin drop.

And then, suddenly, the spell was broken as Michele jumped up, arms in the air, shouting, "Tinkerbell!"

Though the audience laughed, I was mortified. Sandy Duncan, however, didn't bat an eye. Pointing directly at Michele she announced, "That's it! Tinkerbell. Tinkerbell!" and the show continued, as though Michele's part of the production had been planned.

After the show, as we prepared to leave, an usher approached stating that Sandy Duncan wanted to meet us backstage. Delighted, we followed his directions to the stage door where we were admitted immediately. Michele could hardly contain her excitement as she walked up the stairs to the dressing room.

Sandy greeted us warmly. She asked Michele if she'd liked the show. "It was great!" was her quick response. Then Sandy told us that she knew something about vision loss, since she had lost an eye. Michele listened intently, laughing at some funny exchanges made during the conversation. But she had a puzzled look on her face and kept moving closer to Sandy. Finally, Michele blurted out, "Were you Peter Pan??!"

"Uh huh," Sandy responded.

"But, you're a girl!" she said, showing her disappointment.

Sandy, smiling at her reaction, looked at me and said, "I think I've burst her bubble."

When we said goodbye, Michele did so politely. Sandy, taking her program, wrote, "To Michele. Love, Sandy Duncan."

We found Michael and Arnie waiting for us outside. When we got into the car, Michael asked his sister how she had liked the show. "Peter Pan was a girl," Michele grumbled. After some prodding, she admitted that she'd had a good time and showed Michael her autographed program. It became one of her prized possessions.

*Cross-country skiing in Vermont
where they had a snowballfight.*

Michael & Paula on their Wedding Day.

Chapter IX

One day, I turned around and discovered that Michael had grown up. He loved being taller than I, but I laughingly assured him it didn't give him any more power.

"I don't care, I love it just the same," he said, smiling broadly as he gripped my shoulders and looked down at me.

In high school the subject Michael loved most was math. In his senior year his teacher was amazed at his mathematical ability and came up with some college courses for him to attempt. Michael comprehended the material quickly and enjoyed the challenge! This love of math gave us all a clue regarding the career that he might eventually pursue. We knew it would have to include numbers!

Then, something very special happened in Michael's life. He met Paula Valentovic, who became the love of his life. She attended college in upstate New York, and Michael frequently visited her there. Paula was a wonderful girl and we were all crazy about her. She also related well to Michele. One day Paula called and asked to speak with Michele.

"Hi, Paula," Michele said excitedly. "Yes, yes, I'd love to. Tomorrow is fine. I'll be ready." Then Michele announced, "Paula's coming over tomorrow to take me out to lunch!"

"Just you?" I asked with a smile.

"Just me," she declared with a look of self-importance.

Sometime later, Paula and Michael announced their intention to marry. Delighted, we made plans for the wedding. When the day finally arrived, Michael looked very handsome in his light beige tux with dark brown lapels, complete with ruffled shirt and bow tie. Paula was a beautiful bride with her flawless skin, sparkling eyes, and engaging smile.

The newlyweds initially lived in an apartment in Flushing, not far from our home. Within six months they started talking about moving out of New York City to a sunnier climate. After much discussion, they chose Arizona.

We hated to see them move, but it was their life and ultimately their decision. When the day arrived, we felt a great deal of sadness. Arnie was able to keep his emotions in check and I was a close second, but Michele let it all spill out.

"Why so far away?" she asked. "I love both of you, and I want you to stay."

Michael was successful in winning her over by telling her they would talk to her on the phone and come back and spend Christmas with us. "Then you could come and visit us!" he reminded her, something Michele hadn't considered. "C'mon!" he insisted. "A big smile." Michele's resistance crumbled. She gave a reluctant smile and hugged them both.

We walked outside to see them off. After more hugs, kisses, and laughter mixed with tears, they got into their station wagon and slowly pulled away. Michele grabbed my hand and said, "C'mon let's race them down the block!" Aware of what she was doing Michael slowed the car.

"Where are they now?' she yelled as we ran at top speed.

"We're right next to them, Honey," I said while gasping for breath.

Michael and Paula both called to her, "Goodbye, Michele! We'll talk to you soon."

"Okay!" Michele screeched in reply. "I love you, I love

you," she yelled, throwing multiple kisses.

Laughing at her shenanigans, they waved for the last time and the car moved away, picking up speed as it did. I looked after them until they were completely out of sight. My heart was heavy. Two young kids, barely out of their teens, off on their own, with all they owned tucked inside their station wagon.

We were all exhausted with the emotional impact of their leaving. During dinner Michele was listless and dejected and just played with her food.

"What's going on, Sweetie? You miss Michael and Paula already?"

She gave me a wan smile and said, "No, I don't think it's that. It's just that I feel really sick. Maybe if I went to bed, I'd feel better."

Now I was really worried. This child loved to stay up more than anything, and always had a million excuses as to why doing so was a good idea. So, my concern was genuine when she wanted to go to bed so early. The rest of the evening was uneventful. Michele was sleeping soundly when I looked in on her around eleven o'clock.

At midnight I heard a noise and got up to check on her. She was out of bed, sitting on the floor, doubled over in pain.

"My God, Michele, what's happening?" I asked as I knelt beside her.

"I feel very sick and I've got lots of pains in my stomach," she said.

"Okay, I'm going to call the doctor, but let me help you up first. Just lie on your stomach and try to relax. I'll be back in a minute."

I raced down the stairs to the phone. Doctor Solomon told me to bring Michele to the emergency room immediately. Hurriedly, I helped Michele get dressed. Normally she gave me a hard time about going to the hospital, but there was no resistance this time. My fears intensified as I noted how awful she looked.

Because Arnie had to go to work the next morning I decided not to wake him. I figured I could manage by myself. I left a note telling him what happened and where we would be. In retrospect, that wasn't the smartest decision I ever made. As we headed into the chill of the night, Michele cried out in pain. She then doubled over abruptly and, coughing harshly, she threw up, just seconds before she opened the car door.

I made every effort to remain calm as we began our journey. Most of the time Michele remained quiet and dozed on and off. I approached the Queens Midtown Tunnel, having just driven over the incline a few hundred feet from the toll booth. Suddenly I heard a loud noise. Then the car sputtered and died. Frantically, I pumped the gas pedal and turned the key in the ignition. It wouldn't budge. Hearing the screeching of brakes, I realized this was a very dangerous place to be broken down. Other drivers couldn't even see our car until it was almost too late.

I hurried to get Michele out of the car. Desperately, I hoped that someone would slow down so that I could tell them to have the toll booth people call the police. The cars continued to race by. Then more screeching of brakes. Suddenly some guy opened his window. Before I could say a word, he raised his fist in the air, shouted a few disgusting expletives, and yelled "What a place to park your car!"

Park my car? What a jerk! Who in their right mind could ever think that someone would deliberately park their car in such a dangerous spot and then stand by the side of the road with a child freezing to death?! My frustration was so great I wanted to yell, 'Idiot! Idiot! Idiot!' into the still of the night. Instead, I remained calm and held Michele close in an effort to ward off the cold.

Fortunately, appearing on the top of the incline was a police car! A big, burly policeman got out and started to walk down the hill toward us. Looking at me, he shook his head. "If you'd tried to break down in the most dangerous place in New York City you couldn't have picked a better spot."

"I know," I said, "but the car just sputtered and died, and here we are."

"Well, you did the smart thing both by getting out of the car and by standing at the side of the road."

Before I could introduce ourselves, he asked, "What are you doing here at two o'clock in the morning?" I explained our mission and then gave him our names.

"Listen," he responded, "my partner called for a tow truck and I see it arriving now. Just tell the driver where you want your car to go, and we'll wait for you in the patrol car." Because he was kind and gentle, Michele went with him willingly.

I found the tow truck driver uncooperative. He gave me an argument over where I wanted my car delivered. "If I agree to take it there, it will cost a lot more," he said. Feeling I had no other choice, I told him that was fine. I pulled out my checkbook. "Oh, no," he said. "Cash only, ma'am."

"I have no cash on me," I protested, "and I've got a sick child here."

"That's not my problem," he shot back. "No cash, no service," and he reached to unhook the car from the truck.

Walking to the police car, I told the officer what had happened.

"You stay here," he said, "I'll handle this." He approached the driver and put his arm around his shoulder. They talked for a few minutes privately.

Then the tow truck driver addressed me. "I'm sorry, I didn't know all the circumstances. I'll deliver your car to the address you gave me, with no extra charge. And your check will be fine."

The police siren blared as we shot through the tunnel into Manhattan and to the hospital. We arrived in a matter of minutes. The officer had called ahead, so staff awaited and wheeled Michele inside quickly. The cops came over to wish us luck and I walked them to the door asking the burly policeman what he had said to the driver to make him change his mind.

"I just appealed to his better nature. He's really a nice fella," he said smiling.

I smiled also and thanked them both for making life a lot easier.

After looking at Michele's pallor, listening to her symptoms, and examining her, the doctor concluded that she was suffering from drug toxicity.

"What would cause that?" I asked.

"It looks like a drug she's taking is acting like a toxin, or poison, in her system. We need to admit her, do some more tests, and probably change her medication. By the way, the fact that she vomited was the best thing that could have happened."

In a matter of hours, Michele felt and looked much better. Medication adjustments were made and she was released a few days later. Once home, she was back to her old self.

What an ordeal, though. We will always remember that trip to the hospital. However, the one thing that holds true during these difficulties is faith in the belief that things will get better. Having a positive attitude has seen us through many tough times. It has become my overriding coping philosophy. Do I flounder? You bet. But, fortunately, I'm able to pull myself out of the doldrums pretty quickly.

A child like Michele brings enormous challenges to a family. In our case, we didn't even know what we were actually dealing with yet. I couldn't wait for the disease to be diagnosed because I felt that once we knew what it was we'd have a better chance of fighting its dreadful onslaught. Until that happened, our job was to meet Michele's needs and keep her as happy as possible. Perhaps not the simplest task in the world, but its rewards were second to none.

Michele returned to school, happy to be back. When she came home she excitedly reported that her teacher, Mrs. Walker, had gotten a new dog, and how much fun the kids had playing with it.

"That's wonderful, Honey," I said. "What's its name?" I asked that without thinking and I was immediately annoyed with myself because I knew Michele was having difficulty with that kind of retrieval, but wouldn't be satisfied until that name was recalled. Finally, I could almost see a light bulb go on in her head.

"I know," she said, pleased with herself. "What's the name of your friend at Cresthaven?"

"What friend, Michele? I have so many over there."
She thought a little while longer and then said. "The one with the bunk beds."

"You mean Mrs. Burns?"

"Yes!" She said, enthusiastically. "What's the name of her little girl?"

"Katie," I told her.

"That's the name of Mrs. Walker's dog!" she said triumphantly.

I hugged her and we both laughed at her successful retrieval. As usual, she had figured out a way.

It was at this time that the transportation issue was heating up with both city and state. I sent a letter to Louis Grumet, Assistant Commissioner for the New York State Education Department informing him of the city's lack of compliance with the law. Grumet's responsibilities included overseeing and reviewing problems concerning handicapped children. Roger Walker, Director of the New York Institute of the Education of the Blind, told me he was also sending a letter to Grumet supporting our position.

Another lawyer we consulted told us that since the law was already on the books the best thing to do was to have a brief written for the court (or courts) to review. If the issue was declared moot by the judge, our argument would be strengthened automatically. We took his advice and his predictions came true. This encouraged me to push even harder for city compliance.

Within a month I got a call from Ben Birdsell from the State Education Department. He told me that the state was very concerned about the situation and assured me that he would pursue the matter with the City of New York after he researched how many other residential schools were not receiving appropriate transportation. Ultimately, this issue became a saga to beat all sagas.

Despite the pressure from the state, the city staunchly refused to provide Monday/Friday transportation. We didn't back down, and I continued the pressure for compliance through the commissioner's office. The last I heard from Ben Birdsell was that if the city continued to refuse, the state could withhold all transportation funding until it complied. Now that was leverage! I don't know if that threat was ever made to the city, but shortly after my conversation with Birdsell we received word that transportation would be provided, with children being picked up and dropped off at their usual scheduled time.

Everyone was elated, of course, but I wasn't ready to celebrate just yet. Not even when Roger Walker called to say that when the buses rolled in on that particular Monday he wanted to call a press conference because it was so incredible.

"Do you realize" he said, "this school is over a 100 years old and this will be the first time the children will be bused from all the boroughs? As many times as this issue has been fought over the years, no one has ever been successful, until now, in achieving the desired result! This is a momentous occasion, Kathleen. I want you to be there.

I listened intently to what he had to say and while I was flattered by his nice remarks I was still cautious. "Roger, I have an uneasy feeling that the city has something up its sleeve. They agreed too quickly for my liking," I said.

"What could possibly go wrong?" he asked.

"I have no idea, but I'd like you to postpone the press conference until this success story plays itself out. At any rate, I don't want to participate right now.

"Well, you may be right," he said. "Postponing is no problem."

As for Michele, she would not travel by bus at any time. I planned to continue driving her to school and picking her up. This was because of her seizure condition. For that reason I was still at home when the calls started to come in from parents on the first day of pick up. All with the same lament. The bus drivers would take the children but refused to take the suitcases containing their clothing. Taking the children without their luggage was pointless. Lack of space was not the problem, but the drivers claimed taking luggage was not in their contract. This left the parents stranded, bags in hand.

This was a deliberate, well-thought-out plan by the city to bring buses to a screeching halt. It had been planned well in advance because every bus driver throughout the five boroughs reacted in exactly the same way. It was like a script being read to me over the phone as the calls came in from parents throughout the city. Each thought it might only have happened to them, but after several calls, I knew it was a deliberate effort to sabotage the program.

I drove Michele to school and then called another emergency board meeting. No one could believe that the city would pull something like this. The parents were enraged and who could blame them? Upon arrival they interrupted the board meeting, demanding an explanation. I told them I had no answers because it was too early to call the state and we were meeting now to discuss the issue.

"Why didn't you take the first offer with the children arriving later in the morning?" one parent demanded. "I'll bet luggage wouldn't have been an issue then!"

"Yes!" others chorused. "This is ridiculous. If they don't take the luggage, they might as well not take the children!."

"Look, I feel for you. But, don't you see, this roadblock thrown in our path today is just like every other roadblock that we've already overcome. We have to just keep fighting. If we give in now all we'd be doing is playing into their hands. I didn't anticipate this. No one did. It's the element of surprise they're hoping will devastate us."

Despite what I said, the parents refused to be placated, continuing to be critical. Eventually, I threw up my hands and said, "Look, enough is enough! These outbursts are getting us nowhere. I am not your enemy here and neither are the others in this room. Your anger is misdirected. A lot of hard work has gone into this transportation issue, and we can't fall apart because they've thrown another obstacle our way. Look at obstacles as stepping stones instead of deterrents and we'll win this thing. In my case, Michele won't even be taking the bus. I'll be driving her as usual because of her seizure condition, so what have I got to gain? Nothing except some headaches and who needs that? If you people feel you can do a better job, I'm willing to turn it over. Just say the word."

Their frustration ebbed some and it became clear they didn't want to take over the reins. Rising and approaching them in the doorway I said, "Things will work out, believe me. Appropriate transportation is just around the corner, but we just have to weather another storm before it becomes a reality."

So, back to the drawing board we went. The bus drivers' refusal to take luggage was a new wrinkle. Could they defend their position since it wasn't in their contract? Assuming they could, we had to find out when their contract expired.

After a couple of hours, I finally reached the commissioner's office and their reaction was similar to ours. They agreed that the drivers probably had a legal right to refuse the luggage. So, when was the contract due?

Norm Doctor from the commissioner's office in Albany was to be my contact now. Reaching his office in the city would be easier than calling long distance to Albany. The day after my call to the commissioner's office I got a call from Doctor with some good news. He told me that the contract for the bus drivers would be up in a couple of months and that negotiations for a new contract would get underway over the summer, which was just around the corner.

During those negotiations Norm Doctor and I kept steady company over the phone. The state was determined to include the luggage clause in the contract when it was ready for signature. During this time Norm Doctor received his doctorate degree and from then on I called him Doctor Doctor, which he found amusing. He did his job well, as did Ben Birdsell. On Tuesday, September 19, 1978, an agreement was finally reached between the schools involved and the NYC Board of Education. A firm commitment to take full responsibility for the transportation of weekend students was made by the city.

When the buses actually started rolling, one of the children who lived in Brooklyn wasn't picked up. The Bureau of Pupil Transportation claimed she lived outside their boundaries. I was so aggravated, I told them "Stretch the damn boundaries!" and insisted that the transportation clause included all children from all boroughs, period!

One call to the state took care of that and the child was included without any further delay. Whew! What an ordeal! It felt good to have finally and actually won. The parents were happy, as were the members of the board and the administration. We all celebrated! We never did hold a press conference, though. I think we were all too exhausted after such a trying experience. What we really needed was a vacation! But a vacation was out for me.

I had registered for college and my classes were at night, keeping me very busy. My ultimate goal was to become a lawyer, which I figured was what these kids needed. I contacted the Bar Association, and was told that I needed to first obtain a bachelors degree. And so, I became a matriculated student at the City University of New York!

Chapter X

Michele was one of the children selected for a study of the new seizure medication called Depakene. Used in Europe for years with good results, it was finally up for testing in the United States. The only hitch was that the ophthalmologist chosen for this study was none other than the neuro/ophthalmologist I had had a run-in with at the New York Hospital clinic. I told Doctor Solomon about my confrontation with him and his vow that he would never see Michele again. She merely replied that the Federal Drug Administration (FDA) had chosen him and he would be the only doctor involved with the study.

I sighed heavily driving home, but I knew I had no choice but to call the number Doctor Solomon had given me to make an appointment for Michele. When I told Arnie about this new development he asked me what I was going to do.

"Make an appointment," I said.

"Without talking to him first?"

"Yep. I'm just going to act as if nothing ever happened."

"Suppose he refuses to see her?"

"I'll cross that bridge when I come to it. But the way I see it is this: Michele is part of a study required by the FDA in order for this medication to be approved. And he's the doctor selected by them to monitor the children involved. It's that simple. So, we'll just see what happens."

A short time after our arrival we were called into the examining room where the doctor was perusing Michele's file. He looked up and we exchanged a few pleasantries and shook hands. Studying me, he asked, "Have we met before, Mrs. Morton?"

"I'm wondering that myself, Doctor," I said with a smile. He smiled back and then turned his attention to Michele.

Nothing more was ever said and we got along well during the length of the study. Depakene was ultimately approved by the FDA and it soon became one of the most effective medications given to Michele for seizure control.

Several years later, it was this very same neuro/ophthalmologist who finally diagnosed Michele's illness. Ultimately we were indebted to him. While attending a medical conference in Europe there was some discussion concerning a unique image seen behind the eyes. He kept wondering where had he seen this before and then it hit him. When he got home he called me and made a simple statement, "Mrs. Morton, I think I know what's wrong with Michele."

I was absolutely speechless. After all these years, could it be true? I didn't know whether to laugh or cry.

"She has to be admitted to the hospital for a biopsy," I heard him say.

"I'll bring her in today," I said and called out to Arnie as soon as I hung up the phone. "You'll never believe what just happened," I said, walking into the living room from the kitchen. "The neuro/ophthalmologist just called stating he thinks he knows what's wrong with Michele."

"He does?" he said, jumping up and hugging me. Then we shouted for joy as we were overtaken by exhilaration.

"She has to be admitted to the hospital today for a biopsy." We were both standing in the middle of the living room hugging when Michele came downstairs.

"What's going on?" she asked.

"Michele, Honey, we got some news from a doctor, and he wants to see you at the hospital."

"I'm not staying there," she immediately insisted.

"You may have to, Honey, but only for a day or so," I said, bringing her close to me. "And just think, with this test we might find out what's wrong with you."

Pushing me away, she looked at both of us wide-eyed, "There's nothing wrong with me!!" she exclaimed.

Astonished, Arnie and I looked at each other. Here was a kid who was blind, took severe seizures, lived in hospitals, and had motor and speech problems. Yet, she saw herself as A-OK. There was certainly nothing wrong with her self-esteem. She was unbelievable and her stamina was extraordinary. Laughing, we pulled her towards us, hugging her from both sides..

"Sweetheart, you know we believe you are one terrific kid, right?"

"Yes, but I hate hospitals."

"I know, Michele, they are anything but fun. However, this test will probably give us a lot of information that the doctors can use in the future, so please cooperate with us, okay?"

"Oh, I guess so," she said, devoid of enthusiasm.

Because the biopsy had to be done in the OR, it was scheduled for the next morning. Michele was nervous and wanted me to be with her. That went over like a lead balloon when I proposed it to one of the doctors making his rounds. I then asked to speak with the surgeon, and he came to Michele's room. After talking with me he admitted that, because of Michele's blindness, her comfort zone was definitely with me. He proceeded to say that while he did not want to put Michele under completely, the biopsy required that she remain still and that my presence might be just the stabilizing factor needed. Looking at me inquiringly, eyebrows raised, he asked, "Do you think you can handle this? It won't be easy."

I promised him I wouldn't faint. He smiled, nodded, and told me to accompany Michele when they came for her.

Once that happened we wheeled Michele downstairs and I started to suit up. The rest of the OR staff immediately took exception to having a mother in the operating room with her child. The surgeon didn't budge, however, so I became part of the OR team. My job was to keep Michele calm and still. And no, it wasn't easy, particularly when the surgeon cut into the calf of her leg and the blood spurted out. I'd never seen so much blood in my life! My stomach was doing somersaults. Fainting started to look like a good idea! I barely flinched and succeeded in keeping Michele from squirming. The next day, when the surgeon stopped by, he told us that we had both done a great job. Michele squeezed my hand and smiled.

We had to wait a couple of weeks for the results, so were on pins and needles every time the phone rang. I was glad Michele was in school when the call finally came from Doctor Solomon, who requested we meet with the doctors at the hospital. Arnie left work and met me in the lobby.

When we went upstairs, the doctors looked so somber, leading us to think the news would not be too good, but never did we expect what we were about to hear.

"Mr. and Mrs. Morton," the doctor began, "we do have a diagnosis for you. Michele is suffering from a rare, neurological disease which includes vision loss, seizures, and gross and fine motor problems. Unfortunately, the future is not bright because, in addition, she will also eventually lose cognitive functioning and verbal communication skills. Following that, she will suffer a general progressive deterioration to a vegetative state. We're sorry, but there is no known treatment or cure, and no child has ever survived."

We both sat there motionless, staring at them. I felt that I had been punched in the stomach so hard as to take my breath away, leaving me unable to speak. Not one syllable would pass my lips. Arnie, the first to recover, asked the doctors if this disease had a name. They immediately said something that sounded like a foreign language. When we continued to stare at them, they repeated it. Finally, I found my voice, and said, stoically, "Please write it down." When he handed me the piece of paper, it read, "neuronal ceroid lipofuscinosis." I felt numb all over. Whoever heard of that, for God's sake?! I'd have to take lessons just to pronounce the damn thing!

"I need to tell you, Mrs. Morton," Doctor Solomon said, interrupting my thoughts, "that you have done an exceptional job with Michele. Considering the type of disease she has, she's doing great."

Those words were not reassuring because the devastation I felt was unrelenting. What I had really wanted to hear was: "Here's what it is and this is what we can do to attack it."

But time and time again I'm reminded that I don't write the script. What it had taken the doctor about two minutes to say would ultimately change our lives forever.

We drove home in silence. We couldn't trust ourselves to speak without completely falling apart.

Arnie went to work the next day but any normal activity for me was out of the question. The smallest task seemed insurmountable and all I did was cry nonstop. It seemed I had lost control of any emotional stability. The doctor's statement that: "No child has ever survived," continued to haunt me.

I tried to pull myself together, and called Arnie. But once he got on the phone, I lost all control again and could not speak without gut-wrenching sobs. Because he was at work, he tried desperately to control his own emotions while trying to comfort me. Arriving home early, he found me sitting on the couch staring into space. He sat next to me and put his arms around me. And there we sat in deafening silence, locked in an embrace. No words needed to be spoken.

When I finally stirred, several hours had passed. Arnie asked me how I was feeling.

I smiled wanly. "Once I get over this feeling of helplessness, hopefully I'll be able to cope."

"I know, I know," he said and tightened his arms around me.

I knew I had no choice but to pull myself together because Michele would be home in a couple of days. I couldn't let her see me like this. We decided not to tell her about the disease and its horrendous prognosis. It wouldn't serve any purpose except to thwart that bubbly spirit of hers. Besides, who knew what might happen in the future? There could be a medical break-through. I knew I needed to find out as much as I possibly could about this disease. I smiled imperceptibly when I realized that these were the kind of thoughts that ultimately propelled me into action.

"What are you smiling about?" Arnie asked.

"I'm trying to think of ways to combat this dreadful disease," I replied decisively.

"That's what I like to hear!"

"Are you hungry by any chance?" he suddenly asked.

"Yes, I guess I am a little. I haven't eaten anything all day."

"Let's go out to dinner tonight," he said.

I wholeheartedly agreed. Rather than take the car, we decided to take a leisurely walk up to Bell Boulevard in Bayside to our favorite restaurant. Cozy and quiet. Just what we needed. Long and invigorating, the walk increased our appetites. The cool air and gentle breeze were also very inviting. After dinner, we arrived home exhausted, yet felt that we had overcome the worst of the devastating news.

I knew we could never project with Michele. Projections would drive us crazy. We had to live day by day. My job would be to meet her needs medically, educationally, and emotionally, so that she could derive as much happiness out of life as possible.

Once I felt more emotionally stable, I called Michael in Arizona and told him the sad news. He talked with both Arnie and me, and while his voice broke a few times, he managed to keep a stiff upper lip. "Call me any time you need to," he said and we promised we would.

I felt very comforted having talked with Michael. That evening when I went to bed my overwhelming exhaustion won out the moment my head hit the pillow. I was immediately lost in a deep sleep.

I spent the next several weeks calling around the country to major medical institutions to see if I could obtain any more information on neuronal ceroid lipofuscinosis (NCL), all to no avail. The libraries yielded the basic symptomatology already given to me by Michele's doctors. Doctor Solomon, aware of my quest to seek out information, tried to be as helpful as possible. She learned of a Doctor Leon Wolfe from Canada who had been involved for some years in researching NCL and was now considered an expert on the disease. I asked Doctor Solomon to forward Michele's medical history to him, stating that I would call Doctor Wolfe directly.

When I reached him at the Montreal Neurological Institute, where his research was being conducted, we talked at length about the disease and its deleterious effects on the body. He did not hold much hope for a cure anytime in the near future.

"Doctor Solomon sent me Michele's records," he said, "I understand you would like to have her evaluated here in Montreal. I'd be happy to see your daughter, Mrs. Morton, but, of course, I can't promise anything."

"I realize that," I said, "but I feel I should follow up every lead, no matter where it takes me. Will someone at the hospital be able to stay with Michele while I'm meeting with you and the other doctors?"

"Yes, or she could be with us during the conference," Wolfe replied.

"No, I don't want that. We don't talk about the disease and its consequences in front of Michele at any time."

"But she wouldn't understand," he protested. "I have her file in front of me and she has a full-blown case of NCL."

"That may be so, Doctor Wolfe, but Michele understands everything, believe me and if she heard something really negative, she'd probably object, get up, and walk out."

"It's incredible to me that she's still walking, and talking." Wolfe said, with obvious surprise.

"I'm really looking forward to meeting this young lady. Let me put you through to my secretary, Mrs. Clark. She'll set up an appointment and also make reservations at a nearby hotel for you and Michele."

"Thank you very much, Doctor." I said. "I'm really looking forward to meeting you."

When I told Michele we were going to see a doctor in Canada, she immediately told me she wasn't going. "All doctors are stupid, and they're ugly too," she said in defense of her brave stance. "All they do is stick needles in me and take blood. I think they sell it!"

I couldn't keep from smiling. This was her comical way of

protesting. In her heart, however. she knew this was something we had to do. "We won't be there long, Michele. Only a couple of days. I need your cooperation, okay?"

"Okay," she said, conjuring up a smile. "I like the idea of eating out. Can we do some shopping, too?"

"You bet, Michele. We'll find time to do it all."

When we arrived at the Montreal Institute we were met by Doctor Wolfe. "Good morning, Mrs. Morton," he said, greeting me warmly with a smile and a handshake. "And this must be Michele. How are you, Michele?" he asked cordially and with a distinct English accent.

"Fine, Doctor," she replied, extending her hand.

"How was your trip?"

"Great!" she replied happily. "And the hotel is nice too."

"I'm glad to hear that, Michele. Now, why don't you go with Mrs. Clark, and she will take you to a recreation room while I talk with your mom."

I then joined Doctor Wolfe and a few other doctors who were waiting in his office. Once seated, we immediately launched into an in-depth discussion about Neuronal Ceroid Lipofuscinosis.

"We've been involved with the research of this disease for several years," Doctor Wolfe explained, "but we still have a long way to go."

"How many children do you know with NCL?" I asked.

"I believe there are about 40 in the Newfoundland area."

"Wow!" I said, shaking my head. "I find it so incredible that with a disease like this so little has been done to combat its devastation. I couldn't even find anything written about it in New York!"

"I know what you mean, Mrs. Morton. Even with concentrated effort at our center, it's a slow process."

"Let's meet with Michele. We'll examine her, run some tests, and then talk some more," he said.

Michele's tests were extensive and thorough, and she was cooperative throughout the day. I was so proud of her. Later that afternoon I took her to the recreational area, returning to Wolfe's office alone.

"Mrs. Morton," Wolfe began, "as you know, there's no doubt that Michele has NCL. Doctors Andermann and Kirkham, who also examined Michele, will write full reports regarding their findings. You will receive copies of those reports, along with my own. The preliminary findings are that the disease process seems to have been delayed, especially the expected mental deterioration. I suspect that your involvement with Michele has had a lot to do with that. Tell me about her usual routine."

"Well, she attends the N. Y. Institute for the Education of the Blind, an excellent residential school. She is very happy there. She attends their camp in Vermont, Camp Wapanacki for three weeks every summer and enjoys it tremendously as well. After camp, we, along with my friend, Marilyn Butner, and her daughter, Donna, drive to the Poconos to a dude ranch for a week, where she rides horses and enjoys playing video games at a quarter a shot! She loves the action and sound of the machines.

"In addition, she's learned how to swim and how to skate in a roller rink to dance music. She even wanted to learn how to hit a tennis ball, which she also accomplished. All of these things were Michele's own ideas after she lost the vision. I arranged for lessons for each activity, which she took until she mastered the particular skill. Then we celebrated!"

Doctor Wolfe laughed. "That's really quite amazing!" he said. "Keeping her that busy and active has certainly helped her maintain a higher functioning level. There doesn't seem to be any other explanation."

"Thank you, Doctor. My goal is to meet Michele's needs so that she can be happy. But, what I'm really looking for is a cure. I know the research is slow and a cure elusive, but that will not stop me from hoping and striving for a break-through."

"No, I'm sure it won't, Mrs. Morton," he said, shaking his head and smiling. "You are a remarkable woman. I'm glad we had the opportunity to meet and if anything develops I'll be sure to let you know."

"Thanks so much, Doctor. Difficult circumstances brought us here today, but you and your staff have made it a very pleasant experience," I said, shaking his hand, as our meeting came to a close.

Michele cheerfully said her goodbyes to the staff. She had had such a good time in the recreation room and was now looking forward to going shopping as promised. And so, we did!

Several months after our return from Canada I received a call from a friend.

"Have you seen the New York Times today?" she asked.

"No, I haven't, why?"

"There's an article about your research."

"What research?" I asked, perplexed.

"On Health and Light. Everything you told me about is in there. The researchers are two medical doctors."

"Thanks," I said. I immediately picked up the Times. It was amazing. The headline read: "From Fertility to Mood, Sunlight Found to Affect Human Biology." Dr. Richard Wurtman and Dr. Alfred Lewy were the researchers. It was an in-depth study of the sun filtering through the eyes and having a positive effect on the biological system. Any doubts I had harbored about picking up stakes and moving to a sunnier climate were instantly erased. We had taken some steps to make this a reality. Arnie had already flown to Arizona to look for a job, but hadn't been successful, so we had placed the potential move on the back burner.

Additionally, my college graduation had taken place just a couple of weeks before Michele's illness was diagnosed. Just before graduation, I was offered a doctoral program in sociology from my undergraduate studies. It was a tempting offer, but I declined because I wanted law, and I was making preparations to take the law boards. However, my direction immediately changed once the pronouncement of NCL was made. Total concentration moved to the disease and how to combat it.

Now I called Arnie to tell him about the N.Y. Times story. "I'm on my way to see Doctor Solomon," I said. "What do you think of meeting me at the hospital and having dinner out tonight?"

"That sounds good. Bring the article so that I can read it."

"Oh, that's what I plan to do, just in case Solomon hasn't seen it yet."

"Good. I'll meet you in the lobby at 5:30."

When I got to the hospital, I ran into Doctor Solomon in the hallway. "I think I know why you're here," she said. "We've been discussing that research article most of the day."

"Well, you can imagine my surprise. It's what I've been saying all along."

"I know, Mrs. Morton, I know."

"So, what do you think now, Doctor?"

"Well, I know Doctor Wurtman very well and he's a highly respected physician."

"And you do agree that Michele gets better in the summer?"

"Yes, I do. I've seen some positive changes in her functioning level. But I'm reluctant to say that it's due to exposure to the sun."

"Well, I'm not, Doctor Solomon. In fact, I'm making arrangements to leave for Arizona. I don't see that we have a choice at this point."

"That's a major decision, Mrs. Morton, particularly since it may not help Michele at all."

"Maybe not, but I'll never find out by staying in New York."

"Well, if you go through with this, I wish you all the best."

"Thanks, Doctor. I'll see you before we leave so that Michele can have a final check up."

As I left Doctor Solomon, I looked at my watch. It was almost 5:30. When I got downstairs, Arnie was already in the lobby. Once at the restaurant, Arnie read the article.

"I'm really surprised. It covers everything you discovered in your research – and a lot more. What did Solomon say?"

"She doesn't know what to think. She admires Doctor Wurtman, but cautioned me against putting too much stock in this as far as Michele is concerned. But, do you know something, Arnie? I don't think Michele should spend another winter here."

"I agree, but first I've got to get a job out there. I can't quit here before that's accomplished. If I did that, we'd have no income and especially no medical insurance. That would be a disaster!"

"You're right, of course. But, maybe we're looking at this all wrong. Why don't I go with Michele? Michael and Paula said we could stay with them temporarily until we get Michele settled in school. Then I could get a job and you could follow us out there."

"Oh, I don't know," he said. "I'm not exactly crazy about that idea."

"Well, neither am I. But, if we're going to act in Michele's best interests, what choice do we have?"

Arnie stared straight ahead. "None, I suppose. That's the hard part," he sighed. "That's the hard part." He repeated the statement, almost to himself.

Reaching over, I placed my hand on his. "Arnie, things will work out. We have to believe that."

He responded with just a hint of a smile. He wasn't happy but, like myself, he was willing to do what needed to be done.

In the days that followed, we went about the business of preparing to leave New York. There was so much to do but eventually, it all came together. Having already been in contact with the Arizona School for the Deaf & Blind in Tucson, I flew out with Michele to discuss admission. We were well received and I was told to contact them when we arrived in Arizona.

Adjacent to the school was the Arizona Diagnostic Treatment and Education Center, commonly known as ADTEC, which many of the children attended until their individual diagnostic education plan was developed. I was impressed with this system.

Returning to New York the schedule was hectic as we tried to bring some kind of closure to every area in our lives. There were friends at St. Kevin's, friends within the neighborhood, the parents at the school for the blind, and Cresthaven Country Club. I was suddenly involved with a whirlwind of goodbyes. Michele was dazzled by all the attention and enjoyed the excitement it created.

In a few weeks, Michael flew into New York, accompanied by his cousin, Alex, for the purpose of picking up my car and driving it back to Arizona. "You can do without a car in New York, Mom," he said, "but not in Arizona." Prior to Michael's marriage, Alex, originally from upstate New York, had stayed with us while working in the city. As a result, he and Michael became very close friends. Michael was always available when we needed him, and

Alex was never far behind.

"How's the car, Mom?" Michael asked. "Did you have it checked out?"

"Yes, I did everything you asked me to do. It's also got a full tank of gas."

"Good, now all we have to do is load the U-haul and we'll be on our way."

When they had finished, Michael turned to me smiling and said, "See you soon, Mom, – in Arizona!"

"Yes, in about ten days." Everyone hugged each other and off they went.

That evening we decided to go to Cresthaven for dinner with some friends. A couple of hours later, in walked Michael and Alex! We almost fainted.

"What happened?" I asked.

"Nothing that a key to your gas tank wouldn't fix," he said.

"Oh, Michael, I'm so sorry I forgot to give it to you."

"Alex discovered it when we stopped to put air in the tires. I thought he was kidding when he said that he sure hoped I had a key. We were lucky we were still in New York!"

"Oh, I feel terrible about this, Michael. You must have wanted to kill me!"

"The thought did occur to us," he said teasingly, while Alex nodded his head in agreement. As they were leaving, Michael waved to a lot of members who knew him well.

The decision to leave New York became harder as the time to do so drew near. I repeatedly shook off questions and doubts about this being the right thing to do. Arnie not being able to come with us, of course, was the most difficult of all. When we arrived at the airport and it came time to say goodbye, Arnie hugged and kissed Michele and said, "You be a good girl for Mommy, Honey, okay?"

"I will, Daddy. I promise. Oh, I'm going to miss you so much," she said, trying to hold back the tears.

"I know, Sweetheart. I'm going to miss you too. But we'll both be brave, right?" he said as he cupped her face in his hands and wiped away her tears.

Then he hugged and kissed me. Neither of us wanted to say much because our brave stance was precariously close to crumbling. Michele and I walked away, then turned for one last wave. There he was, standing alone, looking so forlorn. He waved back and smiled, struggling to hide his true feelings and the ultimate sadness that engulfed him.

Donna & Michele at the
Dude Ranch in the Poconos.

Chapter XI

Michael and Paula met us at the airport with smiles and hugs. "Welcome to Arizona!" they chorused.

"How was your trip?" Michael asked.

"Everything went smoothly."

"And I loved the food," Michele said smiling.

"What else is new?" Michael asked. "I've never seen anyone with an appetite like yours. Beats me how you stay so thin," he declared. Just one look at Michele told us how happy she was to be with her big brother.

Michael and Paula owned a three bedroom house in Glendale and Michele was happy when she learned she would have her own room. We were greeted at the door by their dog, BeeGee. Michele fell in love with her immediately.

After we got settled in I asked if I could do anything but Michael responded, "No Mom, just sit back and relax."

"Okay, you don't have to tell me twice," I said, sinking into the recliner, then pushing it back and putting my feet up. "It feels so comfortable, Michael, and to tell the truth, I feel a bit bushed now that the excitement is over and the adrenaline has stopped coursing through my system."

"Great," he said. "I'm sure you'll be busy soon enough."

"Where's Michele?"

"She's out on the patio with Paula and BeeGee having fun."

Then the phone rang. It was Arnie. After talking to him for

a few minutes and assuring him everything was okay, Michael handed me the phone.

"Hi Honey," I said, a bit subdued.

"Hi," he replied. "Don't tell anyone, but I miss you already."

I laughed and said, "I miss you too. It was not easy to leave and I felt for you, standing there waving and knowing you were going home to an empty house."

"I admit, it wasn't the best night I've ever had, but don't worry about me. I'll be okay. Just concentrate on Michele's needs. I'll do fine just sitting here all by myself, lonely and depressed."

"Oh, stop it," I said chuckling. "You'll be here at Christmas, which is only a few months away."

"Yeah, you're right. Of course, that's if I'm not too lonely and depressed to enjoy it," he persisted, this time with laughter. "Okay, okay, you know I'm just kidding. Remember, I still have Casey. But, the problem with him is that he doesn't do dishes."

"He doesn't?" I feigned surprise. "Then you didn't train him right!"

"That's for sure! If anything, he trained me! Well, I guess I'd better go. Give Michele my love. And try to relax a bit. You've been on quite a merry-go-round."

Taking Arnie's advice, I gave myself a week to unwind. The next week I took Michele out to a swimming pool in Glendale every day, where she swam for hours while I sunned myself and did some reading. The weather was always beautiful, something we certainly weren't accustomed to in New York. We never had to cancel anything here!

Michele needed new clothes for this type of weather, so we went shopping. She selected shorts and tops by feel, informing me which colors she wanted. I then selected by size so she could try them on. This kid was having a ball. It was like an extended vacation!

I knew, however, that I had to get things rolling for Michele. I called Noel Stephens, Director of the Visually Handicapped for the Arizona School for the Deaf & Blind (ASDB). I had already completed and sent the application and Michele's records, before we left New York. "I guess you know why I'm calling," I said, when we connected. "I'm here in Arizona. Did you get all the material and Michele's enrollment form?"

"Yes, I did. We've already had a meeting concerning Michele's placement. The committee feels she would benefit by being placed in ADTEC first. That way we could get a good solid diagnostic educational prescription, appropriate to her needs."

"Well, I was impressed with ADTEC's approach when you first discussed it with me a few months back. I think an initial enrollment in that type of program would be a very good idea. When do classes start?"

"ADTEC's not on the same schedule as public schools. The program won't begin for a few months yet. Meanwhile, my suggestion is that you enroll Michele in the local Glendale public school. Then, over the next few months, we'll gather as much information on her as possible. She'll be videotaped throughout the school day as well as at home and at play. All of this with your approval, of course."

"Sounds great, Mr. Stephens. You certainly are thorough. I'll call the principal in the Glendale school this week to determine registration procedure for the special education program."

"Good!" And in the future, Jim Heriot, the Director of ADTEC, or his assistant, Jerry Maddox, will keep you updated. Okay?"

"That'll be fine, Mr. Stephens. Thank you very much for

everything."

I hung up the phone feeling very good about Michele's program.

"Was that the school?" Michele asked, as she came downstairs.

"Yes, it was."

"Am I going there?"

"Yes, but not right away."

"Why?"

"Their program doesn't start for a few months yet. Meanwhile, you can go to the local public school."

"Good. It's so boring at home."

"What! Are you saying I'm boring?"

"Yes," she responded laughing, then holding up her arms to stave off any imaginary blows.

"Then no more swimming for you," I told her.

Floundering a bit, she said. "You know I was only kidding."

I couldn't keep up the solemn front any longer. "I know Honey. I'm just teasing. So, what are you waiting for, kiddo? Are we ready to go swimming or not?"

"Yes," she replied with delight, and quickly went upstairs to put on her bathing suit.

Obtaining the information I needed from the school secretary, I took Michele to register her for classes the next day. I brought Michele's school records along, and after some discussion about the school calendar and the bus schedule, an IEP (Individual Education Plan) meeting was set.

The IEP approach, according to P.L. 94-142, The Education of the Handicapped Act enacted by Congress in 1975, must be used in order to meet the individual needs of the child placed in special education. Because Congress decided that a year in the life of a handicapped child was too long a time to determine whether the program was working, short term objectives had to be established, after which the child would be re-evaluated. It's a very comprehensive law, and even includes a residential component, at no cost to the parent, if it has been determined that the educational needs of the child require this structured approach.

I drove Michele over to a friend's house while I attended the IEP meeting. When I entered the conference room one of the men approached me with hand extended. "I'm Rob Hutchinson, the principal," he said enthusiastically. "You must be Mrs. Morton."

"Guilty as charged," I said, smiling.

"Good. Let's get started." Seated at the conference table were a physical therapist, a speech therapist, a teacher for the visually impaired, and the teacher in whose classroom Michele would be. We talked at length about Michele's needs, including which approaches did and did not work.

Rob Hutchinson said, "We've all read Michele's records, Mrs. Morton, and we agree that we should establish short term objectives now and then re-evaluate sometime in the near future."

"That sounds like a good idea," I said.

"Is there anything else you'd like to bring up?" the principal asked.

"Yes, I'd like to let you know that I can be available anytime to assist with Michele's response to her new surroundings. Transition is not always easy for her, especially with the vision loss. Since she's not familiar with the school, she'll have to be watched carefully, particularly since your classrooms have outside access. She's used to walking in one door and finding every classroom within the school building."

"Don't worry, Mrs. Morton. Michele will have someone with her at all times," Mr. Hutchinson assured me.

"Good. In conclusion, I'd just like to say that Michele is generally a happy youngster. She has a good sense of humor, but is not afraid to take a stand on something she feels is unfair."

"Mmmm. Pretty spunky, huh?" one of them said while everyone laughed.

"That she is!" I said and the meeting ended on that high note.

When I picked up Michele, I told her about the new arrangements. She was happy to be involved with school activities again. As we got into the car, Michele asked, "Can we go check out the new program you were talking about this morning?"

"You mean ARCH, the one that starts in the afternoon?"

"Yes!" Michele said eagerly.

"Well, I guess we could," I said slowly, while checking my purse for the address. ARCH, the Arizona Recreational Center for the Handicapped, enjoyed a good reputation. When we arrived we received an enthusiastic greeting from the receptionist. I introduced Michele and myself and asked what kind of programs were available.

"Well, we have all kinds of different games for the children to play. We also have a pool table, music, dance classes, outdoor fun, and occasionally go on trips."

"That sounds great!" Michele replied happily.

"An important factor for the staff to know," I said, "is that Michele is blind and would need someone to help her until she became oriented to the facility."

The receptionist seemed surprised to hear this.

"I know she doesn't look it," I said, "and when it first happened she didn't want anyone to know. Eventually she got over that."

"Don't worry, Mrs. Morton, we'll take good care of her."

"Thanks, I appreciate that. What's the procedure for signing her up?" I asked.

"She can stay here now and you can pick her up at 6:30, if you want. We send out for food and the kids generally eat here together. The cost is between $3.00 and $4.00, depending on what she orders. Or, she can eat at home, if that's her preference."

Someone had already begun showing Michele around. "I didn't expect to leave her here today," I said. "Nothing is ever that simple. Aren't there a thousand forms for me to fill out?"

The receptionist laughed, "No, this is a drop-in center. All we need is her name, which we already have, and a phone number where we can reach you."

"Sounds good to me!" I said, smiling as I wrote down my phone number. "This is a refreshing change. I'm not sure that I can handle it," I said laughing. I walked over to where Michele was standing with a staff member and asked if she was ready to go home.

"Can't I stay?" she pleaded. "I'm having fun."

"I guess that will be alright. I'll pick you up later," I said, kissing her cheek. I left the facility and went shopping nearby. Although closing time was around 6:30, I couldn't wait that long. I went back within the hour just to check on Michele. But I needn't have worried. She was doing great! I left money for food and told the receptionist to tell her that I'd come back for her at 6:30. "If I know her," I said, "she'll want to eat here."

"She's already told us that," the receptionist replied with a smile.

The first several weeks at the Glendale school seemed to go well. But one day Michele came home extremely upset. She told me that her teacher had said she needed a wheelchair to get from one class to another. "I told her I could walk, but she said I was too

179

slow. I don't want to use a wheelchair!" she said with frustration.

"Are you sure, Michele, that you didn't misunderstand?"

"No! She made me use the wheelchair today. Also, she says I can't bring a tuna fish sandwich for lunch anymore, because I'm too messy. I try not to drop any, but sometimes I can't help it."

"Don't you spread out the wax paper that I wrap it up in, so that it can catch any mess?"

"Yes, but she still doesn't like it."

"Okay, I'll call her." When I reached the teacher, she told me the wheelchair transported Michele to class on time and more safely. "Isn't there someone always with her?" I asked.

"Yes, but the wheelchair is faster, and makes life that much easier."

"For you or Michele?"

"Mrs. Morton, I'm not going to argue with you. I know what's best for Michele, and that's how she's going to get around campus."

I couldn't believe her arrogance. Remaining calm, I said, in a slow, measured tone, "I want you to listen very carefully, because I'm only going to say this once. Michele will not be transported *anywhere* in a wheelchair, including your campus. No program schedule will ever determine whether Michele walks or does not walk. Remaining ambulatory is extremely important to her. And as long as she can do it, that's the way it'll be. Do you understand?"

"Yes, of course. But I still intend to do what I think is best for her here at the school. I need to go now," she said, and hung up.

I couldn't believe this. I hadn't even had a chance to touch on the tuna fish issue. I picked up the phone immediately and called Rob Hutchinson. The secretary said the principal was not in his office. "Can you tell me the name of the Special Ed Director for your schools?"

"Yes. It's Dave Roels," she said, spelling out his last name. Then she gave me his phone number.

I dialed the number and asked to speak with him. I didn't have to wait long before he answered. "Dave Roels speaking."

"Hello, Mr. Roels. This is Kathleen Morton. I'm the mother of Michele Morton, who was recently enrolled in the special education program of the Glendale school. There's a problem with her teacher that I think you should know about." Once I explained the situation, he reacted with surprise.

"Why would she do that?" he asked. "Does Michele have her own wheelchair?"

"No. She has never used one. But, because the whole facility is new to her, she's naturally hesitant in her step. If you take her by the hand, her confidence returns and she walks fine. Someone has to be with her anyway, wheelchair or not, so I don't understand the teacher's thinking. When I told her that Michele would not be transported in a wheelchair on the campus or any other place, she was not very receptive."

"I'm sorry, Mrs. Morton. I'll get to the bottom of this. I haven't met Michele, but I have reviewed her record. If my memory serves me correctly, Michele is blind. Is she not?"

"Yes, she is. Oh, I almost forgot. The teacher also told Michele today not to bring anymore tuna fish sandwiches for lunch, because they're too messy. Where is she coming from? I'll go over and clean up after Michele if she wants."

"No, that won't be necessary, Mrs. Morton. Send Michele to school in the morning as usual, with tuna fish for lunch if you want, and I'll be there to see what's going on."

"Thank you very much, Mr. Roels."

"Dave, call me Dave."

"Okay, Dave. Will you get back with me tomorrow?"

"Yes, I will. I'll call you after school is out."

I had to coax Michele to go to school the next day. "Don't worry, Michele," I assured her. "A Mr. Roels will be there and he'll talk to the teacher. I think everything will be okay." So, off she went with her tuna fish sandwich tucked inside her bag.

I busied myself around the house. Then I gave Arnie a call to tell him the latest, and wrote some letters to my friends in New York. I missed them all so much. My friends at the school for the blind in the Bronx, the ones at St. Kevin's, as well as at Cresthaven Country Club, all wanted me to stay in touch so they could remain up-to-date on Michele. The day passed quickly. Suddenly I heard a bus stopping outside and realized Michele was home.

I jumped up, and opened the door, hoping I would find her happy. I wasn't disappointed.

"Hi, Mom," she said, grinning. "Guess what?"

"What?" I asked smiling. "Good news I hope."

"Yes! Your friend, Mr. Roels, did come to school today. He walked with me to my classes, holding my hand. He even walked with me down to the pool, and back. Then, we walked over to the cafeteria and he sat down and had lunch with me. I was a little afraid about the tuna fish, Mom, but he said I did fine. He also liked the way I walked, and said not to worry about a wheelchair. He was so nice!"

"Oh, that's wonderful Sweetheart! I'm glad everything turned out so well."

"Can I go to ARCH, Mom?"

"Sure, but I'm waiting for a phone call. Then I'll drop you off."

"Okay, call me when you're ready," Michele said, and went up to her room.

Within fifteen minutes, the call came in. "Hello, Mrs. Morton," Dave Roels said, as I answered. "I'm calling to report what happened today."

"You don't need to," I laughed. "I've already been informed." Then I told him everything Michele had said. "You made a big hit with her."

"I'm glad to hear it! She did a good job of reporting, and I agree with you, Mrs. Morton, Michele can walk fine. And, I mean, I walked her long distances, and she was unfazed. She kept right up with me chatting away. I've met with the teacher, so hopefully everything will go well in the future."

Everything did go well until several weeks later, when Michele fell and hit her head. She required medical attention at the ER where she received multiple stitches. When I arrived at the hospital, I asked, "What happened, Honey?"

"I don't know," she replied. "I was standing there waiting for someone to take my hand and walk with me. All of a sudden I felt a push from behind and I fell on my head."

"Are you sure it was a push, Michele? Couldn't someone have just brushed against you by accident?"

"Maybe, but I don't think so. It sure felt like a push to me."

"Okay, Michele, I'll see if I can find out what happened."

"No, Mom! I don't want to go back to that school," she said, gingerly touching her head.

"Why?" I asked.

"Because, I don't feel safe there."

"What about ARCH? You go there practically every day after school."

"Oh, I love it there, Mom," she quickly said smiling. "They would never let anything happen to me at ARCH."

"Why do you say that?" I persisted.

And she simply replied, "Because they care about me, just like the school for the blind in New York."

I looked at her standing there with her chin set, and with that look of determination, which I had seen many times before when she was making a point important to her. Even her stance showed she wasn't going to give up easily. I finally said, "Okay, Michele, if that's how you feel, you won't have to go back."

She put her arms around me, "Oh, thank you Mom!"

I called the school the next day and told them Michele would not be returning. They were concerned, especially since she had been hurt at the school. "You needn't worry," I said. "Michele will recover from the injury. But, she still feels that someone pushed her from behind. She doesn't feel safe at your school and was emphatic about not returning. That's why I'm removing her from the program.

"Also, the holidays are coming. After, that she'll be going to ADTEC, where fostering independence for blind children is a top priority. That's really what she needs. So, I've decided to just wait until their program starts up."

As soon as I hung up the phone rang again. It was Arnie. "Hi Honey," he said cheerfully. How are things going?"

"You don't want to know."

"Yes, I do," he said. "What's happened?"

I told him about taking Michele out of the Glendale school, and why.

Arnie seemed surprised. "I don't remember her ever saying she didn't feel safe before."

"No, that's a first. And, as you know, she's been in a lot of new places in her young life."

"Is she still going to ARCH?"

"Yes! She loves it there. Tuesdays through Fridays, she's one of the first kids at the door."

"What else is going on?"

"What else? I miss you, and my old lifestyle. Going from being very busy to zero involvement isn't easy to take. As active as I was back east, my life still had a balance to it. Here, I feel like the solitude is all-encompassing, and there is no escape. Now, aren't you sorry you asked?"

"No." he said seriously. "You left behind everything that's familiar and comfortable. That's going to take some adjustment. How are Michael and Paula doing?"

"Fine. They're incredibly supportive. But, of course, they go to work every day, and on weekends they have their own social life, which is the way it should be."

"Why not join a private club with a restaurant, tennis programs, a pool, and social activities?" Arnie asked. "You know you love tennis and you can meet new people that way."

"That thought did occur to me, Arnie. But, right now, I'm trying to avoid any added expenses. I'll eventually be getting my own apartment, which means we'll be maintaining two households."

"That's true," Arnie said. "But, I still think the club membership is important. We'll manage. First thing tomorrow, check the various clubs in the Phoenix area, and join the one you like best."

After that call, I felt energized again. Arnie was probably right. But right now I had to contact a pediatric neurologist. A Doctor Allen Kaplan had been recommended and I had already placed a call to him. I hoped he would call me back sometime that day. Although Michele had been doing very well since moving to Arizona, I needed her to be seen by a specialist so he would be familiar with her case if something happened. She also needed prescriptions for ongoing seizure medications. I was about to call again when the phone rang. It was Doctor Kaplan. I told him about Michele, her rare neurological disorder, and our recent move to Arizona.

"What's the name of the disease?"

"It's called neuronal ceroid lipofuscinosis."

"I'm so sorry, Mrs. Morton. Neuronal ceroid lipofuscinosis has a dreadful prognosis. I guess you know you have a rocky road ahead of you."

"Yes, I do. That message came through loud and clear upon diagnosis. But we don't talk about the prognosis in Michele's presence. I must tell you, Doctor Kaplan, I'm very much involved with Michele's care. I consider myself a partner, not just a recipient of information."

"That's great! Why don't you bring Michele in to see me? I'll put you through to my secretary so that you can make an appointment."

When the appointment day arrived, Michele called down from her room. "Do I really have to go? I'm not sick. I feel fine."

"Yes, you do have to go, Michele. We need to have a doctor here in case you get sick. But he can't treat you unless he sees you first."

"Oh, alright," she said with resignation. "I'll get dressed."

"Atta girl. You'd better hurry up though. Breakfast is almost ready."

Kaplan's office was located at 12th Street and McDowell on the campus of the Good Samaritan Medical Center.

We had only waited about fifteen minutes when we were called in. The doctor was already in the examining room. He was medium height with dark hair, in his forties, and had a very pleasant demeanor. He strode forward with a big smile saying, "Hello

Mrs. Morton, I'm Doctor Kaplan. How are you?" We shook hands.

Turning to Michele, he said, "I bet I know who you are. You're Catherine, right?"

"No, I'm not," she said, with some indignation.

"Then you must be Mary. Or is it Nancy?"

"You're silly," she responded laughing. "My name is Michele – with one L."

"Michele, with one L. That's a funny name," he said.

Her shoulders dropped. She shot him a look, then finally threw up her hands in amazement wondering what to make of this guy.

Kaplan laughed and said, "I'm just kidding you, Michele. You're a real good sport, you know that?"

"Yep," she said nodding her head in agreement.

The way Kaplan introduced himself to Michele made her very relaxed and cooperative. The exam was completed quickly and Michele went out to the reception area while I talked to the doctor afterwards. "Here are Michele's recent medical records from New York," I said.

Doctor Kaplan smiled. "Good. These will be very helpful."

"If you need more information, you can call New York Hospital, Cornell Medical Center, and ask for Doctor Gail Solomon, Michele's former neurologist. The phone number is right there with the material."

"Fine. Michele is really doing very well for the type of disease she has. She also seems to be quite happy."

"That's her nature, Doctor. She doesn't let many things get her down."

"That's wonderful. I'm sure that's due to the way you've been working with her."

"Thanks, Doctor Kaplan. I appreciate your saying that. Oh, before I go, I need two prescriptions. One for Celontin and one for Depakene, her seizure medications."

After he finished writing the prescriptions, he shook my hand warmly and said, "Remember, call me if a problem comes up." I told him I would and then I was on my way, contented that I had found not only a good doctor, but one with an engaging sense of humor.

The next day, Michele and I began our hunt for a club. We enjoyed ourselves at a different place each day. This went on for a week. We swam in the pools, ate in the restaurants, and checked out the tennis. It was like a vacation! We finally settled on the LaMancha Racquet Club, on 23rd Avenue between Northern and Dunlap Avenues. It had a fitness program, a pool that Michele could access and exit without a problem, a nice restaurant, and tennis with clay courts, which was a big plus. This was the type of surface I'd had at Cresthaven. In addition, the owner, Chuck Griffin, introduced himself to us, and was very nice and personable. He especially paid attention to Michele, making her feel very comfortable. So, we signed up, and the club became a pleasant way of life for a long time.

Two weeks before Christmas, Arnie flew out to spend the holidays with us. When he got off the plane, I told Michele her dad had arrived and she was truly ecstatic. He engulfed her in his arms, hugging and kissing her as the rest of us gathered around, taking turns laughing and hugging him. This was indeed a happy moment. Once we got back to the house, and while Arnie was unpacking, he asked Michele about Doctor Kaplan. "He's nice and he's funny," she said.

Arnie looked at me quizzically, eyebrows raised. I nodded my head in agreement. "She's right. I was quite impressed. He's also very knowledgeable about the disease process, and he listens well."

"And how about the club? Did you join one?"

"Yes. And that's working out well, too."

"I love it," Michele chimed in.

"Ah, you would love anything that had food and a swimming pool," he said, pushing her head teasingly.

"No, really, it's a great place," she replied laughing and returned the push. "Honest!"

"Okay, I believe you," he said laughing as she continued to come after him. Catching her in his arms, he said, "I'm really glad everything seems to be working out well for you and Mom."

I smiled as I watched Michele's playful antics with her dad. Chronologically, Michele's age was now fifteen, but the anticipated deterioration of her cognitive functioning level was slowly taking its toll. All we could really be sure of was our unconditional love for her. Hopefully, this would lighten the burden she carried so valiantly.

Some researchers have indicated that these children suffer from a dementia similar to Alzheimers. And although Michele was aware she was not functioning on the level of her peers, it was still very important for her to be perceived at that age. Despite the slowly evolving mental setbacks, Michele saw herself as a child first, then growing up to become a teenager. The day she attained the age of thirteen, she was absolutely delighted, and nothing could have taken that joy away from her. Now, here we were two years later in Arizona getting ready to celebrate Christmas, her favorite holiday.

During the next few weeks, we were caught up in the excitement of Christmas shopping, wrapping gifts, and showing Arnie the sights, all of which led to having a memorable Christmas, and New Year. Then Arnie had to return to New York. Sadness accompanied his departure. But it would only be for a short while, we convinced ourselves, which made the separation more tolerable. Little did we know that many Christmases would come and go before we were all permanently together again.

Michele and Mom at Christmas time.

Chapter XII

Before Michele left the Glendale school, ADTEC video-taped her in both the educational setting and at play. They also gathered together her prior educational and medical records, which gave them a complete picture of her level of functioning up to the present. Then, after assembling everything we were invited to Tucson, where they were located. It was about a two hour drive from where we lived.

When we arrived, Michele was told to wait in the reception area, while I attended a meeting. I hesitated leaving her alone but the staff convinced me that they would be observing her to see how she handled this situation. She did well, sitting very quietly and patiently, until a staff member came for her.

At the end of the day, when the Individual Educational Plan was compiled, everyone in attendance made every effort to meet Michele's needs. The end result was a very effective and comprehensive program for the start of Michele's entrance into ADTEC in mid-January. I felt very relaxed with all the staff members, especially Ellie Terzieff, who was going to be Michele's teacher. Then Doctor Herriot, the director, came into the room. "Hello, Mrs. Morton," he said extending his hand. "How's the day going?"

"It's been pretty busy. You are all very thorough. I'm impressed."

"Good," he said smiling. "I'm glad we were able to put together a program that will benefit Michele while she's here. Her file reveals that she has been through a great deal in her life for some years now, yet there is no evidence of any emotional disturbances. That's surprising. She actually appears very happy. Is she always like that?"

"Yes, by and large, she is. Michele loves life and takes her problems in stride. She's very courageous. My goal is, that despite her infirmities, Michele derive as much happiness from life as she possible can."

"Well, I want you to know we're in your corner, Mrs. Morton," Heriot said as he stood to go.

After that all-day session in Tucson, with the holidays behind us, and with Arnie safely back in New York, I busied myself making preparations for Michele to start at ADTEC, only a week away. Michele was excited, which was a good sign. The next day on her way to ARCH she asked. "How will I get to the school? Will you drive me, Mom?"

"No, they'll provide bus service from Phoenix to Tucson and then back to Phoenix on Fridays. I'm waiting for a call from Jerry Maddox to tell me where the pick up point will be. However, the first day I could drive you there and then you could come home on Friday by bus. What do you think?"

Grinning, Michele replied, "I think that's a great idea, Mom!"

"Okay, then, that's settled." I said.

I thought I would relax and read for a while when I got home. Just as I settled into the recliner, the phone rang. "Hello, Mrs. Morton. This is Jerry Maddox. I just wanted to tell you that Michele will be picked up at the Phoenix Day School for the Deaf, located at 19th Avenue and Hayward. Do you know where that is?"

"Yes, I do. But, for the first day, I'm going to drive her to school. Will she be dropped off at the same place when she returns at the end of the week?"

"Oh no, Mrs. Morton," Maddox said, surprised at my question. "Michele won't be coming home every week."

"She won't! Why not?"

"None of the ADTEC kids go home on weekends. They stay at the school for a period of nine weeks, and then they go home for three weeks. Didn't someone explain that to you?"

"Yes, the nine weeks in session and the three weeks at home were explained to me. But no one said anything about her staying there on weekends. Michele thinks she's coming home every week. One day when I was out there I saw some buses picking up kids on a Friday. What was that all about?"

"That was for the kids who go to ASDB. They go home every Friday. But the children attending ADTEC have a whole different schedule. I'm sorry, Mrs. Morton."

"I'm sorry, too, Jerry," I replied feeling more and more downhearted. "Tell me, are the ASDB children dropped off at the Phoenix Day School for the Deaf?"

"Yes. Why?"

"Well, I thought maybe Michele could come home with them. ASDB and ADTEC are on the same campus. Would that be possible?" I asked, hopefully.

"No, I'm afraid not. Again I'm sorry that the schedule wasn't clearly explained to you."

I sighed audibly. "Okay," I said, "I guess that's it then. Just take Michele out of the program."

"You're not serious!"

"Yes, I'm afraid I am, Jerry. It would be terribly upsetting to her to have no home contact every week. She's still adjusting to the move from New York. That was hard for her, particularly since her dad is still back there. To introduce another unexpected change could jeopardize any stability we're trying to achieve."

"But you're welcome to be with her here whenever you want."

"I know, and I'd intended to drive out during the week sometimes and take her out to lunch or dinner. But that wouldn't be enough. She loves to come home. It creates some excitement in her life. No matter how good the program is I just can't take that away from her. I know it's never been done before, but couldn't you just inquire about the possibility of her coming home by bus on Fridays?"

"Alright, Mrs. Morton. I'll discuss it with Doctor Heriot to see if anything can be done. But I wouldn't count on it if I were you."

"Okay, I appreciate that. Thank you very much for calling," I hung up feeling a sense of helplessness. I walked back into the family room, but I didn't feel much like reading. There always seemed to be a glitch. Then I threw my hands up in the air and screamed, penetrating the silence of the moment. "Will it ever end? Dammit! Will it ever end?" I muttered through clenched teeth and then fell into the chair, physically and mentally exhausted. BeeGee came running over and sat down in front of me, cocking her head to one side, looking at me dolefully. I smiled and petted her while she licked my hand.

Although I felt thwarted, deep inside I knew I was overreacting. Withdrawing from ADTEC, although disappointing, would not be the worst thing that had ever happened to Michele. Not by a long shot. As a matter of fact, this setback was minor when compared to the challenges we'd already faced.

Yet, I let it get to me. Why? I guess stress plays tricks on us. Each setback just chips and chips away at our defenses, ultimately challenging any coping mechanisms we might have on reserve. And many times it's not the big things that throw us but the little ones. In the end, it's like the old adage: "The straw that broke the camel's back."

I jumped up when I saw the time. I suddenly remembered I was playing tennis at LaMancha at 6:30 and I needed to pick up Michele from ARCH earlier than usual.

"Let's go Michele," I said when I arrived. "I'm playing tennis tonight, so I'm in a hurry."

"That's right. I'll get my things. Why can't I go with you tonight?"

"Because this is my night out. Paula and Michael will be home with you. Besides, most of the tennis will be during the day, and you'll be with me then."

"Will I be able to go swimming?"

"Sure. After I play tennis. You can listen to your music while I'm on the court. But you can't bug me," I said smiling.

"Oh, I know, not when you're playing tennis," she said rolling her eyes.

You'd better watch it, kiddo," I responded laughing.

A few days later, I received a real pleasant surprise. Jim Heriot met with Noel Stephens, Director of the Visually Handicapped for ASDB, and discussed my request about Michele coming home on Fridays and they concluded that, all things considered, returning home every week was probably in Michele's best interests. They agreed to make an exception! Jerry Maddox, passed this wonderful news on to me and I was elated! I guess Heriot meant what he said when he told me he was in our corner.

The first day of school was very informal with arrival set for one o'clock in the afternoon. This schedule was designed to get the kids acclimated to their living quarters before classes started the next day. It was fun. Michele met a bunch of people who all made her feel welcome. When it came time for me to go, Michele felt very contented and didn't mind my departure. I felt great leaving her in such good hands. The realization that she was happy was all I ever needed to make my day.

Five months later, Michele was still doing extremely well. I visited often during the week, taking her out as planned, usually for dinner. She loved the Holiday Inn, where I had initially stayed, so that's where we ate on a regular basis. ADTEC had an apartment on campus and when the staff learned I would be staying over frequently, they allowed me to use it, which was great. I stayed over so many times that they facetiously dubbed it, 'The Morton Apartment.' ADTEC represented a wholesomeness that was unique and I had the greatest respect for Jim Heriot and his staff. During this time I enjoyed the entire experience so much that if anyone had tried to convince me that ADTEC would eventually turn into one of my worst nightmares, I would never have believed them.

Chapter XIII

Michele had indicated to me in January that she wanted to go to Camp Wapanacki that summer. I told her I didn't think that would be possible because she no longer attended the New York Institute, but she insisted upon asking Joe Ingram by letter because she was convinced that Joe would let her go. And she was right! He wrote to say that she would be welcome at Camp Wapanacki any time. He said tell her mother to put her on the plane, that he would meet her at the airport.

I knew Joe meant well, but I would never put Michele on a plane by herself. Never! I would be a basket case before the plane got anywhere near Kennedy Airport.

Now that school was out for most of the summer, I had two surprises for Michele. One was that we were moving into a new apartment and the other was that she was going to Camp Wapanacki. She was thrilled with the news. "How will I get there?" she asked.

"I've already made arrangements for us to fly to New York in a couple of weeks."

"Does Joe know?"

"Oh yes, I talked with him first, and you'll be able to go to the camp on the bus with Joe and the other kids when we arrive in New York."

"Oh, thanks, Mom," she said, hugging me. "Does Daddy know?"

"You bet," I said. "He was in on this little secret from the beginning."

Wapanacki was now the conversation of the evening. When Paula and Michael got home, Michele talked of nothing else. Finally she left the room. Michael turned to me and asked with amusement, "How do you turn her off?"

I smiled. "Not very easily, as you can see. She's practically overcome with excitement."

"It's unbelievable how she keeps her enthusiasm so high," he said, "when you think of all she's been through."

I told them. "I think there may be a lesson here for all of us."

When the time came Michael drove us to the airport. As we approached the gate he placed his hands on his sister's shoulders and said. "Have a great trip and a wonderful time at the camp."

"Okay, Michael, I will," Michele assured him. "I'll tell you all about it when I get back."

Rolling his eyes, but successfully suppressing laughter he said. "I can't wait. I just can't wait."

"M i c h a e l!" Paula said, directing a punch at him. "Be nice." Turning I caught Michael holding his arm in feigned shock over this obvious flagrant husband abuse. I shook my head, waved and laughed, and boarded. We were off!

The plane touched down at Kennedy after a smooth ride, and we passed two flight attendants standing by the cockpit door. Hearing a male voice, Michele turned and asked. "Are you the pilot?"

"Yes. Why?" he asked.

Putting out her hand she replied, "It was a nice trip. Thanks."

"Why, you're welcome, young lady. My pleasure!" he said

smiling as he shook her hand warmly. Those within earshot appeared to find the exchange very amusing. Then the pilot continued, "Oh, wait a minute, I have something for you." He handed Michele a pair of wings.

When she realized what they were, she smiled and accepted them gracefully, thanking him for his kindness.

Driving on the Belt Parkway, in a rental car, memories came flooding back. Having been away for a while made the surroundings loom larger than ever. It was a nice day, not too humid, as it usually is in New York during the summer months. I felt a sudden elation at returning. One glance at Michele confirmed how happy she was.

I had called Arnie from the airport, so when we drove up, he and some neighbors were waiting outside to welcome us. Once inside, Casey bounded down the stairs to greet us. As he happily jumped on me, I made a big fuss over him, while Arnie got Michele safely seated on the sofa before he went after her. Michele's shouts of glee were delightful, as she tried to stop Casey from licking her face. Arnie and I just stood there hugging, kissing, and wiping away tears of joy. It was an emotional homecoming.

Then the phone rang.

"Oh, no, not already," Arnie said. "You just got here."

It was Faith Gioella, one of my good friends from Cresthaven.

Surprised, I said, "How did you know I was in New York?"

"It was rumored at Cresthaven that you were coming in, so I thought I'd call to see if it were true. How about playing tennis this weekend at the club?"

"I'd love to, but I'm not sure I can play there. Let me check it out and I'll call you back."

I walked into the living room. Arnie and Michele were sitting on the couch and she was animatedly telling him about ADTEC. "They even have a pool," she declared.

"I'm happy to hear that, because you sure love the water." Then he turned to me and said, "We've decided what we're going to have for dinner tonight."

"Oh? I can imagine what that is, with the two of you collaborating."

"I bet you think it's pizza," Michele called out.

"No, I don't *think* it's pizza, I *know* it's pizza." I replied.

The next morning I called Cresthaven, gave my name, and asked to speak with Rita Haff, manager of the Club.

"How are you, Kathleen?" Rita asked.

"I'm fine. I'm going to be in New York for a month and I was wondering if I could have a short term tennis membership while I'm here."

"Of course, we'd love to have you. Just come over, and play with your friends any time. No charge."

"Thanks so much, Rita. I can't wait to see everyone again. Faith has already asked me to play this weekend. How will I get past the guard at the gate?"

"Oh, don't worry about that, I'll tell Bob to expect you."

"So, Bob's still at the gate. If I remember correctly, he wouldn't let a fly through without the proper credentials!"

She laughed, "You're right about that. But believe me, you'll have nothing to worry about."

The next day, Michele left for Camp Wapanacki. Arnie took some vacation time and we both enjoyed being alone together for a while. Tennis at the club was great and seeing everyone again brought back some wonderful memories. As usual, when fun is the name of the game, time passes quickly. Before we knew what was happening, it was time to return to Arizona. Our lives had become a series of hellos and goodbyes.

Before I left New York, I had an opportunity to talk in person with Joe Ingram about Michele and her camp experience that year. He told me that she had been her usual happy self, enjoying everything familiar to her. When she experienced some difficulties, they allowed her to do what she could at her own pace. But it had been a good camp experience.

"What else at Wapanacki?" I said laughing. "I've learned to take each day as it comes, and encourage her as much as possible. However, I do want to thank you for agreeing to let her attend the camp this year. The joy this brought her cannot be expressed in words. This will undoubtedly be Michele's last hurrah at Camp Wapanacki, but the wonderful memories she carries with her will last forever and we have you to thank for that. If you had not persisted that day many years ago, we would have taken her home. But there was something about your sincerity that got through to us, which led us to make one of the best decisions in Michele's young life. We are very grateful to you for that, Joe," I said, extending my hand.

Smiling, he shook my hand and said, "Michele has endeared herself to all of us at Wapanacki and we'll never forget her. We wish all of you the very best. Have a safe trip back to Arizona."

I never saw or spoke with Joe Ingram again. Several years later I got a letter from the New York Institute stating that after 50 years of serving blind children, Camp Wapanacki would be closing its doors. The letter went on to say, "....Undoubtedly, you have many warm memories of your experiences at Camp Wapanacki and you will feel an inevitable sense of loss...." No truer words were ever spoken.

Michele was really looking forward to attending ADTEC

when classes began again. She got on the bus contented and happy on Day One.

However, by the end of the week I got a call telling me that Michele didn't feel too well. When I got her home, she was out of it. Some kind of odd seizure. I couldn't put my finger on exactly what it was. The next day she seemed better, and by Sunday she was fine. I called Doctor Kaplan to see what he thought.

"It's hard to say what she's reacting to," he said. "But, since she's doing fine today, by all means, send her back to school. And keep me posted."

Michele was anxious to return, and seemed to have no awareness of her recent problem. I put her on the bus as usual and she cheerfully kissed me goodbye.

Two days later her teacher, Ellie Terzieff, called and said. "Mrs. Morton, Michele is quite ill today and isn't responding well to anything. We contacted Doctor Michael Cohen, our Medical Director, and he's with her now."

"My God, I can't imagine what this is!" I said with exasperation. "When Michele got on the bus she was feeling fine. I talked to Doctor Kaplan over the weekend and he was just as baffled since she recovered so quickly. I will call him again and then I'll get back to you."

Obviously troubled by what I reported to him, Doctor Kaplan said, "I really need to see her, Mrs. Morton. As a matter of fact, I'd like to admit her to Good Samaritan Hospital in Phoenix for observation. Do you think they would drive her to Good Sam?"

"I think so. If not, I'll go get her. In any event, make preparations for her admission within the next few hours."

Much to my relief, ADTEC arranged to have Michele transported directly to Good Samaritan.

When she was admitted Doctor Kaplan checked her right

away. "I want them to observe her overnight," he said. "Will you be staying with her?"

"Yes, I'll be here throughout the night."

"Okay, then. I'll see you tomorrow morning."

The next morning, Friday, brought the exact same results as before. She was responsive. By the next day, Saturday, Michele was not a sick child. Doctor Kaplan looked at her and shook his head. "She looks great," he said, pleased with her rapid recovery. "I assume you checked to make sure she's getting the Celontin medication for seizures?"

"That's the first thing I did. Nursing assured me she's getting the Celontin without fail and I believe them. ADTEC is an excellent program, well supervised and managed. They have a very good attitude and are just as eager as we are to find an answer to this recurring medical dilemma."

Turning toward Michele, Doctor Kaplan asked. "Well, now, what are you doing in the hospital, young lady, when you look so good?" he asked, showing his usual humor.

Shaking her head and shrugging her shoulders, she replied, "I don't know."

"Okay, you're out of here," he said smiling.

While Nursing helped Michele get dressed, Doctor Kaplan and I talked a little more. "What do you think is happening here, Doctor?"

"It's a puzzling pattern," Kaplan said. "I don't believe it's deterioration due to NCL. If it was, she wouldn't recover like this. The big question is, why is this happening?"

"Should I keep her out of school?"

"No, I don't think that's a good idea. She needs the stimulation and she seems to like it there."

"In that case, would you call Doctor Michael Cohen? He's

the Medical Director for ADTEC. He's done his best to figure this out too. He's also been sympathetic and very helpful whenever I've spoken with him."

"Sure, I'll be glad to call him," Doctor Kaplan said. "Let's hope this is the end."

But it wasn't the end. Far from it. Several times Michele was taken to St. Mary's hospital in Tucson with the same symptoms. A day after she arrived, she was better, and the next day well enough to be discharged. The abnormal became routine. And the bills from St. Mary's were piling up because we were responsible for a percentage of those hospital stays.

As this medical nightmare continued, strained relations developed between the administration and myself. I was looking for a solution, while they were only looking to throw her out. Doctor Cohen, however, remained steadfast in his resolve to find an answer. He worked with me throughout, always seemingly aware of my feelings and of how tough this situation was.

And then, one day after Michele came home, I opened her suitcase and found Celontin, her seizure-control medication, packed away with her personal items and clothing. This was unusual because Nursing knew better than to send her medication home, since I had my own supply. But a substitute nurse, unaware of the procedure, had been on duty that day. I opened the bottle to give her one then sat back in stunned silence, trying to catch my breath. The pieces of the puzzle were rapidly falling into place. The small kapseals in my hand should have been dull and cloudy. They were now transparent. This meant only one thing: They were spoiled! I quickly put a paper towel on the table and emptied the contents of the Celontin bottle, examining each and every one. Each kapseal was the same.

No wonder Michele always got sick in school. Giving her

this medication was tantamount to a quick withdrawal of the anti-convulsant medication, the worst thing that could happen to a seizure-prone child. Even if seizure medication is being discontinued, it can never be stopped abruptly without dire consequences. That fact is well-known throughout the medical community and to parents of seizure-prone children.

I felt rage welling up inside of me. When Nursing said that Michele was getting her Celontin, it never occurred to me to check the medication itself. This was something Nursing should have noticed immediately!

I went to Walgreen's, the drugstore that filled Michele's prescriptions and spoke to the pharmacist. When I explained the problem, he took the bottle from my hand and looked at the kapseals. "You're right, these kapseals are spoiled. And that's most unusual because the expiration date is several years away. My guess is that they were exposed to excessive heat or light. Let me remove a few and send them to the pharmaceutical firm, Parke and Davis for analysis. I'll have them contact you."

When I returned home, I called Doctor Kaplan. He was shocked when I told him what I had discovered.

"Well that would certainly explain the unusual episodes she was experiencing. Have you told the school?"

"No, not yet. But I think I know how they'll react. Initially, ADTEC was one of the best programs. They had a great attitude and were very supportive – until all this happened. Now, I think they'd be delighted if Michele and I would simply disappear."

"I hope it's not that bad," he said.

"Really, I'm not kidding. My relationship now with administration and Nursing has become extremely strained. No, they're not going to take this well." Before hanging up I asked Doctor Kaplan to call in another prescription for Celontin.

Neither Doctor Cohen nor Doctor Heriot were available over the weekend, so I wrote to Cohen telling him of my discovery regarding the Celontin sent home from school. I sent a copy to Heriot. Then I met with Doctor Heriot and Nursing. Heriot remained impassive while I explained how I'd discovered the spoiled medication, but the nurse was more vocal. "It's not our fault. You gave us the medication that way," she blurted out defensively.

"It's not your fault?" I retorted, shocked at the quick denial. "Not your fault? Think about what you're saying. Let's suppose the medication was spoiled when I picked it up from Walgreen's. This medication was turned over to you, intact, in a stapled pharmacy bag. One of you should have recognized that the medication was spoiled. A quick glance was all I needed to determine that. So, either way, you are still responsible for what has taken place here. Also, the Celontin I use at home comes from the same pharmacy, and I've never had a problem with it. Anyway, we're not here to point fingers, but to make sure this doesn't happen again." The meeting ended with our relationship more strained than ever.

I was exceedingly disappointed with the administration at ADTEC, directed by Doctor Heriot. He was in charge of an excellent program, but when the chips were down they showed their true colors. None of them would even consider the possibility that Nursing may have been derelict in their duty, even with something so obvious. No, it had to be the disease of NCL that created the problems for Michele. That, they could handle. As a result, the administration had no desire to discuss the issue and there was certainly no apology.

Doctor Cohen, on the other hand, called as soon as he received my letter. "Mrs. Morton, he said, "I'm so sorry about what happened with the Celontin medication, I hardly know what to say. The sample kapseals you sent me certainly should never have been used. I've told Nursing to refrigerate the new supply you sent out to them. How is Michele now?"

"She's still having some problems, especially with her speech. It's become unintelligible, but we're hoping this will clear up in time. This was quite an assault on her system."

"That's for sure. Let me know, Mrs. Morton, if I can help you in any way now or in the future."

"Thanks very much, Doctor Cohen. You've always been very supportive and I really appreciate that."

The on-again, off-again, medication regime, unwittingly played out in this saga, weakened Michele so much that it placed an enormous strain on her system. Doctor Kaplan, believing that the medication was now attacking her system rather than aiding it, slowly withdrew the Celontin. Finding another medication to control Michele's seizures was not easy, and within a couple of weeks she was back in the hospital, where she remained for several months. She never returned to ADTEC.

But I did feel that the State should be responsible for Michele's bills at St. Mary's and I requested that they pay them. They refused without comment. So I sought legal help. Sitting in a conference room, flanked by three lawyers, I asked them to intercede with the state.

"Seems to me they owe you a lot more than the hospital bills," one of the lawyers said.

"I don't want to make any money on this," I responded, looking around the room. "I just want the medical bills paid."

"Mrs. Morton, filing a lawsuit against the State of Arizona, or any state for that matter, can be difficult and costly. What we'd have to do, in this case, is sue the doctor."

"Sue Doctor Cohen?" I said increduously. "No way!"

"Why not? He's the medical director of the school and therefore ultimately responsible."

"Look, there is, I repeat, no way I would ever sue Doctor Michael Cohen. He was the only one who had a heart and showed a great deal of empathy for what I was going through."

"But filing a lawsuit against him doesn't mean he's going to be hurt by it. After all, he has malpractice insurance, and it is the only way to go."

Rising to my feet, I collected my belongings. As I pushed away the chair I said. "Thank you, gentlemen, for your time."

"Go home and think about it, Mrs. Morton. Then call back and let us know if you want to proceed with the case."

I nodded my head in silence and left, thinking 'Where's the justice in this world?' At this point I was sick of the whole thing. It was a tough time we were going through, especially with Michele not responding well while in Good Samaritan. But I knew with certainty that I would never sue Doctor Cohen.

The next day I called St. Mary's and spoke with April. "I want you to know that I'm not ignoring the bills from St. Mary's," I told her. "I wonder if you could do me a favor and help me sort them out. Could you list all of Michele's admissions, the full cost, total it, then deduct what insurance has paid, and what balance is my responsibility?"

"Yes, I'm sure we could do that for you."

"Thanks, April, that would be a great help. Also, could you find out the minimum I need to pay each month?"

"Will do. I believe they'll be very understanding, Mrs. Morton, because of the unusual circumstances of your case."

"Now, that sounds like good news!"

The next day April called back and said I could pay a min-

208

imum of ten dollars a month until our situation changed. From that day forward a monthly check was sent to St. Mary's until the balance was paid-in-full.

A few days later, Parke & Davis told me that the contents of the Celontin Kapseals that I had sent to them for analysis via Walgreen's, had obviously liquified and resolidified as a result of exposure to improper storage conditions and should not be used or dispensed. That information came as no surprise, but did validate that my own assessment had been correct.

Whenever we allowed ourselves to think about it, we realized that everything about the disease of Neuronal Ceroid Lipfuscinosis was catastrophic. Because of this, we made a desperate attempt to stay ahead of the expected deterioration, certainly a challenge of enormous proportions. And the challenges were even greater when an assault on Michele's system took place (such as the saga of the spoiled medication) and not allow automatic blame of NCL without a thorough investigation. It was always so easy to fault the disease, and I had to carefully guard against that.

If I was to remain sane, I knew I couldn't dwell on what was to come but rather, what was before me. This approach certainly worked for Michele, keeping her happy and appreciative of the world around her.

I wasn't quite sure what was going on with her at the hospital. She hallucinated a lot, and there were time periods when she was awake all day and night. Sometimes she ate not at all, which was a concern because she was on so much medication. In between these episodes she slipped frequently into a semi-comatose state.

Still, I talked to her every day. Michele had always demonstrated great receptive communication. I hoped she could hear and understand what I was saying. There was, however, no discernible response from her while in that condition. That didn't stop me, though, because there are so many things we know very little about, including much in the medical profession. Half the time it's a guessing game, especially with a child like Michele. I had seen too many doctors scratch their head in amazement at Michele's ability to rebound. She simply refused to be written off.

Much to my dismay, Doctor Kaplan informed me he was starting her on Tegretol, another seizure medication.

"Oh, no, I don't like that idea," I said.

"Why? Has she been on it before?"

"Yes. She did well at first, but suddenly started to react to it. She said the medicine made her feel funny inside."

"But that was a long time ago."

"True."

"Tegretol is one of the best medications for the type of seizures Michele is taking and we don't have many options left. I think we should try it again."

"Okay, Doctor, just as long as you're prepared to have plan B on hand, if she eventually reacts to it."

I was with Michele every day for the next couple of weeks without noting any great change. Then, one morning when I walked in, I saw Kaplan was standing by the nurses' station with a big grin on his face. "What are you so happy about?" I asked.

"Come and see for yourself," he said.

Walking into Michele's room, I saw her sitting on the side of the bed, eating breakfast with the help of a nursing assistant. "Michele!" I said, laughing. "Look at you!" I walked quickly toward her.

"Hi, Mom," she responded, giving me a big hug.

"Hi, Sweetheart. I don't have to ask how you're feeling," I said, enjoying the pleasure I felt watching her down her breakfast with gusto. What a moment! I wanted it to last forever.

"You finish your breakfast, Michele, and I'll be right back."

Kaplan and I walked out together. "When did she come out of it?" I asked.

"Early this morning," he replied.

"Why didn't you call me?"

"Because I wanted to see your reaction when you saw her. I knew you'd be here early, and I didn't want to spoil the surprise."

Later, when I got Michele up to walk, she was initially stiff and unsteady. Then, just as she started to walk with more confidence, her right leg started cramping on her. Dr. Kaplan transferred her to Rehab for physical therapy, to see if she would respond. He also set her up for speech, occupational and recreational therapies. Though very responsive and happy with the program, she occasionally still had some outbursts. The Rehab staff, however, was very attentive and had no problem dealing with her behavior, which improved with time. How encouraging it was to see progress for a change!

One day when I got off the elevator, there was Michele, walking and pushing a wheelchair down the hall with a big smile on her face. A physical therapist stood nearby. "Hi, Michele," I called out to her. Before she could answer, I sat in the wheelchair and asked her to give me a ride.

"Okay!" she said delightedly, and laughed all the way down the hall at the idea of pushing mom in a wheelchair. The physical therapist, nurses, and patients all enjoyed watching us.

That afternoon Doctor Kaplan and one of the residents stopped by. "This is Doctor Bruce Bethancourt," Kaplan said, "who will be working with me for a while."

"Hello, Doctor," I said smiling. "Nice to meet you. I'm Kathleen Morton, Michele's mom." He had a nice firm grip, and a pleasant smile. Of course, he was there to observe, so was very quiet, until Kaplan began picking on me, and jokingly giving me a hard time.

Pointing and shaking his finger at me, Kaplan said to Bethancourt. "This mother is incredible. She says 'Michele needs rehab.'

'No she doesn't,' I say.

'Yes, she does!' she says.

And I respond, 'Absolutely not!' "And, where do you think Michele ends up?----------In Rehab!"

At this point, Bethancourt and I were laughing at his rendition of reality, which, of course, was slightly exaggerated.

"Don't listen to him, Doctor Bethancourt," I said shaking my head. "I admit, initially it was my idea, but we discussed it sensibly like two mature adults, until he finally agreed."

"Yeah, well I don't like to see anyone whine or cry."

"Never happen, Kaplan. You've got the wrong mom. I don't whine or cry."

"Maybe not, but you jumped up and down a few times," he persisted.

"I did not! Get out of here, Kaplan, with your stories," I responded, thoroughly amused by his humor. He always knew how to lighten up a situation and he was great with kids. Michele loved him."

"Well, now that Michele is in Rehab, how do you think she's doing?" I asked.

Doctor Kaplan smiled, "She's responding very well to the program here, I must admit. Are you still working on getting her into a highly structured educational program when she is discharged? Doctor Griffith, Director of Rehab, Mary Carpenter, Director of Social Services, and I, will be writing reports supporting that fact. Has anyone talked to you about this?"

"Yes, Mary Carpenter did. She's been very helpful and informative. Michele responds well to a highly structured, residential program, along with a lot of home involvement, and that's what I'm presently pursuing. I'm getting the impression from Carpenter and some of the others that the state won't make it easy, but as far as I'm concerned, they'll have to abide by the federal law enacted by Congress several years ago."

"So, you know that law, do you?"

"You bet. I committed it to memory back in 1975, when it was first enacted."

"Have you met with anyone yet?" Kaplan inquired.

"No, but, I have a meeting with the school district and the Department of Economic Security today."

"Great. Michele will be here for a few more weeks. Meanwhile, we'll prepare our reports, which will show total support for the educational services she requires."

As they moved to leave, I shook hands again with Doctor Bethancourt.

Smiling with eyebrows raised, he said, "I wish you luck."

"Thanks Doctor. I appreciate that."

Little did I know that, as I began to wage my war against *bureaucracy,* what I really needed was something like a miracle!

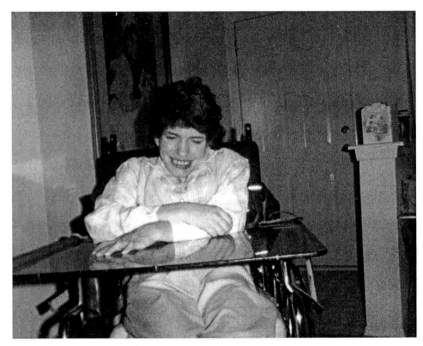

*This is how Michele looked after receiving the
new State formula. She really blossomed.*

Chapter XIV

The knock at the front door jolted me out of my reverie. I was so deep in thought about our lives that for a moment I was confused as to where I was. Then the nightmarish statement, "You must give up your child," made me sit up in the chair fully alert again. The knock came again too, louder this time. I slowly got up out of the lounge chair and moved toward the door. I was pleased to see it was Michael stopping by after work.

"Hi Mom," he said cheerfully.

"Hi. C'mon in."

"What's wrong? You look tired."

"Frustrated is more like it."

"Uh, oh. How did the meeting go with DES today regarding residential placement for Michele?"

"You won't believe what the requirement is," I said with a cynical smile.

He looked at me inquiringly. "Go on, Mom, I'm listening."

"They informed me that, in order for Michele to receive the kind of educational services she needs, I would have to give her up to the state. And they seem to think nothing of it. I was told it was just a simple case of relinquishment."

"My God, that's insane! What are you going to do?"

"Well, one thing's for sure. We're not giving up Michele. Never!" I expounded, hitting the table with my fist.

"Okay, Mom! You don't have to convince ME." He came

over and put his arm around my shoulders, "But to tell you the truth, I'm beginning to feel sorry for the state. Remember, I've seen you in action before!"

Though I laughed at him I recognized that his comments pulled me out of my doldrums.

"The reason I dropped by was to invite you out to dinner. Paula is waiting in the car. Want to go?"

"Sure I'd love to! Just give me a few minutes." What a nice surprise this was! And just what I needed. It was so comforting to know that no matter what happened, Michael was always waiting in the wings.

The next morning before I went to the hospital to see Michele, I spent most of the time on the phone. My efforts were not in vain. I was able to learn that Bill Donovan was the Executive Director of the Governor's Council on Developmental Disabilities and that Douglas Patino was the Director of the Department of Economic Security. I made an appointment with Donovan for the next day, and with Patino for the following week.

When I arrived at Donovan's office I got right to the point. "I came to see you for a very special reason. My daughter, Michele, is a multi-handicapped, blind child requiring special education and related services. According to specialists and a comprehensive report from ADTEC (Arizona Diagnostic Training & Educational Center) she requires residential in order for her educational needs to be met. I'm told by representatives from DES that they agree her needs require the residential component, but in order to receive it I have to give her up to the state. Have you ever heard of this?"

"Yes, I'm afraid I have," he replied, in a somber tone, "and I agree with you. It isn't right."

"I'm glad to hear that someone agrees with me. It's mind-boggling to me that this is an accepted procedure anywhere in the

United States. That's the reason I wanted to meet with you first. Since you oversee programs and deal with issues involving the developmentally disabled, it's important that you're on my side. I would like you to accompany me to my meeting with Douglas Patino next week."

"You have a meeting set up with Doctor Patino?" he asked, an edge of surprise in his voice.

"Yes. I also have a meeting set up with Governor Babbit if I get no satisfaction from Patino."

"You're kidding!"

"No, I'm not. This is a serious matter. Will you come with me?"

He looked at me a trifle ruefully. "I don't know if I can."

"Why?"

"Well, for one thing, I'd have to ask Doctor Patino if it was okay."

"What in heaven's name for? As Executive Director of the Governor's Council, you certainly should be free to accompany a parent to a meeting about a subject on which we both agree. That's why I met with you first. I need support from an organization such as the Governor's Council. Why would you need to get Patino's approval?"

"Because," he said hesitantly, " I report to him."

"He's your boss?!" I threw up my hands in amazement. "How can you effectively oversee what goes on with the children when you report to the one in charge of the special programs they require? It makes for a real cozy arrangement, doesn't it? No wonder nothing works in Arizona!"

Donovan now was showing obvious signs of discomfort. I almost felt sorry for him. He seemed to be a nice guy caught up in an incredibly unwieldy system.

Driving home, I mulled everything over. I knew Patino would now find out what I wanted to talk to him about and no doubt the Governor would too. So what? I decided to write a letter to Patino prior to my appointment so that there could be no misunderstanding about the main issue.

Throughout this time, Michele was doing well in the hospital and I didn't have to worry so much, which certainly eased my tension.

My appointment with Douglas Patino finally arrived. Not surprisingly, his office was in the same building as Donovan's. When I entered he immediately rose to his feet. Perfunctory introductions were made and then he walked around his desk to greet me smiling with hand extended. "So glad to meet you, Mrs. Morton. Here, have a seat," he said, indicating an area of his office that held couches, chairs and a table in between. 'Nice cozy setting,' I thought as I sat down across from him. Donovan was nowhere in sight. Patino asked me if I'd like some coffee.

"Thank you, no," I said. "I'd rather just get to why I'm here. I assume you received my letter?"

"Yes, I did. And the records show that your daughter obviously requires the program you're seeking. However, the process we have to abide by differs somewhat from your expectations."

"You can say that again!" I responded, with a tone of indignation not lost on him.

"Mrs. Morton, what we want to do today is to see if we can come to some sort of mutual agreement concerning Michele's educational needs."

"Doctor Patino," I said, holding his gaze, "Giving up Michele will never be an option. As long as you understand that, we'll get along just fine."

"Okay. You've made it clear. But what you would actually

be doing is filing what we call, a dependency petition through the court system. As a parent, you could still remain involved."

"What you call it, Doctor Patino, is immaterial. The end result is what counts. That action on my part would make Michele a ward of the state. Right?"

"Technically, that's true," Patino admitted.

"And a state bureaucracy would have complete control over my child. No way! The problem here, Doctor Patino, as I told your staff, is that you're completely ignoring the education law covering handicapped children. That's what should prevail here, not your dependency petition.

"I can't believe that this state is in the business of forcing parents to give up their children when their needs require residential educational services. Everyone loses with that approach. And each time I mention the law to anyone on your staff they look at me as if I'm speaking a foreign language."

"That's because they are not familiar with the law you mentioned," Patino pointed out. "And to be perfectly honest, neither am I."

"And do you know why, Doctor Patino? DES is a *service* agency, removing children from homes because of abuse and neglect. It provides welfare to the poor and deals with various other social issues throughout the state. On the other hand, the education of handicapped children is an *entitlement* program, and is bound by legal federal mandates, once the Education Department in each state accepts the Part B funding from the Federal Government. I have a copy of the Federal Register with me covering the Education of all Handicapped Children. May I quote the passage relating to our discussion here today?"

"Sure. By all means, Mrs. Morton. I find this all very interesting."

"Okay, here it is:

Section 121a.302 - Residential Placement
If placement in a public or private residential
program is necessary to provide special education and related services to a handicapped
child, the program, including non-medical
care and room and board, must be at no cost
to the parents of the child.

"That Law was enacted in 1975. Then, the Federal Government gave the states funding and three years to totally implement the new law. It is now 1983, five years after the deadline date
of implementation, and yet all of you still claim ignorance of this
clearly well-written Federal mandate! There it is in a nutshell."

Doctor Patino looked at me with a somewhat bemused
expression. "Very impressive," he said. "I'll tell you what I'm going
to do. I'll schedule a meeting for next Wednesday, March 30, at
10:30am. It won't be in this building, but the secretary will give
you the address as you leave. Can you attend?"

"Of course, I'll be there," I said, feeling good about his
quick action. "Will you also be there?"

"No, that won't be necessary. But, don't worry. Everything
should work out fine. Now then, may I ask you a personal question?"

"What's that?"

"Do you have a job?"

"No, I don't. How could I work? It takes all of my time to
fight you guys."

Patino chuckled at that. "No, I mean once Michele is
placed."

"Which means, in the residential program she needs without relinquishing my parental rights?"

"Yes. And once that's accomplished, will you come to work for me?" he asked leaning forward in his chair.

"I must say, I'm bewildered by all this. Why would you offer me a job, Doctor Patino? You don't even know me."

"Oh, but I do know you, Mrs. Morton. More than you realize," he replied with a touch of amusement. "And I admire the way you work. You present your case well. You're knowledgeable, articulate, and you have an amazing tenacity. We could use people like you in the Department of Economic Security."

While I was basically distrustful of everyone in this state, Doctor Patino seemed to be different. He was certainly very charismatic and charming. I had to admit that I was totally disarmed. While most of these meetings felt more like combat zones, this one had actually been pleasant. And to think that this struggle would soon be over made me feel wonderful.

Patino was studying me and patiently waiting for an answer.

"Doctor Patino," I said, "the reason I came to see you today was to deal with a very important issue involving Michele. I would probably prefer not to digress from that issue right now. I must admit, I am flattered by your offer, and really appreciate the kindness you've shown me today."

Patino stood up when I did and extended his hand. "Of course, I understand. We can talk about this again after Michele is settled."

Immediately I got home, I called Heather McClary. She was my best friend, confidant, and mentor during my trials and tribulations with the state. "Guess what?" I said, when she picked up the phone.

Heather laughed. "I'm afraid to ask."

"Well, don't be. The meeting with Doctor Patino went very

well. I think that appropriate placement for Michele is just around the corner."

"Without giving her up?" she asked suspiciously.

"Yes, I made that clear. Patino was very congenial and I was impressed with his sincerity. He wasn't familiar with the education law, so I read him the portion that applied to Michele and he was very impressed. Then he immediately said he was putting together a meeting the following week, and told me not to worry, that everything would be fine. How does that sound to you?"

"Very encouraging! By the way, did Patino say why the State Department of Education selected his agency to deal with the residential component of the federal law?"

"No, he didn't, and I don't know exactly why either. But I'm willing to wager a guess."

"Which is?"

"Well, it's a bit complicated, but my understanding is that each state must have a law responding to the federal law. In this state, it's ARS:15. The legislature, however, doesn't appropriate enough funding to serve the needs of some of these special education children. So, I suppose it was decided that DES would take care of the residential component, relieving the State Education Department of any financial responsibility for that segment of the law."

"But what's the difference? The cost is the same, isn't it?" Heather asked.

"Yes, but, the funding source is different. The legislature must appropriate a sufficient amount of funds for foster care. And in order for the state to access those funds, a parent must give up their child, after which a judge remands the child into state custody. Then, according to law, the child's needs must be met within three weeks."

"Wow, that's pretty mind-boggling," Heather said

"Exactly the expression I used. Someone burned the midnight oil thinking this thing up. It's a neat little package and a way to circumvent the federal law, which guarantees a free and appropriate public education on a residential basis, when the child's needs require it, without the parent relinquishing custody, I might add.

"But once a dependency petition is filed, the state has complete control over the child. Foster care funds should never be used for providing appropriate education to a handicapped child. Never! But, that's what I believe is happening."

"Boy," Heather said. "I'm surprised you could figure it all out. But it makes perfect sense the way you've explained it."

"And I'm pretty sure it's true. When I tell anyone in the state what I believe is happening, no one argues with me. They just sit and stare and then change the subject."

"Tell me, Kathleen, if you gave Michele up, who would pay for her medical needs?"

"The state! Now isn't that crazy? Her medical needs are enormous even *with* medical coverage, and under the education law that's a parent's responsibility – as it should be. So is buying all her clothes and any equipment she might need in the future, like a walker or wheelchair. But if I file a dependency petition, that's all taken care of by the state. As I said before, foster care funds should never be used for this. But, the state doesn't seem to care about the cost, as long as a parent gives up the child."

"That's incredible!" Heather said. "But, if I were you, I wouldn't celebrate just yet."

"Oh, I agree. Next week I'll see what the committee has to say and go from there. But I must tell you, I feel great after the meeting with Patino."

"Well that's wonderful, Kathleen. If anyone deserves a break, you do. How is Michele doing?"

"Fabulous! We're all pleased with her response."

In high spirits, I arrived the following Wednesday morning at 10:30 sharp at the address given to me by Patino's secretary. The location was also in downtown Phoenix, not too far from the DES building. When I walked in, I was greeted by a receptionist, who gave me directions to a conference room where the meeting was to be held. About eight or nine people were assembled in this room. We each introduced ourselves and the meeting got underway.

As I looked around, I observed that this was not the friendliest bunch I had ever encountered. Most would not make eye contact and they looked very somber. The good feelings I had experienced since meeting with Patino began to evaporate. Then the leader of the group began.

"Mrs. Morton, we're all here to discuss placement for your daughter, Michele, and we're in agreement that she does require a residential program for her educational needs to be met. However, what we are not in agreement about is how to access that program."

I was puzzled. "Didn't Doctor Patino fill you in about our discussion last week, and its ultimate outcome?"

"Yes, he did."

"Well, nothing has changed since then."

"Mrs. Morton, we all realize how you feel, but regardless, we still have only two options open to us. Michele either goes on a waiting list which might involve years or you can file a dependency petition and she'll receives what she needs within three weeks."

"You people never cease to amaze me! Why did we have this meeting?" I asked. "Can anyone tell me that?" Silence followed. "When I left Patino's office last Tuesday, he told me to come here today and everything would be fine. Obviously, this get-together is just a farce."

"But, Mrs. Morton, you must understand........."

"No, I <u>don't</u> have to understand! I will never understand such an incredible demand as relinquishment of custody! You obviously believe the end justifies the means. I don't. This seems to be some sort of game to all of you. Well, I've had it!" As I got up to go, I was enraged. I had fallen for Patino's duplicity. I'm usually very careful about that when dealing with a bureaucrat, but this fellow had been so suave, and he set me up for a fall.

Getting in my car, I drove like the wind to Patino's office. I brushed past the receptionist as she said, "Wait, I have to announce you!"

"Forget it," I retorted, "I'll announce myself." I was on a roll. My adrenalin was pumping overtime. When I opened his secretary's door and strode past her desk heading for Patino's office, she was startled and said, "Mrs. Morton, you can't go in there!"

"No?" I asked without stopping, and then pushed open his door. Unfortunately, his office was empty. I turned to the secretary and asked, "Where is he?"

"At a meeting," she said stiffly.

"Oh wonderful," I said derisively. "He's great at having meetings. I wonder who he's working on this week? Give him this message from me. Tell him that the 'knowledgeable and articulate Mrs. Morton,' who was in to see him last week, *HAS JUST BEGUN TO FIGHT!*" I then turned on my heel and walked out the door, resisting the temptation to take it off its hinges.

What a morning! As I sat in my car, my mind was racing. It was obvious to me now why I wasn't going to get anywhere in this state. The Local School District, the Arizona Education Department, the Department of Economic Security, and the Governor's

Council on Developmental Disabilities were all sleeping in the same bed, effectively setting up a level of bureaucracy almost impenetrable for parents to plod through.

I continued to sit there, absorbed in thought, dwelling on all my efforts to force compliance. I had almost forgotten about the letters I'd written a couple of months ago to U.S. Senator Lowell Weicker, Chair of the U.S. Senate Subcommittee on the Handicapped in Washington, U.S. Senator Dennis DeConcini, and U.S. Representative Bob Stump, both from Arizona, and so far received no support.

But, I must say, after receiving my letters, the staff at DeConcini's and Stump's offices contacted DES on my behalf and tried very hard to get them to reverse their position. Unfortunately, the State bureaucratic rhetoric that followed did nothing to improve our situation.

I also called for a Due Process Hearing, having many witnesses in support of my position lined up to attend. However, I felt I needed a lawyer to plead the case since a mother would have a natural bias which could weaken the case in the eyes of the hearing officer. I knew that the Center for Law in the Public Interest received federal funds to assist in cases like this, but Amy Gittler, the director, turned me down. Through the many phone calls that followed, I determined the Center for Law's funding source. But, before I got a chance to contact them I received an unexpected call from Gittler telling me that she had reconsidered and would represent me at the hearing on the first step only. No representation for appeals or the courts would be available to me through her office. As it turned out, even the first step representation was unnecessary, because the due process hearing was cancelled as a result of what ultimately happened.

While I was wondering what to do next, it suddenly

226

dawned on me – why not get some publicity? Yes, that's it! I quickly put the car in gear and drove over to the hospital. I picked up the pay phone in the lobby and called The Phoenix Gazette, and spoke with Don Warne, one of their reporters. He listened intently to what I had to say and then asked, "Where are you right now, Mrs. Morton?"

"I'm at Good Samaritan Hospital, where my daughter is a patient in their rehab unit."

"Good. I'm coming right over with a photographer."

After this brief conversation I went up to Michele's room to find her sitting in a chair, listening intently to the Wizard of Oz. It was nearing the end, so I didn't say anything until the tape stopped. Then I moved in closer and asked her how she felt.

"Good!" she said with a smile.

"I've got some news for you. A reporter is coming over to do a story and he wants to take your picture. Or maybe a picture of the two of us together. How do you feel about that?"

"Great!" she said with her usual enthusiasm.

When the reporter arrived, he took some more notes as I gave him the names of the people in DES to contact. Then the photographer took a picture of Michele and me sharing a moment of tenderness. The story was published on Thursday, the next day, much to the chagrin of the State bureaucrats. Another positive still facing me was my appointment with Governor Babbit on Monday. My excitement mounted!

Heather called me at the hospital to see how Michele was doing. "She's in therapy right now," I said, "and still responding well."

"So, how did everything go today at DES?"

"It was a waste of time and energy," I told her. "We're right back to square one. Michele either goes on a waiting list, or I give her up. So, I walked out."

"I'm so sorry, Kathleen. What a letdown, especially when you thought success was so near."

"Yes, I know," I said sighing audibly. "They sure know how to jack parents around. I may be down, but I'm not out for the count yet."

"You never will be," Heather replied with fervor.

"I have to admit, I am a little disillusioned. However, I've got a surprise for them. Tomorrow the story is going to run in the Phoenix Gazette."

"What?" Heather exclaimed. "You're full of surprises! I can't keep up with you, never mind them."

"Well, I feel if they can dish it out, so can I. I was furious with Patino, so I drove right over to his office and charged in without waiting to be announced. Unfortunately, he wasn't there."

"Lucky him," Heather said.

I laughed at her remark then said, "I told his secretary to be sure and let him know that I had just begun to fight."

"Good for you, Kathleen."

"Here comes Michele now. I'll call you on Monday after my meeting with Babbit."

After I left the hospital, I was determined to enjoy the weekend at LaMancha, (in between visits with Michele.) Doing aerobics, playing tennis, relaxing by the pool, and having dinner with friends had a very calming effect. By Monday morning I felt ready for my 1:30 meeting with the Governor. Just as I was checking the folder I intended to take with me, the phone rang.

"Hello, Mrs. Morton. This is Governor Babbit's secretary," the voice said. "I'm calling to cancel your meeting with the Governor."

"Oh, that's too bad," I said. "I was really looking forward

to meeting with him today, but I know he has a busy schedule. Could you set up another appointment as soon as possible?"

"No, I can't do that," she replied tersely. "The Governor said he knows what it's about, and will not go against any decision Doctor Patino has made."

When I persisted, she said with exasperation, "Mrs. Morton, there is no room on the Governor's calendar for *you*, period!"

I was stunned. I felt as if I were being clobbered from all sides. The exhaustion I suddenly felt was overwhelming, but I recovered enough to say to this uppity miss, "Fine. Then, you tell the Governor from me that my daughter, Michele, will never become a ward of this State, and she will get the educational programming she requires. *Mark my words!*"

I knew I now needed to contact Washington. Running the risk of getting lost in that maze of red tape, I tried to think of who I could contact to penetrate that huge federal bureaucracy. A direct contact was my only hope. I didn't want to end up talking to a secretary, an aide, or an assistant.

I searched my mind and my contacts in the field of the disabled. After many long distance phone calls, I came up with the name and phone number of Gerald Boyd, Regional Administrator in Washington for the United States Education Department, who made sure that the states he supervised followed the federal mandates of Public Law 94-142, as well as the appropriate use of the Part B funding the federal government provided.

I didn't want to waste another moment. Picking up the phone I dialed our nation's capitol, and then received the surprise of my life. After a few rings, it was answered by a voice saying, "Gerald Boyd here." I was thrown off guard for a few seconds.. Wow! This was great. Another small miracle!

I quickly composed myself and said, "Hello, Mr. Boyd. My

name is Kathleen Morton, and I live in Arizona with my teenage daughter, Michele, who is blind and multihandicapped. In order for her special educational needs to be met, she requires residential programming."

"Well, there's a law that covers that type of programming," Gerald Boyd immediately advised. "Are you familiar with PL 94-142?"

"Yes, I am."

"So, what's the problem?"

"The problem is, unless I give up Michele to the state of Arizona, they won't provide the residential component."

"You mean relinquish custody?"

"That's right." For the next twenty minutes I explained the process Arizona uses when residential becomes an issue.

Boyd took a deep breath and said, "Mrs. Morton, this is what I want you to do. First, put everything you just told me in writing. I can't act until it's in written form. Also, send me copies of anything that supports your complaint and I'll initiate an investigation right away."

"Oh, thank you so much, Mr. Boyd. That's great!" I responded excitedly. "I'll send everything out today, along with a letter providing a detailed account of what's taking place."

"Good. That's what I need. I'll keep you informed."

After I hung up the phone, I sat there thinking that, at long last, I'd talked to someone who spoke the same language. His questions to me had been pointed and encouraging. I knew I had finally come full circle.

I would have to move quickly if I hoped to make the last mail pick-up of the day. I had a lot to do and I needed help so I decided to call Heather. When I told her about the Governor cancelling she said, "Oh, no, won't it ever end?"

"Yes, I think it will," I said surprising her, and then I told her everything that had transpired that day.

And, true to form, she asked, "Can you use some assistance?"

Between the two of us, we accomplished the task in record time. Heather searched the files for the material I needed and then made copies of everything to be sent, while I concentrated on writing the letter to Boyd. We then put it all together and drove over to the post office to mail it.

"Thanks so much, Heather," I said to my friend as we sat back relaxing when we returned home.

"Don't mention it, Kathleen. It was just so important to get this done today. What a great sense of satisfaction you must be feeling right now," she said smiling.

"You bet," I responded contentedly. "This just might be what's needed to finally turn the tide."

Battern Disease Support and Research Association

"A Light in a World of Darkness"

BDSRA
120 Humphries Dr.
Suite 2
Reynoldsburg, OH 43068
1-800-448-4570
website: www.bdsra.org
email: bdsra1@bdsra.org

Michele in her new RED wheelchair and

*she's happy here because she's all dressed up for a
St. Patrick's Day Party.*

Chapter XV

What happened next was one for the history books. The tide moved so quickly in my favor that I constantly had to come up for air. I was overwhelmed to find how fast Arizona could actually move, leaving no doubt in my mind that the right buttons were finally being pushed.

The material was still winging its way to Washington when I got a call at the hospital from Kritina Mohr, Client Advocate for the Center for Law. "Mrs. Morton," she said. "I'm glad I finally reached you. You can have whatever you want for Michele."

"What do you mean?" I asked mystified.

"Just what I said. Whatever you want. Residential at Valley of the Sun School, The Latch Day Program, or anything else she may need. Oh, and relinquishment of custody is no longer an issue."

"Why the sudden change of heart?" I asked suspiciously.

"I have no idea. I was just told to contact you today without fail and to give you that message. I've been trying to reach you since early this morning. I called you at home, at LaMancha, where I left messages, and then I finally reached you here at the hospital."

Well I'll be damned! I thought. Boyd couldn't have received the material yet, much less acted on it, so what gives? I wanted to talk to Boyd right away, but it was late afternoon on a Friday and I knew that because of the time difference his office would probably be closed. So I contacted him the following week. When I got him on the phone, I said, "You couldn't have received my material yet, or did you?"

"It may have come in, but I haven't looked at it yet. Why do you ask?"

"Well, because I already got a call telling me that without giving up Michele to the State I could have residential, the day program, or whatever else I needed for her."

"And, when did that call come in?"

"Friday afternoon. Can you shed any light on the sudden turnaround?"

"All I can tell you, Mrs. Morton, is that you must have some case. On Thursday a member of my staff had to call Arizona on another issue and just before he hung up all he said was, 'Oh, by the way, unofficially, I'm letting you know that Kathleen Morton has been in touch with Gerald Boyd about her daughter, Michele.'"

"Incredible!" I responded. "The very next morning, they were ready to do whatever was needed for Michele. My battle has miraculously ended, thanks to you, Mr. Boyd! I can't thank you enough."

"You're welcome, Mrs. Morton," he said. "You evidently put together a very effective case. I'm so glad everything turned around this quickly for you and Michele."

A couple of days later I got a call from the Center for Law asking me to come down and sign a Settlement Agreement with the State Bureaucracies involved with this dispute. I objected because I thought the request was out of line since this was an issue of entitlement involving an appropriate educational program for a child. They, however, insisted the agreement had to be written and signed by all parties. I reluctantly agreed. But as I was driving down there I began to wonder who was behind this and what they now had up their sleeves.

I arrived for the meeting, introductions were made around the room, and I was handed the Agreement to read. The first page was innocuous enough, stating that all parties agreed that a residential facility was an appropriate placement for Michele and that the Glendale School District and DES would share the expense. Then I turned the page and it became very clear as to why they had insisted on this Settlement Agreement. This is what the last paragraph stipulated:

> "Kathleen Morton on behalf of herself, her husband, and Michele Morton, waives and releases Glendale Union High School District, its officers and employees, and the Department of Economic Security from any and all claims they may have against Glendale Union High School District and the Department of Economic Security as a result of this dispute and specifically for the cost of Michele's placement at the Good Samaritan Health Center in Phoenix and for any attorneys' fees."

From the beginning, I'd known my case was strong, but that paragraph said it all. Even the lawyer from the Center for Law, who was *representing* me, insisted that I sign this document. Now, whose side do you think she was on? Certainly not mine. And that's what I kept running up against everywhere I turned. The demand for my signature on this document only reinforced my belief that Arizona wanted to show Washington, if they were ever officially contacted, that there was nothing to the complaint, because the child had already been given appropriate educational services and here was the Agreement to prove it. No problem, no case, no need to pursue.

Another interesting tidbit is that during my struggle with the State I contacted the Arizona Attorney General's Office, thinking that they might be concerned about DES trying to force me to give up my child for educational purposes. But they were no help at all. Actually, they argued me right off the phone. And now I knew why. I read the signatures on the Agreement. Guess who the legal representative was for DES? Why, no other than the Office of the Attorney General for Arizona!

Isn't this a joke? It was hard to keep a straight face. The sleeping bed was getting more crowded every day.

All I'd ever wanted was for Michele's needs to be met educationally, just like they had been before she became handicapped. It would never have ever occurred to me to take any legal action beyond that. I could have saved them a lot of time and money had they only asked.

It was amazing how many people in Arizona whom I had initially approached for assistance now wanted to jump on the bandwagon and take credit for such a successful outcome. One of them actually put it in writing to me. That's the one who had no shame.

Michele was discharged from the hospital and a week later started attending Valley of the Sun School. The first person I met was Terry Aleman, the supervisor of the area Michele would be in. She was a sweetheart – great with Michele and very sensitive to my feelings.

Touching my arm, she said smiling, "Michele will be fine. Don't worry, Mrs. Morton."

"Having someone like you here makes me feel very good," I told her. "Do you have a copy of Michele's Program Plan that we all put together last week?"

"Yes, it's right here. I understand she has a great appetite."

"She sure does," I said. "Nobody knows how she stays so thin. They used to joke about it in New York, telling her the school would have to close down if she continued to eat the way she did. She would smile coyly at them and then ask for more."

Terry smiled and said, "I think that's great, Mrs. Morton. It's so much easier to deal with than those who don't want to eat at all."

After a few hours I left. Michele had settled in nicely and was in good spirits. I had already talked to Medical. They had a list of her medications and knew when to give them to her.

I enjoyed the company of Paula and Michael that evening over dinner. "So, how do you feel?" Michael asked.

"I felt a little sad when I first got home," I said, "but I feel much better now. I called to check on Michele and she's as happy as can be."

"That's great, Mom. You hung in there against all odds and made it happen. Of course, no surprise to us," he said smiling. "Didn't I tell you before you started that I felt sorry for the State?"

"That you did, Michael," I said. "But, remember, both of you were always there when I needed a pick up. Like, just what's happening right now. You knew it was going to be a tough day for me and here I am."

"Yeah, we knew," Paula interjected, "and we're glad you're here relaxing with us."

"Did you talk to Dad, yet?" Michael asked.

"Are you kidding? He gets a daily blow-by-blow of everything that happens. He was the first one I called after talking to Boyd. It was a very happy moment."

"How is he doing?"

"Fine. But, being back there alone is not easy. He never complains, but once everything is settled I'm going to look for work and then we'll get him out here."

"So, are you going to get a job with DES?" Michael asked,

trying to keep a straight face.

"Oh sure, without a doubt," I said. "I can't wait, and I'm sure they can't either!" We had a good laugh over that as we continued to enjoy a relaxing evening together.

The next morning I went to Latch School, the day program Michele was attending. I had already met Sandy Landy, the director, when we all got together for the IEP conference to set up a program for Michele. I was impressed with her enthusiasm and vigor as well as her pride in the educational program offered by the school. Sandy was not only the director but also the founder of the school. She had a reputation for running a tight ship. Her constant focus was on the kids and she kept thinking of new ways to challenge them.

That was the main reason I had chosen Latch for Michele, and I was never disappointed. Everyone at Latch – teachers, therapists, aides, and nurses, all supported and welcomed parental involvement. Over the years many people, myself included at times, disagreed with Sandy's dogmatic approach on issues. But no one could ever fault her on the level of performance her school achieved for handicapped students who attended the diversified classes available. They were second to none.

With everything going so well, I concentrated on getting a job. I worked as a substitute teacher for a while, and I did some temporary work in a couple of legal firms and a hospital. Then I was offered a permanent job with the hospital as a supervisor for one of its support services departments.

Michael and I flew back to New York to help Arnie sell much of the furniture and pack what was left into a U-Haul trailer. All went well until I found out they were going to leave behind two of my favorite lamps. "You can't take everything," Arnie said with a show of exasperation.

"I'm not taking everything. Look what has been thrown away already. But I love those lamps and I want them with me."

"There's no more room in the trailer," he protested.

"Move things around and find room," I suggested. "Where there's a will, there's a way, Arnie."

He looked at me, shaking his head, then picked up the lamps and walked out the door.

The cross-country move created some unexpected setbacks. I flew back with Casey, Michele's dog, and a few hours after my arrival the phone rang. It was Arnie. "Hi, Honey," I said, surprised to hear his voice. "Is everything all right?"

"No," he responded. "We've had an accident. I was driving and the trailer jackknifed and pulled me in front of oncoming traffic."

My heart leapt. "Oh no, are you hurt?" I asked anxiously.

"No, no, I'm fine."

"What about Michael?"

"He's okay, too. We both got out of it without a scratch. That's because all the traffic came screeching to a halt just before contact. We were very lucky. However, some things were destroyed, including your favorite lamps."

"Oh, Arnie, who cares? The only thing that matters is that you and Michael are okay."

Then came the Casey crisis. He became extremely aggressive and started to attack us. We tried everything, but nothing seemed to help. Eventually he had to be put to sleep. That was a very sad day for the whole family.

Michele was now walking with a walker and a wheelchair would soon follow. When I picked her up to take her home for the weekend, I took her to her favorite restaurant, Howard Johnson's, where she loved their fish fry. After she finished eating I brought up the subject. "Do you think it's getting harder for you to walk around now, Michele?" I asked her in a soothing, sympathetic tone.

Making a face, she nodded a trifle reluctantly.

"Maybe we should look for a wheelchair. What do you think?"

"Okay," she replied with downcast eyes.

"Okay, we'll pick one out this weekend. What color would you like?" I asked as cheerfully as I could.

"Red!" she said emphatically.

I couldn't help but laugh. "I don't think I've ever seen a red wheelchair before, but if that's what you want, we'll get one." I told her leaning over and giving her a hug.

It took some doing, but we finally found a place that could make a wheelchair in red. Michele was pleased. She beamed every time someone made a fuss over her new red wheelchair. I think it made her feel that she still had some control.

The Latch program continued to function on the same level of excellence and Michele was doing great there. However, as time passed I realized we were not going to be so fortunate with Valley of the Sun School. Although things went well for a while, it eventually became evident that there were many quality issues, which concerned both myself and some of the staff. Eventually, I suggested that a quality council be formed at the school to identify problem areas and make positive suggestions for improvement. The Board of Directors reviewed the proposal, gave its seal of approval, and I became the chairperson of the committee.

We initially identified the level of each problem area, and then focused on particular major issues. Minutes of the meetings were taken and sent to the Director of the school, who was to submit them to the board. After that, the Board was to take necessary action to correct the deficiencies reported.

After some time, when no effort was made to correct the problems identified by the committee, we figured that the board might not be receiving the minutes. I obtained the list of the Board of Directors and at our next meeting we decided to send the information directly to the members. I was quite surprised to see how large the list was. While I was imagining ten to fifteen names, there was actually a total of fifty-nine! We had our work cut out for us. After we'd copied, collated and stapled together all minutes taken at our meetings, and included a short note explaining why we were doing this, we sat down and addressed the envelopes. They were stamped and mailed that same evening.

A few days later the dam burst and we finally had action. The phones rang off the hook at the school. *At last we had their attention!*

The first action that Al Sanders, the Board President, took was to let me know that my services were no longer required as Chair. Surprise, Surprise! Apparently, keeping the entire board informed of developments was not a very popular decision, even though it was they who endorsed the quality council, *or so we'd been told.* In retrospect, we realized that we had talked only to the board president and school director. What happened next surprised even me. Sanders himself replaced me as Chair. Now it was anybody's guess as to how many staff would open up to the President of the Board of Directors!

In the meantime, I had been working with Al Soenneker, a DES official in the Developmental Disabilities Division (DDD), to find another facility for Michele that operated more on the level of the New York Institute and the Latch day program. When I picked up the phone one day, it was Soenneker.

"I'm calling regarding Michele's transfer to another facility," he said. "I believe I may have found the right one for you. It's Bethphage Community Services. This organization has been around for a long time in other states and has a very good reputation but it's new to the Phoenix area. What do you think?"

"It sounds great, Al. I'm glad to hear it's from out-of-state. That's got to be a plus the way this state functions."

Laughing, he said, "You may be right. We do have many problems to address."

"That's putting it mildly, Al. You haven't been here long enough yet to be influenced by the system you work for. I hope it never happens. We need people like you to bring about some effective changes. So tell me, what's my next move with Bethphage?"

"They're expecting to hear from you, so just give them a call." Giving me the number he added, "Ask to speak with Joleen Glassel. She's the director in Arizona. By the way," he said chuckling, "they love parents, especially involved ones, so you should fit right in."

"Well, am I glad to hear that! I'll call them right away before they change their minds!" When I got Bethphage on the phone, I made an appointment to meet with the director the following week.

In the meantime, Michele was attending a summer program at Gompers. Because I liked what they had to offer, I signed her up for it. When she was picked up that first morning she was fine, but by the time she was dropped off at Valley in the afternoon she was very upset and combative. Michele's speech was now very limited and it was difficult for her to articulate what the problem was, so I decided to follow the van the next morning and stay with her during the day. I was impressed with the program and the interaction with staff was very positive. Michele was obviously enjoying herself. So, what could the problem possibly be? It was very perplexing.

Lunchtime arrived and lunch boxes were passed out to each child. I decided to have a quick sandwich at a nearby coffee shop.

When I got outside, I could hardly breathe. The heat was unbearable. I recalled that the temperature was supposed to hit as high as 115 degrees. I gingerly opened the door of my car, and quickly turned on the ignition, then the air conditioning full blast. 'Thank God for air conditioning,' I thought. Turning on the radio, I heard that the temperature had already soared to 117 degrees. That made me feel worse. What a day! I thought of the vans sitting in the parking lot waiting to transport the children after class. Right now, they had to be like furnaces inside.

After I'd eaten, I drove back into the parking lot. I could hear Michele screaming. Running towards her, I asked a staff member, "What's wrong?"

"I don't know," she replied. "She's like this every day when it's time to leave."

Then I saw that the vans were still closed up tight. "You can't put the kids in those vans until you've run the air conditioning for a while," I said. "Why, it must be 150 degrees in there!"

She looked at me a trifle sheepishly. "Mrs. Morton, there's no air conditioning in those vans."

"No air conditioning!" I exploded. "It's 117 degrees out here. No wonder Michele's screaming. I stayed with her all day today in an effort to isolate the problem, and it looks like I have. My God, something needs to be done about this!"

Arriving upon the scene, the director, Bob Thomas, attempted to placate me. "Mrs. Morton, eventually, we may be able to get air conditioning for the vans – perhaps by next year."

"*Next year!*" I retorted. "You can't be serious! Yesterday was too late. How can you justify putting kids into those stifling vans in this heat?" I was beside myself.

By the time I got Michele settled at Valley she had calmed down and was sitting serenely in her wheelchair. Taking her hands in mine I said, "I'm sorry, Honey. I had no idea what you were complaining about. I never dreamed the vans had no air conditioning. I promise you, right now, that you'll never travel in a vehicle without air conditioning again."

She smiled and squeezed my hands saying with some effort, "Thanks, Mom." Then she squeezed my hands again, nodding her head contentedly.

When I got home, I called DES. They were the ones who sponsored the summer programs. I asked to speak with Liz Francotti, the person in charge of the Family Division. After I told her what had happened, Liz responded by saying. "I'll see what I can do, Mrs. Morton." At least she had the good sense not to feign shock, because I'm sure she was already aware that vans without air conditioning were being used.

"What I would like you to do, Liz, is take a thermometer over there this afternoon and just see how high the temperature registers in the rear of those vans. Then call me back."

"Okay, Mrs. Morton. I can do that," she replied, showing her willingness to cooperate.

A couple of hours later, she called me back.

"Well?" I asked inquiringly.

"The temperature registered at 140 degrees, which I agree is intolerable."

"One hundred and forty degrees," I said, slowly enunciating each word for emphasis. "That's not intolerable, Liz. That's criminal! Michele will never ride again in a van without air conditioning. Never!"

"I've already taken care of that for you, Mrs. Morton. Starting tomorrow, Michele will be taken in an air conditioned car to and from the school."

"Oh, she will, will she? How nice. What about the other kids?"

"Well, right now, we're concentrating on Michele, because we know she has a fragile medical condition."

"Liz," I almost shouted, "the most robust person alive couldn't withstand 140 degree temperature! Most of these children have some kind of medical condition. Even if they didn't, there's still no excuse for transporting them with no air conditioning in this suffocating heat.

"Either air conditioned vans need to be leased during the summer months or air conditioning needs to be installed in the present vans. There'll be no need to pick Michele up tomorrow. I appreciate your concern, but she won't be returning to school until all the children are riding in air conditioned vans."

The next morning the phone rang. It was Liz. "Mrs. Morton," she said. "I have tried all over Arizona to find air conditioned vans and I just can't find any."

"You really want me to believe that?"

"It's the truth, Mrs. Morton," she protested. "But I have good news. We opened up the vans for a couple of hours and got the temperature down to 125 degrees."

"Mmmmmm, 125 degrees," I mused. "With that kind of success, the kids will need jackets." She was not amused.

"Mrs. Morton!" she said in anger and frustration. "I'm trying my best."

"I know you are, Liz. I don't doubt that one iota. But, your best is not good enough. Would you like to sit in one of those vans with temperatures of 125 degrees? Tell me, would you? Neither you, nor I, would last five minutes, and you know it."

"Well, as I said before, I can't find any air conditioned vans to lease anywhere in Arizona. So, what can I do?" she lamented.

I thought for a minute, and then replied. "Why don't you call the Humane Society? I know they pick up their cats and dogs in air conditioned vans."

There was dead silence and then a click. I guess I finally got my point across.

I went to the store and when I returned there was a message on my recorder. It was from Liz. "Mrs. Morton," she said. "We've loosened up some emergency funds and air conditioned units will be installed in all the vans at the school on Saturday."

"Yes!" I said aloud, punching the air with my fist. That meant that on Monday morning, Michele and all the other children would ride in comfort and continue so throughout the rest of the summer. 'What a wonderful outcome,' I exulted. 'So Liz came through after all. Good for her! It wasn't easy, I am sure.'

But now knowing that other children in other summer programs were probably going through the same thing, I raised the issue with the Governor's Council. After much discussion and persuasion, the Human Rights Committee for the Governor's Council said they would place the issue on their agenda and investigate. The Chairman of the Committee was a medical doctor. 'That was good news,' I thought, and left feeling quite satisfied. I asked that the minutes of the meetings be sent to me each month so that I could follow the progress of the investigation.

For the next several months, the minutes revealed that the Human Rights Committee was making reports to the full board of the Council regarding the air conditioning issue. Then, all of a sudden, no mention was made of the issue anywhere in the minutes. That bothered me. When I was down at the Legislature one day, I purposely ran into the Chair of the Human Rights Committee.

"Hi, Doctor" I said. "Remember me?"

"Ah, Mrs. Morton, yes," he replied as he strode over to greet me, hand extended.

"I have a question for you. Whatever happened to the air conditioning issue the Human Rights Committee was investigating? It just seemed to disappear from sight."

"Oh, Mrs. Morton," he said looking sorrowful. "You were right, of course, it was an important issue, but we had to drop it, because it was just too expensive."

"Too expensive!" I retorted. "Then it's okay to fry handicapped kids in 140 degree temperatures while you sit in air-conditioned offices convincing yourselves it's a non-issue."

"Mrs. Morton!" he said sharply. "I resent what you're saying."

"I don't doubt it." I said. "But that doesn't change anything." Looking at him, I realized he was just as frustrated as I was. I was sure his committee had tried hard to right this wrong but, as usual, it was like pounding one's head against a stone wall.

Walking away, I realized, the world wasn't going to change overnight. Maybe I could make a difference in some aspect of this when a problem came to light, but the big picture involving all developmentally disabled youngsters needed an organization behind them.

I made an appointment with one of the representatives of the Association for Retarded Citizens (ARC). Appalled that the vehicles were not air conditioned and agreeing there should be a law against it, they promised to pursue it legislatively. They had a good reputation, and their programs for this population were very effective. Impressed with the dedicated staff members I came to know there, I realized that only time would tell how successful they would be with this issue.

There is one thing I must say about New York State. They

did their job well in terms of overseeing the city. When I fought the transportation issue, the city threw unbelievable obstacles in my path and jacked me around big time. But when I reached the State level, those parties investigated and agreed that the city was wrong, and then forced compliance. The State then became my ally and we worked together to get the job done.

That's not how it is in Arizona. On every level: City, County, State, right up to the Governor, they hang together and agree with each other, making the various levels of power totally ineffective. It didn't matter to Governor Babbit that the State was trying to force me to relinquish custody of my daughter for services. Although he refused to see me, he knew what the issue was. And yet he wouldn't go against the decision already made by Doctor Patino. Contacting Washington was my salvation but it should never have been necessary.

Of course, the legislature is also to blame for many of the problems facing Arizona. They don't appropriate the necessary funds to carry out the various programs, leaving agencies like DES in the lurch. Then they pat themselves on the back because they balance the state budget every year. My question is: Who couldn't balance their budgets if they didn't have to live up to their responsibilities? Enough said.

When I had Michele home a couple of days later, she became ill and totally unresponsive. I called Doctor Kaplan.

"You'd better get her down to ER and I'll meet you there," he said. "Also, you'll probably need an internal medicine specialist as well now. If you don't have one, I'd recommend Bruce Bethancourt. He was a resident when Michele was in Rehab."

"Yes, I remember him."

"Well, he's practicing now and I'm really impressed with his ability."

"Okay, great. Can you contact him for me?"

"Sure. I'll call him."

The ambulance came and took us both to the Emergency Room. When we arrived, they took Michele right away. She remained unresponsive, her breathing shallow and her pulse weak. Al Kaplan was there to meet us, and after examining Michele he came out to talk to me looking very serious.

"Kathleen," he said choosing his words carefully, "a preliminary examination seems to indicate that Michele is gravely ill, probably the last stages of the disease."

"But, why?" I protested. "This disease usually doesn't work that fast. She was fine today. She ate well, listened to her music and was full of life, until she suddenly seemed to drift away. It just doesn't make sense."

"Nothing about this disease makes sense. You know that. I just want to prepare you. She may not make it."

"I can't believe that, Al! I just can't! Somehow, I thought I would know. And I just don't have that feeling."

He put his hand on my shoulder and said kindly, "I hope you're right, but I just wanted you to be prepared for the possibility. She will be admitted, of course. They're getting ready to take her up to her room right now. Bruce Bethancourt said he'll be Michele's doctor and will admit her by phone. He'll see you later. Okay?"

I nodded my head. "Okay, I'm glad you got in touch with him. Thanks so much for everything. I know you mean well, Al, but, I just don't think- - - - - -" I let my voice trail off, as I started walking alongside the gurney taking Michele to her room.

Doctor Bethancourt arrived, examined Michele and asked, "Have you ever seen her like this before?"

"No, never."

"Tell me what happened."

"She was sitting in the recliner enjoying her music. I thought she was nodding off so I approached her, asking if she wanted to lie down and sleep for awhile. There was no response. It didn't even look like she was breathing, and her pulse was very weak. Then I called Doctor Kaplan. What do you think?"

He shook his head. "It's hard to say. But it doesn't look good."

"That's what Al Kaplan said."

"I remember you and Michele. But I thought I saw you around the medical center more recently, or was I mistaken?"

"No, you're right. I'm working for the system now."

"That's good. Are you going to stay with Michele tonight?"

"Yes. At least until she pulls out of it."

He looked at me and smiled, "I'll be here about 6:30 tomorrow morning. See you then."

I felt good about having Bethancourt as Michele's doctor. Instinctively I knew she was in good hands.

I sat there wondering how Arnie was making out. I couldn't reach him to let him know about Michele because he was out pounding the pavement looking for a job. However, I did call Michael at work, and I left a note for Arnie when he got home. He joined me at the hospital later and we went to the cafeteria to eat. A few hours after, while up in Michele's room talking about the frustrations he experienced looking for work that day, we suddenly heard Michele stir.

Jumping up to check, we saw her eyes were open and she was smiling.

"Hi!" she said attempting to sit up.

"Wait a minute, Honey," I said. "Don't move just yet. You're in the hospital and I'd like the nurse to check you out first."

"Why?"

"Because you got very sick, so just relax a minute." Arnie had already alerted the nurse, and she was following him into the room.

After checking her out, she said, "This is incredible! Her respiration is fine, her pulse is strong, and obviously she's very alert."

As Michele remained stable the next several hours I decided to go home with Arnie to get some sleep.

I returned the next morning at six. The nurses told me that Michele had had a great night. She was awake and happy. When Doctor Bethancourt arrived, he said, "I can't believe it! Obviously this young lady has her own agenda, despite what I believe. Her recovery is remarkable."

Michele was discharged that afternoon and went back to school the next day without a hint of a problem. Kaplan was amazed when he learned of this. "There just doesn't seem to be any acceptable explanation for what took place," he said. "It's baffling."

Meanwhile, Arnie, got a temporary job at Ticor Title in the Microfische Department, work he'd never done before. After a few weeks on the job, they offered him a full-time position. We went out and celebrated.

That evening the phone rang. The woman on the other end introduced herself as Judy Grant. "I understand you have a child with Batten Disease," she said.

"What's Batten Disease?" I asked.

"Oh, I'm sorry. It's the same as Neuronal Ceroid Lipofuscinosis."

"It is?"

"Yes. It was actually Doctor Batten, an English physician

who identified NCL over 100 years ago."

"Are you kidding? No one seems to have ever heard of it before, including some neurologists."

"Yes, I know. That's what we want to try and change. I'm establishing an organization, the Batten Disease Support and Research Association, BDSRA. We got your name from Doctor Wolfe in Canada. He said you're a very interesting and involved parent."

"That was nice of him. Tell me, Judy, do you also have a child with NCL?"

She hesitated a moment and then said, "Yes, I do, Kathleen."

Excitement stirred within me. "I can't believe it! This is the first time I've talked to a parent who has a child with this disease."

"I know how you feel, Kathleen. But, there's something else I need to tell you. Actually, I have three children with NCL."

"*THREE!*" I said shocked. "My God, Judy, how do you manage?"

"Somehow, it happens," she replied without complaint. "Barbara and Edward are now in a state institution because they require round-the-clock nursing care. Jeffrey is home with us and still functions on a high level. We have a fourth child, Joy Lynn, who's the only one who's escaped this disease."

"That's absolutely incredible," I said. "I just can't imagine how that would be."

"Are you aware that there are four main types of NCL?" Judy asked.

"Yes, I am. Infantile, Late Infantile, Juvenile, and Adult form."

"What does Michele have?"

"Michele has the Juvenile form. What about your children?"

"All three also have the Juvenile form. The Infantile and

Late Infantile children's life expectancy is much shorter than the affected Juvenile children. But, as you know, all are ultimately fatal."

"Yes, I know that. And it angers me to think that this disease was identified over a 100 years ago. My God! And nothing has ever been done. That's appalling."

"You're right. That's why we need to get this organization going in order to get the word out."

We talked, it seemed, for hours. I had many questions and Judy had a lot of answers. In that short period of time, a strong bond developed between us.

"What I also wanted to ask," Judy said, "is if you'd be interested in joining our organization, and being one of its first board members?"

"Absolutely! I'll be glad to help in any way I can."

"That's great, Kathleen. I'll send you a packet about the organization and information about our first annual meeting."

"Thanks, Judy. I'll be looking for it."

Hanging up, I still couldn't believe I finally talked to another parent after all these years. And that was just the beginning. In the years that followed, I met some wonderful parents nationwide at the various annual conferences that were held throughout the country. The programs were great and the guest speakers were caring and informative.

As a board member I became involved in the planning. Every couple of months we held a nationwide teleconference. Judy ultimately withdrew as president of the board of directors, replaced by Lance Johnson. As the years passed, the organization became stronger under his leadership, and through the efforts of the board the National Institute of Health became aware of our existence. As a result, we started receiving funds for research. Of course, millions of dollars are needed to research such a dreadful disease, and although it was identified over 100 years ago, it was the best kept secret on the planet!

This kind of deteriorating, devastating disease carries a multi-million dollar price tag, simply by addressing a child's medical needs (which, in some cases, can continue through young adulthood). Wouldn't it be better in the long run to provide up front the necessary funding for research in order to find a cure? NCL can destroy families along with affected individuals because the emotional strain is tremendous – not only for the parents, but also for the siblings.

The fact that the children are normal to begin with adds another touch of sadness. After Michele attained the age of eight, it was as if we had stepped on an out-of-control treadmill. And we had no idea how to get off.

That's why the Batten Disease Support and Research Association is so *important* to the cause of trying to find a cure. Hopefully, with the help of the United States Government, and fund raising activities, that cure will one day become a reality.

Chapter XVI

During this time, we had worked out a smooth transition for Michele to Bethphage Community Services. When we met with Joleen Glassel some time before, we were impressed with what Bethphage had to offer. I had a million questions, all about level of care, and Glassel's answers were honest and forthright. Joleen was both a pleasant young lady and very knowledgeable about the programs.

"We have several residences in the Phoenix area," Joleen said. "The one we are thinking about for Michele is called the Cactus Home. It's community based, and is in a very nice neighborhood."

"We would like to see it," I said.

"Oh, absolutely," Joleen replied. "I can take you there now if you have the time."

I looked at Arnie and asked, "What do you think?"

"I think that's a great idea. There's no time like the present," he responded smiling.

The Cactus residence was very appealing, exuding an inviting warmth. There would be no more than five children including Michele residing there. We were pleased to see that because it would allow for a lot more individual attention. In addition, if they didn't want to be in the common areas each resident was afforded a lot of privacy. Michele had her own bedroom where we could hook up her stereo so she could listen to her favorite recordings –

especially – *The Wizard of Oz*!

The entire residence was tastefully decorated and spacious. Out back was a swimming pool and large patio. Most of the staff, initially, was from their home base in Colorado. This turned out to be a plus, because all were well-trained in dealing with parental concerns and included us in every decision.

When Michele arrived everyone seemed to be available to greet us. Even Dave Mock, the Chief Operating Officer from Colorado, was there. All treated Michele like a little queen. She loved every minute of it.

Dave Mock shook our hands and said, "I'm really pleased to welcome you to Bethphage Community Services." He was so personable that both Arnie and I felt immediately at ease.

"We like what you have to offer," Arnie said, "and I think Michele will be very happy here. That will make Kathleen extremely happy because she works very hard making sure Michele's needs are met."

"Yes, I know, and that's the way it should be. We welcome involved parents."

"I'm glad to hear that," I said smiling. "Your staff has a great attitude, and I'm looking forward to working closely with them."

"I'm sure you won't be disappointed, Mrs. Morton. If any problem arises, you can call the manager of the residence, the director, or me at this number in Colorado." He handed me his card. "And, always remember, our goal is your goal, and that is to meet Michele's needs so that she will be content and happy."

"She's already having a ball," I responded. "They're playing some kind of game in there with her. Listen to her laughing. That does my heart good."

Later over dinner, I asked Arnie, "Don't you feel good

about the kind of programs they have?"

"Yes, and it's a great feeling."

"Now, coupled with Latch, Michele should have the best all-around educational program that meets her needs. You know, Arnie, attitude is everything. Latch has a great attitude and so does Bethphage. That's because they have nothing to hide. Everything is up and above-board. It's so refreshing."

"Definitely. I'm glad Bethphage came along when it did."

"Yes. And that is thanks to Al Soenneker. He's a great guy. We owe him one. I never thought I'd say that about anyone who worked for DES!" I added with a chuckle.

Bethphage never did disappoint us. The programs and care Michele received were exemplary. Her health was stable for a long time and I spent many enjoyable days there – especially during the pool parties. Michele loved the water and when I jumped in with her, she was ecstatic. The ensuing barbecues were also thoroughly enjoyed by all involved.

The next medical crisis that hit us was unexpected and involved me. During a routine mammography suggested by Doctor Bethancourt, now our family physician, they found something that looked suspicious. A biopsy confirmed that I had breast cancer. The surgeon said that while it was small, a mastectomy was in order. I told him I would think about it, and get back to him.

I wanted to check with Bethancourt first to see what he thought. His response was immediate. "Kathleen, I wouldn't delay at all getting it done. It's good news, actually, having it that small. If it was any member of my family, I wouldn't hesitate a second." "Okay," I said with resignation. "Then, that's what I'll do. I'll call the surgeon now and get the procedure scheduled."

"Good, and I'll see you after it's over."

The morning of the surgery I got up early and was ready a

good half-hour before we needed to leave. Arnie and I were both quiet walking around the house like robots. I finally said to him, "I think I'll take a walk around the block before we leave."

Moving slowly toward me, Arnie asked, "Would you like me to go with you?"

I thought for a minute and then said softly, "No, Honey, I think I just want to be alone."

He respected my wishes and didn't insist, which I appreciated.

I walked for some time, deep in thought, recalling when Michele initially got sick. There seemed to be no let-up. First, there were the temporal lobe seizures that took forever to diagnose, followed by blindness, the crazy behaviors, and then the grand mal convulsions. I remembered discussing it all with a friend of mine who was a priest. I was certainly showing my frustration. He replied. "God must love you very much, Kathleen."

"Why do you say that, Father?"

"Because He pays a lot of attention to you."

I was silent for a moment as I thought about this. Finally I said, "Do you think you could ask Him to ease up a little, Father? I really need a break." We both laughed at my feeble attempt to influence God and my frustrations dissipated.

Breaking through the memory, I suddenly thought of Michele's enormous problems and her ability to endure with silent courage. I realized that the big "C" was just a blip on a screen by comparison. That was when I knew I could more readily accept what was about to happen.

Comforted, I recalled how tightly Michele had hugged me when I told her I had to go to the hospital for minor surgery. I had gently pushed her away from me and said, "Why the sad face? I'm going to be all right, really I am, Honey. But, I do need a smile to send me off in a happy frame of mind." Her response was immediate as she laughed and put her arms around me one more time.

Retracing my steps I returned home. Arnie came over and hugged me. "Are you ready to go?" he asked, looking at me with his hands on my shoulders.

"As ready as I'll ever be," I told him.

When we arrived at the hospital, we were greeted by my good friend, Heather, ready to offer her support. I knew she would be good company and a stabilizing factor for Arnie while he waited for the operation to be over.

The surgery went well and I felt surprisingly good. After a few days of hospital recuperation, the door to my room suddenly opened and much to my delight I saw Michele being wheeled in by one of the Bethphage staff members. What a surprise! Since she couldn't see, she didn't know who was there until I spoke.

"My God, you found me, Michele," I said with a laugh, "and here I was trying to hide! How did you do it?"

She both beamed with pleasure and started laughing when she heard my voice. By now I was out of bed and kneeling down beside her wheelchair. She hugged me and kissed me, not wanting to let go.

I looked up at the staff member and said, "Thank you very much. You guys are always so thoughtful."

"Well, this was Michele's day to do whatever she wanted and I thought coming to see you would be number one on her list, so here we are."

At Bethphage the youngsters were given one day a week to do whatever they wanted. A staff member would then devote that entire day to the child. So, this was Michele's day. She was thrilled and we had a great afternoon together.

I was in the hospital for six days. That was before HMO's, and the 'drive-by' mastectomies espoused today, which I find totally insane. Before I was discharged all the tubes were removed. Even then, it was difficult enough to have to deal with the aftermath of some drainage while the healing took place. However, because the cancer was caught in its early stages and the lymph nodes that were removed showed no signs of it, I didn't require any chemotherapy or radiation treatments. That was very welcome news. As a result, my recovery went well and I couldn't wait to get back on the tennis courts again.

After all of the difficulties parents were experiencing in the handicapped community with respect to appropriate programs and level of care, I decided to volunteer my services dealing with issues involving the developmentally disabled. I joined the HRC (Human Rights Committee), set up to oversee this population and to deal with problems involving delivery of appropriate services by schools or agencies. I also joined The ARC. This involved going into the community to monitor residential programs. In addition, I became a Special Education Advocate for parents seeking appropriate programming for their children.

Many parents did not know their rights under the Federal Education Law and when disputes arose with the Local and State Education Agencies, I took their case until the resolution favored the child. As a result, I was offered and accepted speaking engagements on this subject. At Al Soenneker's request I also conducted Human Rights Training for new DDD/DES employees who would eventually be working throughout the State in residential programs.

During my involvement with all these programs I met a lot of DES employees who really impressed me. Also, DES had some very good programs, it's just that there was always so much red tape to wade through, making the application of the programs very difficult. Still, some employees stood out in the crowd and made a difference. Al Soenneker was one. Of course, he came from a position of power with the agency because of his responsibilities, but he handled that power well.

Then I heard that Douglas Patino was leaving. He had accepted another job in California and I received an invitation to a farewell get-together in his honor. I was unable to attend due to a prior commitment, so I called him. "Hello, Mrs. Morton," he said amiably when he picked up the phone. "How are you?"

"Couldn't be better," I replied. "I wasn't sure if you would remember me."

"Without a doubt, I'll always remember you," he responded, chuckling.

Laughing in response I said, "I heard you were leaving and I just called to wish you well in your new job"

"I appreciate that," he replied. We exchanged a few more pleasantries and then he said, "You know, Mrs. Morton, it was a good thing you didn't take the job offer I made the first day we met."

"Why?" I asked, waiting for some facetious remark, but he surprised me.

"Because you accomplished more positive changes on the outside than you ever could have working within the system."

"Well, that's certainly nice to hear."

"I have a lot of admiration for you and your ability to prevail under great odds. Many other people in DES feel the same way."

"Really?" I responded, pleased with his comments. "It's good to know my efforts have not been in vain. Thanks for telling me that. I've enjoyed talking with you, Doctor Patino, and I won't keep you any longer. I just called to wish you the very best." We said our goodbyes and as I cradled the receiver I thought back to the day when I'd walked out of that meeting, which now seemed like an eternity ago, and how angry I'd been with him! But over the years, working with others in DES, I discovered he was able to impact the system in a very positive way. I ended up having quite a healthy respect for Doctor Douglas Patino, and I meant every word when I wished him well.

In my advocacy role, I had some interesting cases. Some took a few weeks to resolve, while others required months. One in particular I remember well. One morning when the phone rang, a young lady asked me, "Is this Kathleen Morton?"

"Yes, it is."

"Well, my name is Antoinette Metzger and I have a son, Nicholaus, who is a multi-handicapped child and requires a special education program. I heard," she said hopefully, "that you help parents when educational problems arise."

"Yes, I do take cases," I responded. "What's going on with Nicholaus?" I could tell from her tone that this mom was very upset.

"Well, the problem is not with Nicholaus as much as it is with the school districts involved. He's tuitioned out from one district to another, and this has worked well for years, but suddenly the districts are fighting about how much the tuition waiver should be. The school he's currently attending called and told me not to bring him in tomorrow, which I find very upsetting."

"You have a right to be upset, Antoinette, because it sounds like they're violating your child's rights. Let me ask you a couple of questions. You said they told you not to bring him tomorrow. What does that mean? Do you drive him?"

"Yes. The district said they were having a problem with transportation."

"Okay, my next question is: Before the dispute arose, was Nicholaus attending the program they now plan to remove him from?"

"Yes, he's been attending that class since the first day of school."

"All right, now let me tell you what the law says:

"No. 1. The school district must provide transportation for your child.

"No. 2. As long as Nicholaus was in this program prior to the dispute, he must remain there until the dispute is settled. They cannot arbitrarily remove him, despite what they tell you. Under PL 94-142, it's called a stay-put order."

"They can't?" she said with surprise. "Are you sure?"

"Yes, I'm sure," I replied.

"But they sound like they know what they're doing."

"That's what they want you to believe. Do you like the program he's in?"

"Oh, yes, I do, and the teacher's great."

"Good. Then he can't be removed and that's where he'll stay. Trust me. However, it'll be interesting to see what method they'll use to attempt to keep him out. How do you feel about driving Nicholaus to class tomorrow?"

"Well, I have to admit it's a little hard since they told me to keep him home, but I'll take him if you think that's what I should do," she answered plaintively.

"Good, Antoinette. You see, the district personnel could always deny that they called to tell you not to bring him in, or they could claim that you misunderstood what was said. It's a lot harder to deny a physical confrontation set up to prevent him from entering. So it's better to take him over there and see if they'll try to pull a stunt like that. Call me and let me know what transpires, okay?"

"Okay," she responded. "Thanks very much."

The next morning, a tearful mom was back on the phone. "Alright,

Antoinette," I said soothingly. "Try to relax and tell me what happened."

"It was awful!" she exclaimed. "I got Nicholaus out of the car and placed him in his wheelchair. I started walking toward his classroom. Standing there was the principal and the assistant principal, both of whom blocked my entrance to the school. And a policeman was there to back them up! Would you believe that? They had no interest in what I had to say. They just told me that Nicholaus could no longer attend that school."

"I'm so sorry it happened that way, Antoinette," I said. "But now we have work to do. The first thing is to get Nicholaus back in class. That means we have to go to federal court, but since I'm not a lawyer, I can't do it."

"Oh no," she moaned. "Most lawyers don't know anything about the education law covering handicapped children."

"I agree, but they have ready access to all those laws and I'll be with you all the way. If more clarification is required after the legal presentations, the judge will take it under advisement."

"What does that mean?"

"It means he'll have his law clerks research the law, and when that happens, you'll win."

"You think so?" she responded somewhat dubiously. "I don't know, they took such a strong stand, and acted like they were well within their rights."

"I know, but that's for intimidation purposes only. Unfortunately, it often works."

"Okay, you've convinced me, I think," Antoinette said and then she started to laugh. "By the way, what do you charge for your services?"

"I don't charge anything, Antoinette. So don't worry about that. But I do have a job, so my volunteer work must be done during the late afternoon hours, evenings, and on weekends."

"Thank you so much," she said, obviously reassured about the things we had discussed.

Because of the show of force the district used to block Nicholaus from entering class that day, I could tell Antoinette was still a little skeptical, even though she said she was convinced. But when we got to court, and after the arguments from both sides were heard, the judge decided to take the case under advisement.

All it took was a couple of days for the judge to hand down his decision:

1. Nicholaus must be returned to his class immediately.

2. Bus transportation must be provided immediately.

3. Then the judge ordered the district to pay the parent's legal fees.

Let me tell you, I had one happy mom on my hands that day and I believe I made a friend for life.

Receiving recognition from Governor Symington's wife Ann and

from Sam Thurmond, State Director for my
involvement with the Developmental Disabled.

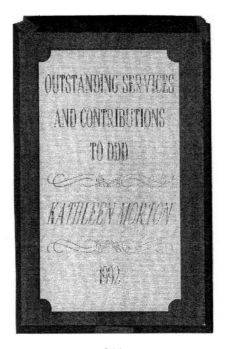

Chapter XVII

When a child's needs required residential, the main problem was the relinquishment issue. The fact that I'd won my fight with the state without giving up Michele didn't mean that the procedures they followed had changed so that other children and parents would benefit. On the contrary, it was business as usual.

Because of this, I filed a formal complaint with the United States Education Department, Office of Civil Rights, against every agency in Arizona that had anything to do with the education of the handicapped child. I felt all these agencies needed to be scrutinized. The Office of Civil Rights that would be handling my complaint was located in San Francisco. I was pleasantly surprised when I received a call from a Gale Frances, from the prosecutor's office.

"Hello, Mrs. Morton," she said affably. "We received your complaint and I've been assigned as an investigator on your case."

"How wonderful" I responded. "That was fast work. If possible, I'd like to receive copies of any letters sent out to the agencies involved."

"Sure. As far as I know, that will be fine. But I'll check to make sure and if you have to submit a request another way, I'll let you know. Also, I thought you would like to know that the Chief Regional Attorney, Paul Grossman, finds the case so interesting that he's assigning himself to it. He usually doesn't handle cases directly, but after some discussion it was felt that this case was going to be very politically sensitive because of how the state has handled the issues, and the number of agencies involved with possible violations."

"Great! You've made my day. It would be so reassuring to know that the 'relinquishment issue' was a thing of the past. Thank you so much for telling me that. I'm elated."

She laughed, "I thought you'd be pleased. If you find you have any further items of interest, address them to John Polomino, Director of the Elementary & Secondary Division of the Office of Civil Rights in San Francisco and mark them to my attention. Also, I'll let you know when we come to Arizona to investigate so we can meet with you personally."

When I hung up the phone, I thought 'Hurray for the good guys! Maybe we'll be able to see the light at the end of the tunnel after all.'

Shortly after this call I received a five page letter detailing my case from the Office of Civil Rights. They did a very impressive job in assembling all the facts relating to my complaint. They also gave each of the agencies they were going to investigate a docket number. Next, letters went out to those agencies informing them of what was about to happen. I was copied on all correspondence and was also told by Paul Grossman that I would be kept informed during the investigation. He also asked me to send him a copy of the Arizona Education Law and some other material.

Everything was progressing well. Unfortunately for the handicapped children and parents, it was short-lived. After some time passed and I had not heard from San Francisco, I called to see when the investigation would begin and when they would be meeting with me in Arizona. I got the classic run-around. I had thought that nothing about this issue could shock me anymore, but this did. I plied the Office of Civil Rights with questions, demanding to know the reason for the change in attitude, but I got no satisfactory responses. Then came the avoidance technique. They were never there when I called, and when I left messages, my calls were not returned.

What happened after that shocked me even more. I got a call from San Francisco one day. "Hello, Mrs. Morton," the voice said. "I'm making this call because you have worked passionately to right a wrong, and I believe you should know the reason why this case will not proceed as planned. However, I must warn you that if you reveal my identity, I will deny everything I'm telling you. Do you understand what I'm saying?"

"Yes, I understand quite well and I'm anxious to find out exactly what has happened. You don't have to worry about my revealing who you are to anyone."

"Very well. The Prosecutor's office of the Civil Rights Division has been told to back off your complaint. This order came from the highest office in the land."

"You mean from the Secretary of Education's office in Washington?"

"No, much higher than that. It came from the White House."

"The White House!" I exclaimed. "What would President Reagan have to do with an issue like this?"

"I don't know. But that's the level it came from. Do you know anyone in Arizona who is that close to the President?"

I thought for a moment, and replied, "No." Then it came to me. "Well, now that I think about it, I guess there is someone who could pick up the phone and get right through to the Oval Office."

"There is? Who?"

"Nancy Reagan's mother. She lives in Phoenix. Nancy's

father, Loyal Davis, was a retired neurosurgeon, but I think he died last year. The only information I have about her mother is that she resides here. "Why? Are you suggesting. . . .?"

"I'm not suggesting a thing," the voice interjected. "But because of your hard work I thought it only fair to give you an explanation."

"So, what you're implying is that the OCR's findings will ultimately produce no evidence of wrongdoing by any of the agencies involved and *that* astounding piece of information will be sent out to all of us."

"Something like that. I'm really sorry. But remember, we never had this conversation." Those were the last words I heard before the line went dead and that was the last time anyone ever talked to me from the Office of Civil Rights.

This was the ultimate disappointment. And, we can draw our own conclusion as to what actually happened. The question, however, will always remain: Did dirty politics get in the way of a much-needed investigation into appropriate services for handicapped children? If so, I will always wonder how those involved sleep at night.

It is interesting to note, however, that President Reagan seemed to smile down on Arizona. For instance, Sandra Day O'Connor from this State was appointed to the United States Supreme Court by him. She also was the first woman ever to serve on the highest court of the land.

In addition, the health program for indigents, AHCCCS (Arizona Health Care Cost & Containment System), which was an alternative to the Medicaid program, was approved under Reagan's reign. I believe Arizona was the *first* state in the union allowed to do that and receive federal Medicaid dollars.

Not too long after this travesty of justice by the Office of

Civil Rights, I received a letter from Thomasina Hardy from the United States Education Department. It stated that she was coming into Arizona for an "on-site visit with the State Education Agency." A meeting was to be held on March 5, which interested parents, advocates and professional groups could attend.

I called numerous parents and advocates knowledgeable about the relinquishment issue so that it could be thoroughly discussed at this meeting. I also contacted a well-known columnist for the Arizona Republic, Tom Fitzpatrick, to write an article about my fight with the state bureaucracy regarding Michele's education. After listening for a while in his office, he responded with genuine interest, "This would make a good mother/daughter story."

"That may be, Tom, but a mother/daughter story will not help the situation. We need my fight with the state to be reported and published on Monday morning, so that I can call Thomasina Hardy at her hotel to let her know that if she picks up the Arizona Republic she can get a good idea of what is happening with the education of the handicapped in this state. It's important, Tom, that the story be published Monday, so she will have a chance to read it before we meet with her later that day. Would that be possible?"

"Yes," he responded with a smile. "It would be possible. Just leave all your material with me and I'll get back to you when I'm finished."

This columnist was a terrific writer and I was confident he would do a super job. He did not disappoint me. He did throw me at first when he called on Saturday to tell me that the mother/daughter story would be published on Sunday.

I reacted immediately. "Tom! I told you that wouldn't help get the point across."

"Hold on a minute now, Kathleen. You didn't let me finish. I'm writing two articles. I couldn't do justice to this story unless I did the mother/daughter part first. That will be published Sunday. Your fight with the state will appear in the Monday morning edition."

"Oh, Tom. That's wonderful!" I said. "Thank you very much. I appreciate the extra effort you've made." I couldn't sleep that night, so I finally stayed up to wait for the newspaper to arrive! When it did, I opened it quickly to page 2, where Tom's column usually appeared, and I was touched. It was a wonderful, poignant rendition of the relationship between a mother and child trying to overcome adversity.

The second article was published on Monday as promised, with the headline screaming: 'KATHLEEN MORTON'S CASE PROVES BUREAUCRACY CAN BE BEATEN.' And, there before me lay a well-written article about my stalwart determination and the incredible bureaucracy I had had to plod through just to obtain the appropriate education guaranteed by law for my child. It was an impressive piece of journalism.

Unfortunately, Thomasina Hardy didn't seem too impressed when I called her at the hotel. Later that day when we met and I brought up the issue of relinquishment, she stopped me immediately. "Mrs. Morton, we're not going to discuss this because I spoke with Gale Frances at OCR and she told me they found no evidence of any policy that parents were forced to relinquish their children for appropriate educational programming."

"That's because they never came in to investigate!" I shot back. "They need to do an investigation before they release any findings. It's a sham!"

Before she could answer, the representative from the ARC interjected. "Mrs. Morton is absolutely right. What she is saying about having to give up custody for educational services has been taking place here for years. At her suggestion I called Gale Frances to tell her that I knew of several cases throughout the Valley where residential and relinquishment of custody was a factor. But Frances wasn't interested in taking any names except for those in the Glendale Union High School District where Michele Morton resided. So what's that all about? Since when do they all have to be in that district? This is happening all over the Valley and all of you should be very concerned." Several parents echoed what she said and Hardy made some notes.

Then one father spoke up, complaining bitterly about the lack of appropriate services.

"What district are you in?" Hardy inquired.

His reply showed the depth of his despair. "Oh, just keep walking all along Glendale Avenue," he said with a sigh, "and when you come to a big pile of manure, you've found it."

An awkward silence followed. They may have thought I had arranged to have that parent attend, but I'd never met the man in my life.

It would have been easy to be discouraged but I was determined to continue to make as much noise as I possibly could. I wrote articles on the issues of relinquishment, discriminatory attitudes by the state, the incredible bureaucracy parents are forced to wade through, and the air conditioning issue. They were published in the Maricopa Advisory Council on Developmental Disabilities' monthly newsletter. The column heading "Tell It Like It Is," included the by-line Kathleen Morton. By way of example, the last paragraph in the article on the air conditioning issue, I wrote:

"This intolerable situation, which borders on atrocity, came to light last summer simply because there was one brave multi-handicapped youngster. . . .

who can't see
who can't write

who can't walk

who can't speak

was able to complain to her mother."

Now, even with everything going for them, how many bureaucrats do you think would be able to get their point across so well? Zero, would be my guess.

I think that of all the infirmities that afflicted Michele, the loss of speech was the hardest to deal with. When a problem arose and she could no longer tell us what was wrong, her level of frustration was high. I had to be extremely diligent in trying to find the right answer, while also avoiding quick-treatment solutions, such as that suggested at Latch one day. The director called and said, "Kathleen, Michele is having a bad day."

"Really? What's going on, Sandy?"

"She won't stop screaming, no matter what we do."

"Has nursing checked her out?"

"Yes, but they can't find anything wrong. The psychologist on staff was consulted and after observing Michele, she believes it's just a behavioral problem. She's with me right now and would like to discuss some behavior interventions with you."

"Hello, Mrs. Morton," the psychologist said when she got on the phone. "I think I'd be able to help Michele, but I need your permission."

"What do you plan to do?"

"Well, it's a process we've used with some degree of success. It entails placing earphones on Michele. When she screams, I hit a button on the small box attached to the earphones with wires. This shocks her with a loud, high-pitched sound in the ears."

"Are you serious?" I asked in a shocked tone of voice. "Suppose it's not behavioral and she's really hurting? Generally, Michele doesn't have behaviors like this unless something is really wrong."

"Mrs. Morton, believe me, I know this is a behavioral problem," she said, slowly emphasizing each word. "I've seen these behaviors too often not to know what's happening."

"Maybe you have," I replied, "but you're assuming it stems from an emotional base, when it may be pain-related, which would create a bigger problem. However, I have to tell you that even if the cause was emotional, I find your procedure very disturbing. It presents more than a suggestion of cruelty to unsuspecting students. I know you mean well and you're only trying to help, but this is not the answer, especially for Michele. Out of the five senses Michele has, hearing is the only one left that works well, and you expect me to give you permission to assault it? There's no way. I'm sorry. Tell Sandy I'm coming right over."

When I arrived at Latch, Sandy met me at the door. Falling in step we walked to Michele's classroom. "Sandy, do you endorse this zapping procedure suggested by your psychologist?" I asked.

"Well, she's a good psychologist and it seems to have worked for her before. But I told her she could never touch Michele without your permission."

"I appreciate that. It's good to know I can always trust you to do what's right by Michele." As we neared the classroom and opened the door I could hear Michele, obviously very upset. "Hi Honey, what's the matter?" I asked as I went over and hugged her. She held me tight. "Are you hurting some place, Honey?" I whispered in her ear. Her grip tightened in response. "Okay, Sweetheart, just try to relax and don't worry. I'm going to take you home and together we'll find out what the problem is."

I turned to Sandy and said, "Could you get her wheelchair for me? I'm just going to take her home."

"Are you sure that's what you want to do, Kathleen?"

"Yes, I'm sure. We'll be fine. I think I need to put on my medical detective hat to find out what's bothering her."

"Then you don't think it's just behavioral?"

"No, I don't Sandy. See how her face is grimacing? That's from pain. I believe she's hurting somewhere."

"Okay. Then I wish you luck," she said encouragingly. "What about Bethphage?"

"Oh that's right, Sandy. Could you call them for me and let them know I'm taking Michele home?"

"Sure, no problem," she replied, eager to cooperate.

When we arrived home I put Michele in her dad's recliner. It was her favorite chair too. She seemed to relax and grew calmer. Leaning toward her I said, "Are you a faker or what?"

She laughed and vigorously shook her head.

I heard the garage door open and knew her dad was home. When he walked in the door, he said surprised, "Michele, what are you doing home? Are you playing hooky?" He kissed her, then turned to me and asked, "What's going on? Is she okay?"

"I don't know exactly," I replied with a shrug of my shoulders. Then I filled him in on what had transpired at Latch. "Dinner's almost ready, but I thought I'd give Michele her's first to see how she does."

"Fine," he said. "And if she's not eating, we're in bigggggggg trouble."

Michele chuckled at that remark and nodded her head.

Her dinner plate ready, I tried to sit her down on a straight back chair, but she screamed and clung to me, shaking all over.

"What is it, Honey?" I asked as she shook her head. "Arnie, help me here," I said. "I need to check her all over. Let's carry her into her bedroom."

When we'd laid her gently on the bed, she seemed to relax.

"Okay, I'll take over from here, Arnie," I said.

"What are you going to do?"

"I'm going to check every inch of her body." Arnie left and I closed the door. Michele had always valued her privacy when she was in control and that had not changed now that she was dependent.

"Let's see what we have here, Honey," I said to her. I methodically removed her clothing and inspected her from head to toe. I also pressed on her abdomen and sides with both hands, without reaction. Then I checked her legs, arms and ankles, asking each time if anything hurt. She shook her head each time. I was puzzled as to why she had objected so strongly when I went to put her down on the dining room chair.

I sat there in deep thought, studying her. Then I said, "Honey, I'm going to check the vaginal area just to make sure everything is okay." When I put on the plastic gloves and started examining her, I couldn't believe my eyes. I was looking at the worst case of vaginitis I had ever seen. The area was fiery red, surrounded by pus-like lesions.

Now it all made sense. Sitting in her dad's recliner with her feet up took the pressure off the area, as did lying down in bed. But once she was placed upright on a hard chair, it hurt like the dickens, and she screamed. I looked at her and she was smiling.

"I guess you know I've found the problem, huh kiddo?" I asked. Her face, now wreathed in smiles, was all the answer I needed.

I knew I had to call the doctor. Then I remembered that Bethancourt was away, so I called Kaplan. I gave him a rundown of the problem. He laughed and said, "Well it's not quite my specialty. In fact, it's the opposite end," he said jokingly. "But, sure, I can give you a prescription for Nystatin to treat it."

"I appreciate that, Al. She'll need the vaginal suppositories along with the cream for around the external area." I gave him the name and number of our pharmacy. A half-hour later the prescription was ready.

I kept Michele home until the pain subsided and she could move around with ease. She was happy as a lark returning to school. I told Sandy Landy that her psychologist needed to be more circumspect before she used the zapping method on anyone. I shuddered to think how horrible it would have been for Michele if I had given the okay. "Snap judgments should never be made when they can't tell you what's wrong," I said and Sandy was quick to agree.

To get back to the relinquishment issue: Some time after Arizona was 'exonerated' by the U.S. Civil Rights Division (because, supposedly, no evidence of wrongdoing was found involving the education of handicapped children) it was interesting to find out that the Legislature introduced the following paragraph into law:

"A developmentally disabled child has the right to appropriate services that are consistent with the child's written individual program plan. These services do not require _the relinquishment or restriction of parental rights, or custody_ . . . . . " Then the last paragraph of the law stated: "These services are _subject to available appropriations, if they are not mandated by federal law._" (emphasis supplied). So, since federal law mandates these services under the Education of the Handicapped Act, now called IDEA (Individual with Disabilities Education Act), which covers residential programming, no parents in the future should ever be forced to give up their children for services. Changing the law to add that paragraph is really interesting behavior from a state that was found innocent of all charges. This is what I would have expected had Arizona been found guilty and told to clean up their act. That's politics for you. It really does make strange bedfellows. The new law, my friends were quick to insist, should have been called "*Michele's Law.*"

When it comes to the education of any child, political bureaucracies should never be in the business of dictating the terms of the learning process. A red flag should have been raised immediately when DES became involved with the education of handicapped children. It's not unusual for a welfare agency to have the 'relinquishment' mind set because taking children away from abusive or neglectful parents is what they do. However, when the circumstances were different and the parent was not neglectful or abusive, the mind set did not change.

Many DES directors would come and go between the time Douglas Patino left and a man by the name of Charles Cowan was hired. Cowan was a retired Army colonel and after only a few months on the job the Arizona Republic reported that he told the legislature in a scathing report that the State Department of Economic Security was fouled up from A to Z, running on "a constant roller coaster ride from crisis to crisis. . . ."

The article also mentioned that he told legislators his agency was so wrapped up in red tape that it was a "social service mayhem. . . ." He further reported, "That the agency expected to be fined more than six million dollars for inaccurate processing of food stamps for one year alone. . .!"

That's *millions* folks not hundreds, or thousands of dollars, but *MILLIONS*! How many children do you think that would educate appropriately? Mismanagement always comes with a hefty price tag.

Quoted in the same article was Matt Salmon, R-Mesa, Assistant Senate Majority Leader at the time. He stated: "That (DES) bureaucracy is the stereotypical bureaucracy gone mad.

Hopefully, he (Cowan) can bring some sanity back to that place, if there ever was any. . . ."

Cowan also said, "The good people and good programs at DES are enslaved by processes and policies, rules and regulations, systems and services of Byzantine complexity." His answer was to introduce a five year program wherein, "Within nine months, improvement will be apparent, within eighteen months, improvements will be obvious, and within three to five years, there will be a dramatic transformation of DES."

Fascinated by such encouraging rhetoric, we looked forward to a new enlightened DES. Unfortunately, Cowan resigned within the year, another victim of a system considered by many as totally out of control.

Chapter XVIII

The next afternoon at work the secretary buzzed. "Kathleen there's a call for you from the nurse at Latch School. Can you take it right now?"

"Yes, sure. Put her right through."

"Hi Lynn," I said as I picked up the phone. "Is everything okay?" It was really unusual for Latch to call me at work.

"I'm not sure, and that's why I called you, Kathleen. I can't put my finger on it," she said, "but Michele didn't look like her old self today."

"Is she still with you or has she returned to Bethphage?" I asked.

"She was okay to travel, so she returned to Bethphage, but she just wasn't as responsive as she usually is. I thought I should let you know."

"Thanks, Lynn, I appreciate that. I'll be leaving work within the half hour. I'll go over to Bethphage and check on her right away."

When I arrived I was greeted warmly by the staff. Kim Brooks, who worked with Michele on a regular basis was there, along with a couple of other staff members interacting with the other young residents. Obviously relieved to see me, they described Michele's unresponsiveness much as Lynn had.

Kim accompanied me to Michele's room, where I quickly looked her over. Her color wasn't good and she had a slight temperature. "What about her urine output?" I asked.

"Not very much at all," Kim told me.

"I thought so. She looks a bit puffy-as if she's retaining fluid. I'm going to call Doctor Bethancourt."

One terrific aspect about Bruce Bethancourt was that he made sure I could always reach him day or night. This gave me a great sense of relief, especially at a time like this. I dialed his direct line right away and he answered on the first ring.

"Hi Bruce, this is Kathleen. Michele doesn't seem to be doing too well today. She's lethargic and not very responsive. She seems to be getting worse as the day goes on." I told him about the possibility of fluid retention.

"How's her breathing?"

"A bit shallow."

"You'd better bring her into ER right away and let them take a look at her. We can never know with Michele until we check her out thoroughly."

Kim immediately jumped into action and soon Michele was in the car. I adjusted the passenger seat so she could lie down next to me with a pillow under her head.

Arriving at the emergency entrance, I signaled a security guard and told him I needed assistance and a gurney. Immediately two people came running out with the gurney, lifted Michele onto it, and pushed her quickly into the hospital's emergency unit. Nurses drew her blood, applied oxygen, and began an IV drip.

A little while later, the doctor in charge came out and asked, "Are you Michele's Mom?"

"Yes, I am."

"Who's her doctor?"

"Bruce Bethancourt."

"Michele is very ill," he told me. "Whatever it is, it's systemic. Her whole system is affected and she's losing ground fast. Your daughter needs intensive care, so she's being taken to ICU right now. I'll let Doctor Bethancourt know."

I swallowed hard, wondering what was in store for Michele now. She had been fine over the weekend – responsive and happy. I didn't believe this onslaught was the result of NCL either. The disease just didn't move that fast. I quickly left ER and made my way to ICU.

Standing on the sidelines, I watched the nurses and doctors attend to Michele. By the time they had finished, she had tubes coming out of every part of her body and could no longer breathe on her own, so she was placed on a ventilator. I hardly recognized her because she was now about three times the size of her normal weight due to fluid retention.

A surgical procedure was performed right there in the room, and a large segment of tubing was inserted in her side. That was connected to a plastic bag hanging over the edge of the bed for excess fluid drainage. I shook my head and leaned against the wall watching Michele. Tears were not far behind. The whole scene was so gross. I felt nauseous. Moving to her, I picked up her hand and kissed it. Her entire body was limp. She was now unconscious.

Doctor Bethancourt walked in. I looked up and gave him a wan smile. "Hi," I said. "What do you think about this?"

"It's incredible, Kathleen. I just read Michele's chart and it seems her whole system is shutting down since we talked on the phone."

"I know. She can't even breathe on her own now. She's also totally unresponsive and no one seems to know why."

"It's hard to tell until the results of all the tests come in. Has Al been in to see her yet?"

"No, I haven't even had a chance to call him. Everything

happened too fast."

"Neurologically, I'd like to know what he thinks. I'll call and talk with him. How are you holding up?"

"I'm okay, thanks."

"Where's your husband, Kathleen?"

"He's on his way. Actually I'm expecting him any minute."

"Good. Try to relax. I'll see you in the morning."

The next day, Michael left work early to come to see Michele. I was by her bedside when he walked into the room. When he saw the ventilator and all the tubes, he immediately turned away with tears welling up in his eyes. Then he walked out of the room without saying a word. I followed him and told him to wait.

Shaking his head, he said, "Even though you told me yesterday what had happened, I was unprepared for what I saw. I just can't look at her that way, Mom, I'm sorry. It's too painful."

"That's okay, Michael. I'll walk you out." When we got off the elevator on the first floor I said, "How about having a cup of coffee with me? You can sit down at one of the tables while I get it."

"Okay, but make mine a Pepsi," and we walked downstairs to the basement where the cafeteria was located.

When I brought the coffee and Pepsi over, he was deep in thought. He looked down, and picked up the soft drink almost in slow motion and started sipping it. "It's unreal, Mom, to see Michele like that," he said, fighting back the tears. Then he leaned the back of his head against the wall, and closed his eyes.

We sat in silence for some time, but it was a comfortable silence. Then he spoke. "I feel I'm letting you and Michele down, and there doesn't seem to be any way out of this."

"Well, you're not letting us down, Michael. Stop thinking

that way. You know anytime over the years when we've needed you, you were right there. I never had to ask twice, so get that out of your head. Besides, there will be plenty of times in the future I'll need you to rally to the occasion, so don't think you're off the hook completely," I said smiling.

He grinned and responded, "Okay, Mom. Thanks."

In the weeks to come, every conceivable test was done and at least a half a dozen specialists were in on the case, but all findings were inconclusive. Kaplan was there every day, along with Bethancourt, and we conferred each morning.

The ICU nurse, Kathy McKenna, attended Michele most of the time. She was great with Michele, very supportive of me, and had a wonderful sense of humor. For that matter, most of the nurses in the ICU were very helpful and compassionate, which helped me to cope. One day I brought in Michele's very large soft furry bear and placed him on the window sill.

"Who is this intruder?" Kathy demanded when she walked in and saw the bear.

"Why, this is Mr. Bear," I said with a smile. "He's going to supervise Michele's care when I'm not here."

Placing her hands on her hips, she exclaimed in mock indignation, "What?! I don't need anyone looking over my shoulder."

I laughed and said, "Sorry Kathy, he stays. As a matter of fact, he'll give me a report when I come in tomorrow."

"Well, we'll see about that," and with a straight face and a haughty look she turned on her heel and left the room.

The next morning I came upon the funniest scene when I walked into Michele's room. There was Mr. Bear still sitting on the window sill, but with a slight change in appearance. He was bound, gagged and blindfolded! It was a scream and the nursing staff got the reaction they expected. I couldn't stop laughing. What a way to relieve stress! When I took Michele's hand at her bedside, I felt as if she were laughing with us.

And then, one day, in the late afternoon while I was holding her hand, Michele opened her eyes, turned her head toward me and gave me a feeble smile. "Well, look who woke up!" I said startled. She squeezed my hand hard. "I'm going to tell the nurses on you," I told her and her smile widened a little.

When the nurses came in, they were surprised and happy to see how responsive she was and made a big fuss over her. Doctors Kaplan and Bethancourt also registered their surprise. "This is a good sign, Kathleen," Kaplan said, "but she's not out of the woods yet."

"I know, Al, but she's out of the coma!" I said with a smile.

"You're right about that," he replied looking pleased.

"As I told you before," Bethancourt added, "Michele comes with her own agenda, while we doctors stand around in wonderment shaking our heads."

Almost immediately, everything started working well within Michele's system. The next day the surgeon came by and removed the tubing from her side. She had no more fluid retention and her weight was back to normal. The other tubes were removed one by one and by the third day the doctors talked about removing the ventilator. This they did gradually until she was breathing well on her own. By the fourth day, Michele was off the ventilator completely.

The discussion now focused on transferring her from ICU to a private room on a regular floor. The crisis had run its course, having ended almost as quickly as it had begun. Still, as Doctor Kaplan had said, she wasn't out of the woods yet. She remained in the hospital for another few weeks while the nurses and doctors attended to the complications of vitamin deficiency, colitis, lactose intolerance and malabsorption, and severe weight loss. Normally, she weighed about a hundred and five pounds. She was now down to sixty-five. A doctor specializing in nutrition was called in.

"Mrs. Morton," he said after examining Michele, "your daughter needs to follow an aggressive nutritional program which I can set up for her. I'm going to use a nutritional supplement that comes highly recommended for cases such as Michele's. She will continue to be tube fed for a while, even after discharge, until we can get her condition and weight under control."

We all realized that Michele's medical needs were much greater than before and that she would require more intensive care upon discharge. Although it saddened us to even think about moving Michele out of Bethphage, we finally agreed with the doctors that her present medical needs did require around-the-clock nursing care, which Bethphage was not able to provide.

The big question was what to do now. I called Al Soenneker at DES. The secretary put me right through.

"Hi, Al," I said when he picked up the phone. "I need some assistance in finding a facility with around-the-clock nursing care. It's for Michele."

"I'm sorry to hear it" he said. "I knew she was in the hospital, but I thought she was doing better."

"She is, but the illness has left her so medically challenged that she now requires this type of support. I hope you can help me."

"I think I can. An Intermediate Care Facility with around-the-clock nursing has just opened up not five minutes from Good Samaritan, where you work. Your timing couldn't be better."

"Wonderful!" I said. "What's the name of it?"

"Windsor. It's located on 16th Street, just south of Thomas. I'll have someone contact you so that you can take a look. If you like it, the necessary arrangements will be made for Michele's transfer from Bethphage."

"Okay, Al, and thanks a million. You've really made my day."

"Good! I'm glad this has worked out so well for you."

In my advocacy role, Soenneker and I frequently found ourselves on opposite ends of the issue, myself arguing passionately in favor of the child's needs. When any particular case was over, there always remained a strong professional relationship, mutual respect, and often an expressed genuine appreciation of my efforts. For this I was ever thankful.

The next day the phone rang and a voice said, "Hi, Mrs. Morton, this is Joleen from DES. Remember me from Bethphage?"

"Joleen, oh, yes! You were the former director. Are you handling Michele's transfer to Windsor?"

"Yes, I am."

"Well, then I know we're in good hands."

"Thanks, Mrs. Morton. I think you're going to like Windsor very much. Can we get together today for you to see the facility and sit down to discuss arrangements?"

"Absolutely!" I said.

After I had checked out the place and determined that I liked what I observed, we sat down and discussed the details. With Joleen handling the process, everything went smoothly. No enormous amount of red tape to wade through, just good common sense prevailed.

On the day of the transfer, Doctor Bethancourt carefully wrote out all the orders for Michele's medical needs. The hospital gave us enough medication to last her a few days until Windsor ordered the new supply. The food supplement she required was ordered and shipped directly to Windsor. Michele had a private room with an adjacent bath which we were told we could decorate and personalize in any way we wished. The manager, Rhonda Barr, came into the room and said, "Mrs. Morton, I would like to introduce you to Edie Kahn, who will be Michele's primary care-giver."

I looked up to see a very pleasant-looking woman in her early forties with hand extended. She was about five feet six inches tall and slender, with dark hair, sprinkled with gray.

"Nice to meet you, Mrs. Morton," Edie said as we shook hands. Michele dozed so we left the room, sat at a table, and talked about issues relating to her.

"As for her likes and dislikes," I said, "she generally has a good disposition, and likes to laugh a lot. Having a good sense of humor is definitely one of her strengths. As you know, Michele is blind, so she doesn't like it when she's sitting in the wheelchair if someone comes along and starts to push it without telling her what's happening. Also, she doesn't like anything tight around her waist, so please make sure the wheelchair belt isn't too tight. She loves music and there are some TV programs she listens to – especially Batman."

"Does she have her own TV?" Edie asked.

"Yes she does, and she also has a tape recorder. I have those with me in the car. I'll bring them in before I leave."

Just then the door opened and in walked Arnie. "Oh, here's my husband now," I said to Edie. Arnie strode in and greeted us.

"How's everything?" he asked.

"So far, so good. This is Edie Kahn, Arnie. She's going to be primarily involved with Michele's care. Michele's resting right now and I've been talking to Edie about her likes and dislikes."

Shortly thereafter Arnie went out to my car to bring in Michele's TV and recorder. Edie and I decided to go in and check on Michele. She was fully awake, lying quietly.

"Hello Michele," Edie said. "My name is Edie, and you and I are going to have a good time together. Would you like that?" she inquired, gently stroking Michele's arm.

"Yes," Michele replied smiling.

"Good!" Edie exclaimed. "That's what I like, someone who agrees with me. Will you agree with me all the time?"

Michele laughed and gave a resounding "Nooooo!" while vigorously shaking her head.

Before Edie could respond, Arnie walked in with the TV and recorder. Edie showed him where the electrical outlets were and he set up the TV and plugged it in.

Then he went over to Michele and kissed her. "Hi," he said. "You look happy. Are you feeling good?"

She nodded her head, still smiling.

Edie got Michele up to go to the bathroom. She transferred her from the bed to the wheelchair with ease and wheeled her in, closing the door behind her. When they came back out, Michele was washed, and her hair was nicely brushed. She looked great. It was obvious that Edie was a real pro with a very gentle touch. Instinctively, we both knew that this woman was going to have a very positive impact on our lives, especially Michele's.

The Central Arizona Special Services (CASS) program is what Michele would now be attending during the day. It was set up in another building adjacent to Windsor, very convenient for all the residents. No busing necessary.

The first day at Windsor was a great success and before we left I asked Michele how her day had gone.

She responded with a smile and a look of contentment.

"Okay, then we're on our way, and Edie will call me right away if there's any kind of problem. Right, Edie?"

"You bet," Edie replied. "Try to relax. Michele will be

fine."

For the next few weeks everything continued to go well at Windsor until I got a call from Al Soenneker.

"It's about Michele," he said, "but no big deal, so don't be concerned. Remember the formula the doctor ordered and sent over to Windsor for Michele?"

"Yes, I do."

"Well, we just found out that since Michele is no longer a patient in the hospital, the insurance won't cover it. Believe it or not a thirty day supply runs around a thousand dollars."

"A thousand dollars! My God, that's incredible! And she's supposed to be on it for several months."

"I know and that's why I wanted to talk to you. I'd like to have the State Nutritionist look at the formula, then research other formulas, and possibly come up with another similar one that would produce the same results. I'd never compromise Michele's health, Kathleen, so I want to be sure you talk to the doctor and see what he says."

"Sure, I'll do that right away. And you go ahead and have the State Nutritionist do her research. In the meantime, do you want me to send you a check for. . . . . . "

"No, don't do that yet," he interrupted. "We'll pick it up this time, and hopefully the problem can be resolved within the next week or two."

I left word for the doctor who ordered the formula to give me a call. He returned my call the following day. I filled him in on the problem confronting us and then asked if there was another formula that was less expensive, which would still afford the same result.

"Absolutely not." he responded without hesitation. "That's the only formula effective enough to accomplish the results we're seeking for your daughter. You don't want to jeopardize that, do you?"

"Of course not. I just thought I would call and ask. That's all."

"Fine," he said somewhat abruptly, and then hung up. I took the receiver away from my ear and thought, 'Well he wouldn't get any points for courtesy, that's for sure.' I didn't know this guy. He was just called in because he was a nutritional specialist and had placed Michele on this formula. I decided not to call Soenneker until his nutritionist finished her research.

About a week later and at Al's request, I met with the nutritionist. She had a can of formula with her and was quite excited. "Mrs. Morton, look what I found. A nutritional formula that is almost identical to the one Michele is currently on. All the ingredients are the same, except one, which I don't believe is of any great importance. The best news is the price. The formula runs about $250 to $300 a month. Maybe even less, because the state may get a discount."

"That's unbelievable!" I said. "Are you sure this could have the same results?" I asked dubiously.

"Pretty sure," she replied. "Here take this formula to the specialist and ask him. The only difference I can see is the price."

"Okay, and thanks for all your hard work. I really appreciate your efforts." I admitted to myself that I was skeptical. Before I called the doctor, I decided to discuss the matter with a friend of mine who was a nurse nutritionist at the hospital. She was in her office when I arrived.

"Hi Kathleen," she greeted me. "How's Michele?"

"She's doing very well right now, but I have a question to ask you. You know the doctor who specializes in nutrition here?"
"I do, yes."

"Good. I have with me the formula that he recommended, as well as another one recommended by the State. I would like you to compare them and tell me what you think before I call him. The last time I spoke with him, he was adamant about not changing it. However, the price difference is enormous."

Comparing the labels as I talked, she looked up at me. "Kathleen, in my opinion, the State formula will be as good as this formula. But before you call him, I think you should know something. The doctor in question, along with another doctor, own the company that produces the formula he so highly recommends."

"No!" I said shocked. "I can't believe this. What a conflict of interest! And unethical too. I mean, he knew I would never want to jeopardize Michele's health, so he played on that. How disgusting," I said jumping up out of the chair. I turned to my friend, "Thanks, I owe you one. I'll take it from here." Still reeling from the information I'd received, I returned to my office, and called the 'King of Nutrition.'

"Hello doctor, this is Kathleen Morton. I need to talk to you again about the formula."

"What about the formula?"

"You'll be happy to know that the State Nutritionist found another formula identical to the one you ordered, except for one small ingredient, and it's only a quarter of the price of what Michele is on now."

"What!" he demanded. "I can't believe you're willing to compromise your daughter's health just to save a few extra dollars a month."

"That won't work any more, Doctor. You know I'd never compromise Michele's health. But I have a formula here that's identical except for one small ingredient and you won't even consider it. The big question is why? And, *of course,* the price is a huge factor when the difference is over seven hundred dollars a month! To most people that's a great deal of money. What makes you so unyielding?"

"Because what I ordered is the best formula for Michele and that's final. I will not consider anything else."

"Okay, then just let me ask you one more question, Doctor. By any chance, would your strong stand have anything to do with the fact that you and another doctor *own* the company that makes this formula?"

"What? What!" he sputtered. "How dare you. . . .!" he expostulated seething with anger. "I'm off this case," he shouted and slammed down the receiver.

Now I had my answer, although, I had hoped it would go the other way. But since he had been so insistent, I had had my doubts. However, when he yelled in anger that he was *off this* case! I knew that Lady Luck was finally looking out for us.

Chapter XIX

Michele thrived on the new formula. Within a few months she blossomed, and went from sixty-five pounds to ninety-five. She looked much better and her health greatly improved. The G-tube was removed. She loved sitting at the dining room table once again, eating her favorite foods.

One night, Arnie and I had just finished eating dinner when Michael and Paula dropped by. "Hi, come on in," I said as I opened the door. After everyone was seated Michael said, "We have a surprise for you."

"Great, I love surprises. Does it include both of us?"

"Yes, it does, but it's really more for you because of all the stress you've been under this year. You hardly got a chance to recover from the major surgery before Michele got so sick. And the changes and problems after that were phenomenal. Right, Dad?"

"You can say that again. She's been on some roller coaster ride."

Paula sat next to Michael, smiling. I looked at both of them intrigued, wondering what was coming next. Still grinning, Paula rose to hand me an envelope and said, "Here, this is for you."

I paused, then opened it. To my delight, I held two tickets announcing a 3-day cruise to the Mexican Riviera on the Norwegian Cruise Line. "I can't believe this!" I said. "You're right, Michael, this *is* a surprise. You two are wonderful. Did you know, Arnie?"

"Yes, I did, but they came up with the idea. I told them I thought it was a great plan and that you'd love it."

"You got that right," I said. Then reality set in. "But what about Michele?"

"She's stable now," Arnie said.

"Yes, but you never know with her."

"Mom, it's only four or five days at the most," Michael said. That includes getting there, taking the cruise, and returning. You need some change of scenery and relaxation."

"But. . . . "

"No buts. We've all decided you need this, so, it's settled."

"Oh, it is, is it?" I said laughing. I was quickly warming up to the idea. We hadn't been away for so long and the change of pace was really appealing. It was exciting just to think about it.

"When would we leave?" I asked.

"In about two months," Paula told me.

"That's not far off."

"No, it isn't," Michael replied, "But we've actually had the tickets for quite a while and didn't tell you because Michele was so sick."

"Michele will be in your hands while we're gone, huh?" I said.

"No, I'm afraid not," Michael responded with a slight smile.

"Why not?"

"Because we're going with you."

I looked at him, momentarily speechless, waiting to be told there was a joke in there some place, but he was dead serious. "Well, of course," I said, "It would be great fun for all of us to go, but now I have an even bigger dilemma."

"No, you don't. Talk to the doctors. I'm sure they'll support this. Also, I'm certain your friend, Heather, would be willing to help out while we're gone."

"You're probably right, Michael. The more you talk, the more right it sounds."

"Good. That's what we want to hear!"

Arnie and I both thanked them again before they left. I paused as the door closed behind them, pleased with their thoughtfulness. Of course, Michael was right. Doctors Bethancourt and Kaplan wholeheartedly agreed that the trip was a great idea and Heather said she would be very happy to take over for me while I was gone. Neither of us had any problem getting the time off, so no obstacles were in our way.

Before we knew it, the departure date was upon us. The day before we were due to leave, Michele came down with a slight fever. Doctor Bethancourt made a trip to Windsor to see her. This was a big help. After he'd checked her out, I said, "We're scheduled to leave tomorrow on our cruise, so what do you think?"

"I think you should go and have a great time," he said smiling. "Michele will be fine. There's nothing to worry about. I'll come here to see her if necessary. And you know Al Kaplan is also available in the event of any neurological problems. So, just enjoy yourself and don't even think about NCL."

The next morning we rose bright and early and were ready when Michael and Paula picked us up. Because we were driving to California, all our luggage had to fit in the car. I was a bit skeptical but surprisingly, with a few pulls, pushes and twists, the trunk of the car closed.

The ride was enjoyable. When we arrived, Michael was directed to park his car in a certain place and cruise staff took charge of our luggage. While boarding the ship, Michael said. "Oh Mom, you'd better close your eyes."

"Why?" I asked, but doing as he suggested.

By now all three were laughing. "What's going on?" I asked as I opened my eyes and quickly looked around. And, then I shook my head in astonishment. There before my eyes in very large letters, were the initials N C L. "God, I can't believe this. What are the odds?"

Still amused, Michael asked, "Do you know why?"

"Yes, I do now. They're the initials of the Norwegian Cruise Line, and none of us thought about that." There was no escaping them. The initials were everywhere. On matchbook covers, napkins, glasses, you name it, NCL was in evidence. "Wait until I tell Bethancourt," I said and we all laughed at the irony of it.

"Michele had no intentions of letting us forget her," Arnie said smiling. "It's actually very funny. I bet she's laughing at us right now!"

This was a first cruise for all of us and we enjoyed it immensely. Gourmet food and red carpet treatment all the way. It was easy to relax. I could feel the tension melting away. It also felt good to be surrounded by family members determined that I would enjoy myself or else! The combination of the trip and their thoughtfulness left me feeling rejuvenated and highly energized upon my return.

Michele was fine while we were gone. She enjoyed the Day Program on campus directed by Becky Johnson. Becky was a very creative individual, well organized and upbeat. Michele responded well to such a cheerful environment. After the school day ended, Edie Kahn was on duty. Michele and Edie had become fast friends. Edie had a delightful sense of humor that matched Michele's, so there were lots of happy moments.

I can't say, however, that my life was totally blissful after Michele went to Windsor, because that would not be entirely accurate. The "relinquishment mentality" of the State which prevailed in the minds of some staff members resulted in resentment of an involved parent from those used to being totally in charge. Al Soenneker was a big help in sorting all this out and things were turned around. Also I had a court decree in my possession stipulating that I was Michele's legal guardian.

When it came time to do the Individual Program Plan (IPP) for Michele about eight people attended. Mike, the case manager conducted the meeting. The team discussed different programmatic approaches, therapies, medical needs, and so on. But at the end I was taken aback when Mike said to the team, "Okay, we're finished now except for one last item to vote on. Is the team satisfied with Michele's guardian and should Kathleen remain as guardian?"

"What!" I interjected shocked. "Where are you coming from with that remark, Mike?"

He ignored my protests and continued to ask for the team's approval of me.

A chorus of, "Yes," "Sure," and "Of course," erupted around the table while I sat there astonished.

"Do you really believe that you have that kind of power, Mike?" I asked with a bewildered look.

"Yes, I do, and so does this team," he said gruffly.

"Well, you're wrong. You're all wrong. Just think about what you're saying. You hardly even know me, Mike, and to top it off, three people at this table met me today for the *first* time. So what qualifies any of you to pass judgment on who Michele's guardian is?" I gave a derisive laugh while shaking my head at the absurdity of it all.

Mike's response was short and to the point. "I have the guidelines right here in front of me which stipulate that I have to determine if the guardian is appropriate."

"That's got to be a misinterpretation, Mike. The State

guidelines are only an interpretation of the Federal Law."

"Then what does the Federal Law say?" he demanded.

"I don't know the exact quote off-hand, but I can assure you a decision like that is not in a case manager's job description, or anyone else's for that matter. Perhaps it's to see if the individual still needs a guardian, which would make sense."

Mike remained unconvinced.

As I left Windsor to go to my car, two of the team members walked out with me and one said, "Mrs. Morton, we attend many IPPs, and everyone of them handles the guardianship the same way. We want to assure you that we would never have voted to have you removed because you're such a good parent." As one spoke, the other nodded her head in agreement.

I just looked at them in amazement, shaking my head. I had a lot of respect for these two team members and I knew they meant well, but they just didn't get it. "That's not the issue," I said thoroughly frustrated now. "The issue is that *none* of you have that *right*! Common sense should tell you that," I continued, while getting into my car.

I drove right to the library and looked up Title 19, which was the federal law I was referring to, and it was what I had thought. Title 19 stipulated in part . . . (to discuss) "if the individual's needs still require the _protection_ of a guardian. . ." Quite a difference from what they believed it to be!

I wrote to Al Soenneker explaining what had happened and asked that the state's interpretation be changed statewide in order to comply with Title 19. A few weeks later I received an apology from the case management supervisor stating, "There was a misunderstanding by the case managers concerning what the guidelines meant," and that I was correct about Title 19 focusing in on the individual still needing the 'protection of a guardian.' "As a result, the guidelines were re-written and the case managers have all been re-instructed as to how the guardianship issue is to be addressed at future IPPs."

Pursuing this issue was very important because most parents are not aware of the federal laws, and would probably believe that whatever the state says was gospel. Certainly, if parents did not know their rights and thought they could be removed as guardians at any time on a whim most would be very intimidated. Not that I believe that was the intention of the State in my case.

A few weeks later, at work, I received a very pleasant surprise. I was going to be nominated by Bonnie Wilson, Director of Education for the hospital, for a community service award.

"I'm impressed with all the volunteer work you do in the community, Kathleen," she said smiling, "and I think you should be recognized for it. Have you heard of Doctor Singer, the Samaritan doctor who had an award named after him because of how much work he did in the community?"

"Yes, I have. It's presented to an employee from each of the Samaritan hospitals annually in recognition of community service involvement. My understanding is that the Samaritan Health System and a group of community leaders called 'The Samaritans' established the award a few years ago. Is that what you're referring to?"

"Yes, it is," she replied. "And I can see you're well-informed."

Laughing, I responded, "Maybe that's because I just read the material before I came over this morning. But I must say I'm very flattered, Bonnie. What a nice gesture on your part."

"You deserve it," she quickly replied.

Over the course of the next few weeks, the people I worked with in the community were interviewed. Then the phone rang one day and the voice said, "This is Bo Larsen from Larsen Productions. Is this Kathleen Morton?"

"Yes, it is."

"Good. Regarding the Paul L. Singer award you were nominated for, I have been asked to videotape you at work, at home, and at Windsor with your daughter, Michele. I thought we could discuss dates and times."

"That's fine," I told him.

After all was settled he said, "I understand you're on the board of a national organization called Batten Disease Support and Research Association."

"Yes, I am. That's the organization that was set up to give parents support and to research the disease Michele has."

"What's the name of the disease?" he asked.

"Neuronal Ceroid Lipofuscinosis. NCL for short."

"Wow! Never heard of that one," he exclaimed.

"You're not alone, Bo. Many medical doctors have never heard of it either. That's what we're trying to change. The organization is named Batten because it's easier to say and Batten was the doctor who discovered it over a hundred years ago. Finally, some progress is being made. We have high hopes of eventually finding a cure or even a way to prevent it. But, like all medical research, it will take millions and millions of dollars."

"When do you meet?"

"We have a conference set up in a different state once a year, and during the year we have teleconferences about every two months. As a matter of fact, a teleconference is scheduled in a few days."

"I'd like to come over and tape it. Do you think that would be possible?"

"I don't know, but I'd be happy to ask if there are any

objections. I'll get back to you."

"Great, Kathleen. In the meantime, let's meet at Windsor tomorrow as we discussed."

"That's fine, Bo. I'll meet you there at 4:00 o'clock."

When I walked into Windsor the next day, Bo had already arrived. "I usually arrive early in order to set up my equipment," he explained. "So, we're ready whenever you are."

"I'm ready. How about you, Michele?" I asked, moving toward her bed. This was not one of Michele's better days. She had been in bed most of the afternoon because she seemed to be very tired. "Do you want to sit between Edie and me and have your picture taken?" I asked, giving her a kiss on the cheek. She showed her approval by smiling and attempting to sit up. Edie and I helped her and the taping began. Then, without warning, Michele stiffened, threw her head back and went into a full-blown grand mal convulsion.

"Turn off the lights," I quickly told Bo and Edie and I immediately attended to Michele. The seizure only lasted about five minutes. I turned around and looked at Bo. He was staring in disbelief at what had just happened. For a minute I thought I was going to have to call the paramedics for him. "The lights probably induced the seizure, Bo, but that wasn't your fault."

"Will she be alright?" he asked with a note of concern.

"Yes," I assured him. "She's resting now."

"How could you stay so calm? I was all ready to panic!" he said wiping perspiration from his brow. "I'm impressed."

"Panic is normal the first time you see this, Bo. And you never really get used to it. I've simply learned to cope."

Just saying that made me realize how coping brought some semblance of order into my life. The only other alternative was to go insane and that just wasn't an option. Fortunately, reason always intervened and I managed to plod along, just like so many other parents who have children suffering from devastating diseases.

"Oh, by the way," I said to Bo, "it'll be okay to tape the Batten teleconference at my home when you come over."

"Excellent, Kathleen. Do you have a speaker phone by chance?"

"Yes, I do. In my office."

"Good. We'll have everything we need."

All taping was completed within a few days. There were a total of twenty-six nominees to choose from. 'The Samaritans' certainly had their work cut out for them, I thought. Only six employees would be selected as winners, one from each Samaritan facility they represented.

No one knew who the winners would be until the day of the luncheon when they were introduced individually on screen followed by their video. It was all very impressive.

I was even more impressed when the last video shown had my name and picture on it, declaring me the winner from Good Samaritan Regional Medical Center!

Actually, I was overjoyed, as were all the other winners. There was a lot of excitement among the group as cameras were flashing taking our picture with Jim Crews, President and CEO of Samaritan Health System.

The award was a sterling silver, delicately-crafted Kachina statuette, positioned on a stand and placed upon a bed of sand inside a mirrored glass dome. It was very elegant. In addition, we each received a check for $250. The same amount would be sent to our favorite charity. Mine, of course, was sent to the Batten Disease Support and Research Association.

What a day! I went directly to Windsor to show Michele.

She knew I was being honored at a luncheon that day with the possibility of winning an award. She was excited when I brought it in and set it down in front of her. Her hands moved over the dome at first and she gave me a quizzical look. Then I removed the dome and she found the Kachina.

"It's okay, Honey. You can lift it out," I said. When she had it in her hands, her fingers started to slowly explore the statuette from head to toe, so no detail would be missed. I could tell from Michele's reaction that just knowing her mom had received an award that day was a pleasurable experience for her. When she discovered the sand she laughed heartily, and we both hugged one another, enjoying another one of our special moments.

KATHLEEN MORTON

Chapter XX

A couple of weeks later, Theresa, the Head Nurse, called me at work. "Mrs. Morton, Michele isn't doing well today. We're bringing her over to ER."

"What's going on, Theresa?" I asked.

"Well, for some reason, she seems to be in a lot of pain and is running a temperature. She's not eating and her color isn't good."

I took a deep breath and wondered, 'Now what?' I did not respond right away.

"Mrs. Morton? Are you still there?"

"Yes, I'm still here, Theresa. What time are they leaving with Michele?"

"They're ready to take off right now."

"Okay. Let the staff know I'll meet them in the ER."

I called Doctor Bethancourt and informed him of this latest development, especially the pain. That was new. "So, what do you think, Bruce? Any ideas?" I asked.

"Well, it could be many things, Kathleen. With those symptoms she will probably be admitted. I'll meet you over at the hospital a little later."

Within ten minutes Michele was brought into ER. Theresa was right, her color was not good. She was taken right away into an examination room. After being checked out by an ER doctor, she was admitted to the hospital. Her fever and pallor indicated a possible internal infection of *unknown origin*. Didn't that sound familiar?

I was pleased to learn that Michele was being admitted to a floor where the nurses knew her well. This was a very important factor since she could no longer communicate her needs. There had been a change of Head Nurses since the last time Michele was on the floor, but I didn't think this would matter. *How wrong I was.*

After trying with nursing to work out an acceptable care plan for Michele, I noted the usual cooperation was not present. Then one of the nurses who knew Michele well and who was a very caring individual came on duty. I was so happy to see her and thought she would be assigned to Michele's case as usual, but she wasn't.

"What's going on here?" I asked her. "It was never like this before," I continued, trying to get some idea of what the problem was.

She shrugged, "What can I tell you, Kathleen? I asked to be assigned to Michele and my request was denied."

I could see she was uncomfortable with continuing the conversation, so in deference to her I dropped it.

As Michele's pain became unrelenting, I anxiously awaited Doctor Bethancourt's arrival. When he did, and after his examination, he shook his head and said, "She's sure in a lot of pain. I'm ordering some additional tests to see if we can determine the cause. In the meantime, I'll write a STAT order for some strong pain medication."

"Thanks Bruce, I appreciate that. I can't stand to see her this way. I feel so helpless."

"I know, Kathleen. Just try and hang in there. We should have an answer soon and the medication I'm ordering should bring her immediate relief."

Despite the STAT order, the medication did not arrive. Two hours later I called Bethancourt at home, something I rarely needed to do.

He was astonished when I told him Michele had not yet received her medication.

"What's the problem?" he asked.

"Their attitude! That's the problem," I said disgusted. "It has changed so much up here Bruce, you wouldn't believe. You know I always wanted Michele on this floor because she got such great care. But now it's a nightmare!"

"Okay, take it easy, Kathleen. I'm going to call nursing directly."

When more time passed and still no medication, I asked nursing what the hold up was now. I was informed the pharmacy had not sent it up yet. Then I thought, 'Could that possibly be the problem? Pharmacy, rather than the nursing staff?' So, I called the Pharmacy Manager, Linda McCoy, at home and related the problem to her.

"Oh, my God," she said. "I don't believe this, Kathleen. Let me call, and I'll get right back to you."

When she did, she said, "There's no medication order for Michele on the computer."

"What?!" I could hardly believe my ears.

"That's right, but don't worry. I've gotten the order from nursing and the pharmacist is making it up as we speak. The medication should be up on the floor within ten minutes."

"Oh, thanks, Linda. Thank you so much. I owe you one."

"No you don't," she quickly replied. "It's unfortunate that something like this happened, and I'm glad I was available to help out. Feel free to call me any time."

Bethancourt was right. Within a short period of receiving

the medication, Michele finally stopped crying out in pain, her body relaxed, and she fell asleep. What an ordeal! Then the phone rang. It was Bethancourt checking to see how Michele was doing. I told him what had happened, and about my having to call Linda. His immediate response was, "I'm transferring Michele out of there tonight."

"Oh, no Bruce. Not tonight, please! She's without pain, relaxed and sleeping. I'd go out of my mind trying to move her right now. Besides, I want to talk to the head nurse tomorrow morning. I'm sure she's not aware of what's going on in her section."

"Fine, if that's what you want, Kathleen. I'll meet you tomorrow morning at 7:00 o'clock in Michele's room."

The next morning at 6:45, the head nurse entered her office. I asked to speak with her for a few minutes and we both sat down. "I need to tell you about something that occurred last night on the floor with your nursing staff. It was very upsetting."

"You bet it was upsetting," she interjected with eyes flashing angrily. "You have no right to tell my nurses what to do. And how dare you call the doctor at home! Just who do you think you are?!" she demanded.

I looked at her stunned. "What?! You mean you actually knew what was going on last night and it was done with your direction and approval? I can't believe this."

"Yes, I knew. Because you have no right . . . ."

"Baloney!" I interrupted. "I have *every* right! You've forgotten what your mission is here. And I, like an idiot, prevailed upon Doctor Bethancourt not to transfer Michele out of here last night, in deference to you. What a joke," I said standing up to go.

"Sit down!" she commanded. I couldn't believe her arrogance. "I'm calling a meeting with you, Doctor Bethancourt and myself,

310

and we're going to get some things straightened out right here and now," she declared vehemently.

"In your dreams, lady," I retorted. "Effective immediately, Michele is off this floor!" Turning on my heel, I walked out the door. When I reached Michele's room, Bethancourt was already there.

"What's wrong?" he asked when he looked up and saw me. "You don't want to know, Bruce," I told him. "But you were right about one thing, Michele needs to be moved out of here."

"I've already taken care of that, Kathleen," he said shaking his head. "She requires better care than this. I'm transferring her immediately to the twelfth floor. You know the head nurse up there, right?"

"Yes, I do. It's Selma Kendrick, and she's great. So are the nurses on that floor. I know them through working in the system, but let's remember that I was also a patient there when I was recuperating from my mastectomy. The care was second to none, so I'm happy that Michele will be there."

"Good! Hopefully everything will go well now. I'll see you later, but in the meantime call me if anything unusual happens."

I smiled warmly and said, "Okay, Bruce, thanks. Thanks very much for everything."

This guy was incredible. Nothing was too much for him. He met with me early in the morning at Windsor or at the hospital, sometimes on a daily basis, or late at night at either place. He was always within reach, even when he wasn't in town. An avid sailor, he had his boat docked in California. One time when I was nervous about something that was going on with Michele, when he was going away for a long weekend, he said, "Don't worry, Kathleen. If anything happens and you need to contact me, here is the name of the place where I dock my boat, along with the phone number, and name of the manager, who can reach me anytime at sea. Okay?"

I shook my head and laughed saying, "That's great Bruce. Thanks." He knew I probably would never use it, but he also knew it would help me to relax. And it worked!

A few hours later I went up to the twelfth floor to see how Michele was doing and I was pleasantly surprised. She had already been bathed and her hair had been washed and nicely brushed against the pillow. The encrusted material that had collected in and around her mouth had all been cleaned out and her dry lips were covered with Vaseline.

Lying on a special air bed that they'd ordered for her when she arrived, she was surrounded by a half dozen pillows. She looked like she was resting on a white cloud. Tender loving care was evident throughout, and my heart surged with gratitude.

This was what the Samaritan Health System was all about, "Excellence In Caring." That was their motto. As managers we heard it at meetings time and time again. And by and large, this level of care was achieved. What had happened on that other floor was an aberration, having taken place simply because I was an employee of the system and was perceived as having no rights.

Steve Seiler, President and CEO of Good Samaritan, found out about this type of attitude in another area one day and was appalled. Taking steps immediately to change that behavior, he called a special meeting of his administrators and adamantly stated that this behavior would not be tolerated anywhere in the system. "Employees are important people," he said with vehemence, "And I want to make sure that doesn't change simply because they require medical care." I knew then it would only be a matter of time for this attitude to be changed system wide.

I walked in and stroked Michele's cheek. She opened her eyes and smiled. "I bet you're feeling better, Honey." I said, bending over to kiss her. Her smile grew wider and she squeezed my hand, which meant a resounding Y E S!

She was in the hospital for a while before they finally found out what was causing her severe pain. One of her kidneys was diseased and had to be removed. After surgery she remained in the hospital for several weeks. As the Christmas holidays approached, I decorated Michele's room and hung up all her cards. She received so many of them! Then I brought in a small lighted Christmas tree and placed it on a counter next to the sink. It made her room very cheerful and prompted many nice comments from nurses who walked in and out of the room. I knew this pleased Michele very much.

The HMO got into the act many times, pressuring me about Michele's discharge. They wanted her transferred to Windsor, which was fine with me except that the nurses were not trained in IV therapy, which Michele now required for fluids and medication. "If that's the only problem," the representative said, "we'd be glad to provide an IV nurse to train the nurses at Windsor when Michele is transferred."

"How long would she remain involved?" I asked.

"Until they were comfortable in doing IVs by themselves."

"That sounds good to me, but I'd have to check with them. Also, they're State nurses, so I would have to contact the State for approval."

I called Al Soenneker right away and he was agreeable as long as the nurses at Windsor were comfortable with that level of care. I then talked with Theresa, the Head Nurse, and after discussing it with the other nurses, they all agreed it would be fine with them since Samaritan was providing an IV nurse immediately upon Michele's discharge from the hospital.

Doctor Bethancourt wrote out continuing care orders for

Michele in great detail in preparation for her discharge to Windsor. It was now New Year's Eve and everyone seemed to be in a festive mood. The ambulance came to transport Michele in the afternoon. Although it was my day off, I went to my office to take care of a problem that came to my attention on the floor, so I didn't get over to Windsor until around 4:30.

Driving over there, I thought, 'Michele should be settled in nicely by now in her familiar surroundings, with Edie by her side.' I smiled just thinking about that. What could be more perfect than to have Edie on duty when Michele's needs were so great?

When I opened the door at Windsor, Theresa was standing there with a shocked look on her face, obviously very upset. "Oh, Mrs. Morton, am I glad to see you." she said shaking her head. "You won't believe this."

"What is it, Theresa?" I asked in alarm.

"Samaritan didn't send out the IV nurse and the meds that are due can't be given to Michele."

"There must be some mistake. I'll call them right away."

"That's what I thought, too, so I called and found out that they're not going to send out an IV nurse."

"That's ridiculous, Theresa. It was a verbal contract. They were the ones who suggested it, for heaven's sake."

"I know," she said, "but, I'm just telling you what they told me. We're very worried."

Throwing up my hands I said, "Let me call them." When I got the representative on the phone, she immediately recognized my voice. "I understand the IV nurse has been cancelled," I said. "Can you tell me why?"

"I don't know why," she curtly responded.

"You don't know why?" I asked, increduously.

"That's right. I'm just following orders."

"Who gave that order?" I demanded.

"The director."

"Let me talk with her."

"She can't come to the phone right now. She's very busy."

"I'll bet she is. When making decisions like this, she must have to fend off the world. Well, you leave me no choice. I'll just have to call an ambulance, and bring Michele back to the hospital."

"No, you can't do that," she quickly interjected. "Effective tonight, Michele is being dropped from the HMO."

"Are you for real?" I asked, refusing to believe what I'd just heard. "You can't drop Michele from the plan just like that. What are we supposed to do for fluids and medications? She's overdue now."

"Call AHCCCS," she retorted.

"AHCCCS! Are you people crazy? Michele has never been processed through AHCCCS. That would take weeks under ordinary circumstances, never mind at five o'clock on *New Year's Eve!*"

"I'm sorry, I can't help you anymore, Mrs. Morton," she said, "I need to go." I heard the phone click in my ear while I sat there stunned. My mind was racing. Everyone was watching me, not knowing what to say or do.

"Theresa," I said finally. "I don't want you or the other nurses to worry. I'm going to have to try and contact Al Soenneker. Since it's New Year's Eve, it'll probably be difficult to do. If I'm not successful, Michele will be returned to Good Samaritan."

"I thought they dropped her from the plan Mrs. Morton."

"Yes, that's what they said, Theresa, but don't concern yourself about that. If Michele needs to go back to the hospital, she will. They can't refuse treatment or care, and as far as payment goes, we can argue about whose responsibility it is after the fact."

I made several phone calls trying to track down Soenneker, and finally succeeded. I filled him in on what had taken place.

"My God!" he said. "They were the ones who prevailed upon us to make this arrangement when Michele was discharged."

"Yes, you're right, Al. But now they've backed out and left us in the lurch. What we need now is a temporary fix."

"Okay. I'll get someone to work on it right away. We'll find an IV nurse somewhere and get her over there as soon as possible."

"Thanks, Al. That's great."

After this call, I returned to Michele's room where Edie was waiting. "Where's your husband?" she asked.

"I told him to go home after work. Who expected this fiasco? It was supposed to be a simple transfer. He's in for a surprise, isn't he?" I said ruefully.

"He sure is. I don't know how you stand all this pressure, Mrs. Morton. I'm amazed at your stamina."

Shrugging my shoulders I said, "I'm not sure myself, Edie. There are times I think, when surrounded by all this craziness, that I'm the only sane person in the world. Does that sound right to you?" I asked smiling.

"Yes." she said laughing. "I'm assuming, of course, that present company is excluded."

"Oh, you bet. Absolutely. Without a doubt." I declared and we both enjoyed the chance to lighten the situation.

When the IV nurse finally arrived, she did her job well. I stayed until Michele was sleeping soundly. The staff seemed more relaxed now that the crisis was over. Edie walked me to the door.

"Okay, Edie, you know the routine, right?" I asked with a smile.

"Ohhhh, yes I do," she said amused. "If anything happens, *call you first,*" she emphasized each word.

"Right you are," I said hugging her. Waving to the rest of the staff, I said, "Goodnight everybody, and thanks for everything. You are all pretty special people." Then I opened the door and stepped out into the darkness of the night, driving off to bring in the dawning of a brand New Year and wondering what it had in store for us.

KATHLEEN MORTON

Chapter XXI

When I got home, Arnie was at the door. "You stayed a long time," he exclaimed. "I was beginning to think I was going to bring the New Year in without you," he said smiling. "Did things go smoothly?"

"Catastrophic would be more like it."

"Oh no," he said disillusioned. "What happened? Why didn't you call me?"

"Because I was caught up in the crazy frenetic activity that followed and time just passed." Then I told him what happened.

"I'm going to write to Jim Crews," I said, "and request that Michele be reinstated to the medical plan."

"The CEO?"

"Yes. I have a lot of respect for him and I think he'll do the right thing."

"So, what about Michael and Paula? Are we going over there to bring in the New Year?"

"No, they're coming here."

"Wonderful. Then I can finally relax."

Several days after I wrote to Crews, I received a phone call from his secretary. "Mrs. Morton," she began, "Jim wanted me to tell you that he hasn't forgotten about your letter. He wants you to know that he is doing an investigation. Once it's complete, he'll get back to you."

"Great! Thanks a lot. I appreciate the update and look forward to hearing from him."

Michele's health seemed to be picking up, so we didn't expect what happened next. I got a call from the nurse at Windsor saying that Michele was seizuring. I went right over to evaluate. By the time I arrived, the seizures were pretty intense. I called Kaplan right away since this was a neurological problem and after I described it to him he asked, "Is she coming out of the seizures at all?"

"No, they're pretty constant, and are definitely grand mal convulsions with a few seconds in between, but no evidence of consciousness. It doesn't look good, does it?"

"No it doesn't, Kathleen. It sounds like status epilepticus, which is very serious. She needs to be hospitalized right away."

"Okay, I'll get her over there without delay. Could you contact Bruce and ask him to try to arrange admission to the twelfth floor? The care is excellent there."

"No problem, Kathleen. I'll meet you at the hospital within the hour."

During this hospitalization, a letter arrived from Crews indicating that the HMO had a clause stating that anyone not living at home was not eligible for benefits, which was the reason Michele had been dropped. However, he felt strongly that because of Michele's many hospitalizations the HMO representatives were aware of her situation and even arranged for an ambulance to take her to Windsor. Because they were knowledgeable about this case for some time and took no action initially, Crews supported my position and reinstated Michele for all medical benefits, effective immediately.

The outcome pleased me, of course, but came as no surprise. This Chief Executive Officer had always been very fair-minded.

Michele continued to have convulsions nonstop with no

sign of consciousness. I took time off from work and sat by her side. She was in the same room as before – 1219. I met with Kaplan and Bethancourt every morning at 7:00 for updates. One morning as I approached them, they appeared to be in a heated discussion. When they saw me, they stopped talking.

We went into the small conference room where we normally met. Kaplan spoke first. "I was wondering if we shouldn't try giving Michele large doses of a medication that may end these seizures."

I looked at him, and then at Bethancourt, who sat quietly, obviously not in favor of this decision. "Could it also end her life, Al?" I asked simply.

Kaplan winced a little and replied, "Yes possibly, but it may not. However, these multiple seizures are very hard on her system."

"Al, I know you mean well," I said, "but no one loved life more than Michele. She's fought with all her might to be part of it, while overcoming extraordinary challenges. Now that the chips are down, there's no way I could ever make a decision that might cause her to die. No, Michele's in God's hands right now, and that's as it should be."

"Okay," he said. "I respect that. I just thought I would ask since there seems to be no relief from these convulsions."

For a few moments we all remained silent and then I said, "What I'd like to discuss is the medication she is presently on. If it's not helping her seizures, why continue to give it to her? Maybe she'd be better off not having any. If she gets worse, you can always put her back on it again. What do you think, Bruce?"

"Not a bad idea," he said.

Kaplan immediately agreed.

After a few days off the medication, there were no changes in Michele's condition. Removal of the medication certainly hadn't

KATHLEEN MORTON

hurt her in any way. When the doctors and I next met, it was Michele's eighth day in the hospital. Both doctors encouraged me to take a day off and rest at home.

"You can't continue at this pace without collapsing," Bethancourt pointed out. "Although Michele is still seizuring, her condition appears to be stable at this point. You need to take advantage of this. Go home tonight and rest all day tomorrow."

"Bruce is right, Kathleen," Kaplan immediately insisted. "Go home and stay home. You can't afford to get sick."

"All right," I said, "I'll see if a friend of mine can come and sit with Michele and I'll take tomorrow off."

I called Heather and told her what the doctors had said. She thought that was a great idea and immediately volunteered to stay with Michele from 7:00 a.m. to 4:30 p.m.

"Wonderful, Heather. I now really can have a day of rest. Arnie and Paula are going to stop by after work and should arrive about 5:30 so the whole day is covered."

During my day of much needed rest I heard from Kaplan, who said Michele was doing well. Later, Heather called to report in before leaving at 4:30. "She's doing fine, Kathleen. Everyone has been very attentive to her and there has been no change in her condition.

I sat back down with my feet up to watch a little TV. Suddenly a funny feeling came over me. I got up and called Bethancourt. "Do you think we are doing everything we can for Michele?" I asked him.

"Yes, of course. Why do you ask?"

"I don't know. It's just this feeling I have. Like something isn't right."

"She's fine, Kathleen. I saw her today and so did Al, and your friend was with her during the day. So just relax, okay?"

"Okay, Bruce. Thanks," I said, feeling better as I hung up the phone. I went back to my TV program. About twenty minutes later the phone rang again. It was Doctor Kaplan.

"I'm so sorry, Kathleen," he said with ultimate sadness. "We just lost Michele."

"Oh, my God, Al. No! No! Don't tell me that, please!" I pleaded as I let out an anguished sob. "How could you have let that happen? You knew I wanted to be with her!" I shouted, sobbing uncontrollably. "I'm coming right down. Don't touch her!" I commanded as I hung up the phone. My head in my hands, I screamed into the eerie quiet of the room. More than anything, I had wanted to be with Michele when she died. I wanted to hold her and hug her as life slipped away. I had promised myself I would be with her right to the end. How could this happen, for the love of God? Was there no justice in this world? "*Oh, Michele, Sweetheart, I am so sorry,*" I sobbed. "*I should have been with you. I'm really so sorry.*"

The phone rang again but I ignored it. I was sobbing uncontrollably and the tears were flowing like a river. I didn't want to talk to anyone. However, it continued to ring incessantly, and I realized it was probably Doctor Kaplan. I knew he would never give up, so I finally answered.

"Now, you listen to me, Kathleen," Kaplan said sternly. "Don't jump in the car and come driving down here like a crazy person. You could get in an accident. You hear me?" he demanded. "Call Michael. Call Michael right now!"

"Okay, Al," I responded in a flat, dead voice. All the fight had gone out of me now. "I'll call Michael as soon as I hang up."

"Good," he said with a sigh of relief. And then said softly, "Try to take it easy. I'll meet you at the hospital."

I called Michael right away, and the receptionist answered.

"He's in with a client right now, Mrs. Morton," she said.

"Interrupt him," I told her, and she knew by my voice that something was really wrong.

"Mom! What's going on?" Michael asked in alarm.

"I'm sorry, Michael," I said trying to hold back the tears, "But, there's no easy way to tell you this. Your sister just died."

"Oh, my God, Mom," he said. "Hold on! I'll be right there."

Next I called Arnie, hoping I would reach him before he left for the hospital. He was just walking out the door. When he got on the phone I said simply. "We lost her, Arnie. Michele died about twenty minutes ago."

"Oh, Kathleen, my God, NO!" he said in anguish. Then trying to contain his grief, he asked, "Are you alright, Honey? Do you want me to come home?"

"No, Arnie. Michael's on his way and he'll drive me down to the hospital. I'll meet you there."

Within minutes, Michael was at the door. Embracing me, he said. "Oh, Mom, I'm so sorry. You tried so hard." Then we stood there and cried together, not wanting to let go.

We finally made our way down to the hospital. When we arrived on the twelfth floor, Arnie came over and hugged me tightly, as did Paula. Then Doctor Kaplan came over and extended his condolences. We stood outside Michele's room. The door was closed. As Kaplan moved to open the door, I stopped him. "I'd like to go in by myself, Al." I said, trying to control my emotions.

"Of course, Kathleen. Whatever you want," he said encouragingly.

"Would you like me to go with you?" Arnie asked.

I turned around and hugged him saying, "Thanks, Arnie, but I really want to be alone with Michele."

They stepped aside, and I opened the door. I turned on the light as I entered and closed the door behind me. I walked over to her bed. They had fixed her up so nice and she looked as if she were just sleeping. I touched her and she was still warm. I don't know why, but that made me feel better.

I lowered the side railing of the bed so I could lift her up to kiss and hug her. I wanted to be able to sit on the side of the bed and just hold her, but the air mattress made that very difficult. Whenever I tried to hold her, she slipped away due to the constant movement of the mattress.

Then, without giving it much thought, I decided to lie down beside her and hold her for a while. As soon as I attempted to do this, we both went crashing to the floor. In my grief I had forgotten that the buoyancy of the bed was related to the weight it carried.

I lay there, shaking my head as I held her in my arms. "I bet you're laughing at what a dumb move your mom just made," I said aloud. I couldn't help but smile at how idiotic I looked. The respect everyone had for my privacy with Michele took on new meaning. I knew I was safe and would not be discovered. Then, as I continued to lie there holding her in my arms, I realized that as a tribute to Michele's sense of humor, it was only fitting that something this comical should happen at the end.

I finally removed myself from the bed, and the mattress bounced back to its original buoyancy. I stood there studying her and recalled a conversation I had had with Doctor Wolfe in Canada about how important the brain was in finding a cure for this dreadful disease. Because so much of the information was located there, they were always looking for families to donate their child's brain.

At the time, I remembered thinking that I could never do that. But now I realized that without the donation of brains, a cure might never be found. As I looked at Michele, recalling her love of life and her wonderful sense of humor, I thought, 'What a waste.'

I gave Michele one last kiss and said goodbye as I walked out the door. Everyone surrounded me, lending their support. Turning to Arnie, I said, "I think I would like to donate Michele's brain for research. I know you always felt it was a good idea. Do you still feel that way?"

"Yes, I do," he said, "but I was leaving it up to you."

"All right. I've made up my mind. Where's Doctor Kaplan?"

"He's on the phone," Arnie said. "I think he just called Doctor Bethancourt."

Then Kaplan approached. "Kathleen, Bruce is on the phone. He wants to talk with you."

I went into the nurses' station, and picked up the phone. "Hi Bruce," I said, still trying to control my emotions.

"Hello, Kathleen. I'm really very sorry," he said.

"I know Bruce. Although we knew this day was coming, it's still so hard! And I wanted so much to be with her at the end."

"That's what saddens me, Kathleen. I feel responsible for that."

"Oh, no, Bruce, please. You were just thinking about me and my health, and you were right. I was exhausted. Even if I'd been here and left for ten minutes to go to the restroom, it might have happened then. Who can say? You certainly have nothing to be sorry about. Without you and Kaplan I would never have survived."

"Well, Kathleen, all I can say is that you're some incredible mother. You just never gave up and your love and devotion intensified as the years passed. I've always thought of my wife as a great mother, which she is. But, fortunately, few mothers are tested as you have been. The challenges you faced were enormous, but you kept on going making sure Michele got the best of everything. She was a very lucky young lady."

"Thanks, Bruce, I appreciate your kind comments. The nicest compliment anyone could pay me is to say that I was a good mother, and it's especially nice to hear it now."

When I hung up the phone, Kaplan was by my side. I turned to him and said, "I have decided to donate Michele's brain to research. I want it to go to Doctor Leon Wolfe in Canada. Can you handle that from this end?"

"Sure, I can. And that's a great decision to make. I know it wasn't easy."

"You're right about that," I sighed.

"I'm going to call Wolfe now and I'll turn the phone over to you to make the arrangements."

When I got Wolfe on the phone, he passed along his condolences to me regarding Michele's death. "I'm very sorry, Mrs. Morton, I know how much you fought for a cure."

"Well, it wasn't to be for us, but maybe someday for someone else. We have decided to donate Michele's brain to research."

"Oh, that's very generous of you. That certainly was a tough decision to make."

"Yes, but I'm ready to make it now. I have Doctor Kaplan with me at the moment. He was Michele's neurologist and he's waiting to talk with you to make the necessary arrangements. Here he is now." Handing the phone to Kaplan, I walked over to where my family was waiting. Heather had also joined them. She came over and hugged me tightly. No words needed to be spoken.

KATHLEEN MORTON

Chapter XXII

The next week was a total blur. The funeral was delayed because of the autopsy. Michael came with us to help select a casket and make the necessary funeral arrangements. Most of the time, I was in a trance-like state, moving mechanically from one situation to another.

"Mom, why don't I take over from here?" Michael said gently. "I think you need to go home and rest"

"That's what I was just telling her," Arnie said.

"I appreciate what you're trying to do," I told them, "but I need to be somewhat involved. Otherwise, I'll go crazy. Resting gives me too much time to think. Although now that we've selected the casket, your taking over the rest of the funeral arrangements would be a big help, Michael. Thanks. In the meantime, I'm going to contact the priest and see if he can arrange for the organist to be there."

I spoke with Father Luke Sylvestri, who was very helpful and supportive. "Will there be a eulogy?" he asked.

"Yes Father, we're planning on one."

"What about you? Do you plan to say anything?"

"Well," I began hesitantly, "at one time I thought I would read a passage from one of Kahlil Gibran's books. But now I'm not so sure."

"Why?"

"Because it's about saying goodbye and perhaps meeting

once again. I'm afraid I might fall apart."

"I bet you can do it," he said gently. "Why don't you bring the reading with you," he suggested, "and then decide when the time comes."

"That's a good idea, Father. I may just do that. Thanks."

I spoke with the organist the next day. I asked if she could start with 'Amazing Grace,' then play two of Michele's favorite songs: 'You Are My Special Angel,' and 'Somewhere Over The Rainbow.'

Do you know them?" I asked. She said she did and promised to play the 'Special Angel' song during the service and end with 'Somewhere Over The Rainbow.'

The Wake was due to begin the next day. It would last for two days to be followed by the service the next morning.

Michael stood ready to take charge after the funeral. He intended to have everyone come over to his office building, which was closed for the day. He also arranged for a caterer to set up food and drink in the large conference room. He had thought of everything! Greatly relieved, I thanked him for all his help.

The next morning, Arnie and I went over to the funeral parlor before anyone else was scheduled to arrive. I approached the viewing with some trepidation because I wasn't sure how Michele would look after the autopsy, especially considering the removal of the brain.

There was absolutely no indication, however, that anything had ever been done. We both felt so relieved. Her hair was combed differently than normal and when I mentioned this to the funeral director he immediately had the beautician return to redo Michele's hair according to my instructions.

Floral arrangements started to arrive from various parts of the country. Heather had taken our Christmas list and called all of our friends in New York, along with a half dozen other states throughout the nation to let them know that Michele had passed away. The response was immediate. Phone calls, Mass cards, and condolences all came pouring in. Some of them had written what they remembered most about Michele, which was so touching.

Contributions to Batten Disease were requested in lieu of flowers, and Heather handled that for me as well. However, an abundance of floral arrangements continued to arrive, until Michele was surrounded by some very beautiful flowers. Then, a blanket of yellow daisies arrived from Michael and Paula with the inscription 'Now you are on your own yellow brick road,' referring to the Wizard of Oz. I was visibly moved and smiled through my tears. Arnie was also noticeably affected when he read this message. After all, no one more than Michael knew about Michele's passion for the Wizard of Oz. He had lived with it!

Greeting people at the Wake seemed to help us cope. There was a lot of camaraderie because many of them were co-workers. Doctor Kaplan was standing talking to a group of people when Doctor Bethancourt arrived. I met him at the door and we both walked to where Michele was laid out. He commented on how good she looked and then knelt down and said a prayer. His next move touched me deeply. He had brought with him a beautiful long stemmed rose, which he placed in her hands, without ever knowing that the rose was Michele's favorite flower.

The next day at the service, Mary Carpenter, Michele's first Social Worker, and now a good friend of the family, delivered a touching eulogy involving all aspects of Michele's life, especially focusing on her ability to "experience life with zest and passion," despite adversity.

When Mary finished, the priest returned to the pulpit, and said a few more words, then looked at me. "I think Michele's mom may want to say something at this time or do a reading," he said.

I smiled inwardly at his approach and made my way to the pulpit. I didn't seem to have much of a choice after all. "Thank you, Father," I said, and looking out at family members and friends I was imbued with a strong feeling of acceptance, which encouraged me to continue.

"What I'm about to read," I said "is a passage from one of Kahlil Gibran's books:

Fare thee well this day has ended.
Farewell to you and the time I have spent with you.
It was but yesterday we met in a dream.
You have sung to me in my aloneness, and I of your
longings have built a tower in the sky.
But now our sleep has fled and our dream is over
and it is no longer dawn.
The noontide is upon us and our half waking has
turned to a fuller day, and we must part.
If in the twilight of memory we should meet once more
we shall speak again together and you shall sing to me
a deeper song.
And if our hands should meet in another dream we shall
once again, build another tower in the sky."

This passage was especially meaningful to me because of the way it touched upon the memory of our lives together. I was amazed that I was able to deliver it without faltering. I am sure that Father Sylvestri's confidence in me had a lot to do with this.

Arnie joined me on the altar and hand-in-hand we walked up to Michele's casket. Arnie bent over and kissed her, and said his goodbyes. Now it was my turn. I stroked her face and her hair whispering, "I love you, Sweetheart." Then, squeezing her hand, I leaned down and kissed her cheek. The knowledge that this was the very last time I would be able to see or touch Michele brought me to tears I could no longer contain.

As Arnie and I slowly turned and made our way back to our seats, two funeral attendants came and closed the coffin. Then "Somewhere Over The Rainbow" was suddenly resounding throughout the chapel, conjuring up a beautiful image of Michele's joy and laughter. We both felt that this was a fitting tribute to our young daughter. Yes, indeed, Michele was now on a journey along her own Yellow Brick Road, where only Heaven awaited.

KATHLEEN MORTON

Epilogue

During the next several months I felt as though I was in a state of suspension. But what bothered me was that life did not stand still with me. It just kept rolling right along to the point where I began to feel some resentment. Dawn rose, and night fell with relentless consistency. The days, the weeks, and the months followed each other with frustrating accuracy. Time was passing but we seemed to be in the same place.

Michael, also profoundly affected by his sister's death, dealt with it by not talking about her anymore. He closed his mind to what had transpired earlier and went about his business. Although this may not have been the best way to deal with grief, it seemed to ease his pain.

Arnie and I approached our grief differently as well. We somehow could not grieve together, so we went about our own way of working through the loss of Michele. Neither of us missed a day of work, both effectively accomplished what we had to do, but we were not living any more, only existing. At home, we moved around robotlike, casually taking care of what had to be done. I was assured that time would heal all, but because of how I still felt, the words sounded hollow.

Then, after dinner one evening, I said to Arnie, "Honey, I think we need to introduce a change into our lives. Go somewhere, do something different."

"You do?" he said surprised. "I don't think that's such a

good idea."

"Why?" I replied. "We can't go on like this forever."

"No, but where is the enthusiasm?" he said looking up at me from his lounge chair. "We have none."

"True, but perhaps that will change. Somehow just talking about it stirs a little excitement within me."

"Maybe so," he reflected staring into space. "Where would we go?" he asked with little interest.

"I don't know, because I haven't given it a lot of thought. Right now, I'm just talking out loud." We both sat there with our own thoughts for a while. Then I turned around and looked at Arnie. "What about a cruise?"

"You've got to be kidding," he retorted. "Spend all that money just to end up being miserable?"

"We don't know that for sure. It may be a bit more expensive to cry on board a ship, but at lease the atmosphere will be different."

He smiled despite himself. "You always have an answer, don't you? I guess what you're saying does make some sense. Whatever you want to do, I'll go along with. You know that. And, besides, I have to admit, I'm warming up to the idea myself."

"Oh, good. I'm glad to hear you say that, Arnie. I have no idea what may be in store for us, but I agree. Let's go for it!"

We contacted a travel agent and plans were made to go on a seven day cruise to the Eastern Caribbean on the Holland America Line. We both busied ourselves buying clothes, shoes and formal attire for our trip. Michael drove us to the airport, and said. "Now, you two had better have a great time. It's not an option. I insist!" We both laughed and kissed him goodbye, as we boarded the plane to Florida where the ship was docked.

Deciding to go on a cruise turned out to be the best decision we had ever made. The food, the wine, the live entertainment were all exceptional. One could not help but feel excited and happy. One evening Arnie and I were standing by the railing looking out over the vast expanse of the sea. It was so calm and peaceful with the water rippling around the sides of the ship. The sun was sinking in the west, laying its truly magnificent golden beam across the enormous body of water.

We stood there, entranced, taking all this in, silently drinking up the beauty of the scene. I took a deep breath, turned to Arnie, and said with a bemused smile, "I think Michele is watching us."

He grinned and replied, "My thoughts exactly. Do you think she approves?"

"You can bet on it," I responded with a satisfied laugh bringing Michele's smiling face to mind. We put our arms around each other and, still gazing over the expanse of the ocean, we decided to take a leaf out of Michele's book and enjoy life to its fullest, despite adversity. That was her legacy to all of us. And, it was just at that moment, we knew that this was not only a new awareness, but also a new beginning. Turning our heads, our eyes met. We hugged and looked outward once again. And we never looked back.